D1529927

The Learning-To-Write Process
in Elementary Classrooms

The Learning-To-Write Process in Elementary Classrooms

Suzanne Bratcher
Northern Arizona University

LAWRENCE ERLBAUM ASSOCIATES, PUBLISHERS
1997   Mahwah, New Jersey   London

Lawrence Erlbaum Associates, Inc., Publishers
10 Industrial Avenue
Mahwah, New Jersey 07430

Library of Congress Cataloging-in-Publication-Data

Bratcher, Suzanne.
   The learning-to-write process in elementary classrooms / by
Suzanne Bratcher.
      p. cm.
   Includes bibliographical references (p. 215) and index.
   ISBN 0-8058-2255-0 (alk. paper)
   1. English language—Composition and exercises—Study and
teaching (Elementary)—United States. I. Title.
   LB1576.B596 1997
   372.62'3'044—dc21   97-8623
                                                              CIP

Books published by Lawrence Erlbaum Associates are printed on
acid-free paper, and their bindings are chosen for strength and
durability.

Printed in the United States of America
10 9 8 7 6 5 4 3 2 1

For Beth, who helped me find the ideas,
and for Greg, who helped me find the time

Contents

Preface

WHY ANOTHER BOOK ABOUT TEACHING WRITING

In the last 20 years, the "traditional" way to teach writing has shifted away from a "product" model toward a "process" model. In fact, the writing process has become so familiar that most teachers can recite it in their sleep: *prewriting* followed by *drafting* followed by *revising* followed by *editing* followed by *publishing*. This awareness of the writing process has had a beneficial effect on how we teach writing; it has helped us take a "how-to" approach with our students. In the last 5 to 10 years, however, writing teachers have recognized that no matter how helpful the writing process is, it is not the whole story of how to teach kids to write. Tompkins (1990) reminded us that we need to balance process (how to write) and product (what to write). Calkins (1983, 1994) reminded us that we need to watch and learn from our children. Graves (1983) reminded us that we need to show children how to write and write with them ourselves. Rhetoricians have reminded us that writing is communication and that children need real readers and real reasons to write. The back-to-the-basics proponents have reminded us that correctness is important to communication, too. Children from a variety of backgrounds have reminded us that culture is part of everything we do, even writing. Running through all of these concerns are the constant questions of how children learn best.

This book is an attempt to synthesize what we know about how children learn, how we write, and what we write into a process of teaching children to write in elementary classrooms. Several themes run through the process, more attitudes than concepts, beliefs that inform actions:

- Writing is communication.
- Writing is a powerful tool for learning.
- Learning to write is a process, different from and greater than the writing process itself.
- How children feel about their writing and about themselves as writers affects how they learn to write.

- Teachers are colearners with students.
- Children from many backgrounds can learn to write together.

WHO THIS BOOK IS FOR

The Learning-to-Write Process in Elementary Classrooms is for classroom teachers and soon-to-be teachers. Although my primary audience is elementary teachers, many of the principles in the book can be applied to and adapted for middle school or even high-school writing classrooms. Experienced teachers can use it to examine what they think about teaching writing: where they agree with what I've said, where they disagree, where they have gone further than I have. Beginning teachers and teachers in training can use it to survey some of the concerns writing teachers face.

The Learning-to-Write Process in Elementary Classrooms can serve as a starting place for developing theories of how best to teach writing. I hope readers will use it to think through the issues I raise. I hope it will help teachers who may feel uncomfortable with their own writing find ways of feeling confident about writing and teaching writing. I hope all readers will go beyond it to find their own ways of teaching writing.

HOW TO USE THIS BOOK

Part I, "The Learning-to-Write Process," introduces theoretical and practical foundations for the comfort–confidence–competence model for learning to write that I suggest. Part II, "Reasons to Write," looks at why we write–to communicate with each other, to learn new things, for the sheer love of writing—as well as the forms of writing we produce and the process we use when we write for different reasons. Part III, "The Teaching-Writing Process," discusses instructional planning, teacher evaluation of student writing, and teacher modeling. An appendix offers a quick review of editing rules for teachers or soon-to-be teachers.

Throughout the book, classroom anecdotes and samples of children's writing support practical suggestions for helping students learn to write. Many of my examples are drawn from classrooms in northern Arizona, where I live and work. I do not include these examples because all teachers need to know how to work with Navajo children; I include them merely as symbolic of the multicultural classrooms in which we all teach. For obvious reasons, a thorough discussion of the writing challenges faced by the diverse students in our classrooms is simply beyond the scope of this book. (Authors who do look closely at the challenges children face when English is a second language are Igoa, 1995; Peregoy & Boyle, 1993; Rigg & Allen, 1989; Rigg & Enright, 1986.) "In the Classroom" sections offer classroom teachers' comments about their own experiences. Readers who are interested in more teacher comments might want to look at Heinemann's "Teacher-to-Teacher" series, especially Glover (1995). "Applications" at the end of each chapter offer opportunities for readers of the book to write themselves, to experience firsthand the kind of writing suggested for students. To *show* rather than *tell* how to show writing, I've included samples of my own writing.

When you have finished the book, you might want to reread chapter 1: you may find more there after you have read the whole book than you will the first time you read it. It may be tempting to skip the "Applications" sections: writing, after all, takes time. Because these writing assignments are designed to reinforce the concepts the chapters suggest, take the time. Use writing to learn about the learning-to-write process.

Sometimes readers want to find particular topics that interest them. The following table may help you locate some of those topics.

if you're looking for	*try chapter*
the communication triangle/rhetorical stance	6
creating a community of writers	2
expository writing	8
genres	7–10
grading techniques	13
grammar/conventions of writing	5
learning theory	1
literary writing	10
modeling	2 and 14
the multilingual, multicultural classroom	2, 5, 7
multiple intelligences	3, 5, 7–10
peer response groups	2
personal narratives	7
persuasive writing	9
revision techniques	4
student ownership of writing	4
student self-evaluation	4
teacher planning techniques	12
the writing process	3

ACKNOWLEDGMENTS

I owe the comfort–confidence–competence model to a happy collaboration with Dr. Elizabeth Stroble, now Associate Dean of the School of Education at the University of Louisville. In 1989, she and I often conducted workshops for teachers all over northern Arizona. We created the comfort–confidence–competence model driving across the Navajo Reservation for a last-minute inservice with administrators in Window Rock. We needed a way to explain how learning to write is like learning horseback riding or rug weaving or skateboarding. I don't know which of us thought of which part of the model, but it found its way into our inservices from that point on because it helped us bridge a gap between writing theory and life experience. Eventually we wrote an article based on this metaphor that appeared in *Research in the Teaching of English* (1994). And because I owe so much of what I know about teaching writing to the rare professional partnership Beth and I shared for 6 years, I dedicate this book to her.

I owe the idea of a learning-to-write process to Charles Rullman, the piano technician for Northern Arizona University. Six years ago now, I asked Charles to take me on as an apprentice because I was burned out from teaching writing and wanted to learn to tune pianos for a living. I finished my year of afternoons with Charles and his pianos, not with sufficient skill to be a professional piano technician, but instead with a vision of a new way to teach writing. Ironically, I learned more from Charles about teaching than I did about piano tuning.

Because I have been out of the public schools and in the university for almost 20 years, I owe the classroom examples and much of the practical grounding of my theory to the teachers of the Northern Arizona Writing Project (NAWP), in particular to Jan Larson, Paula Nelson, Becky White, and Bernadette Whistler. These very special teachers invited me into their classrooms to watch, to participate, even to teach my own ideas once in a while. They shared the writing that went on in their classes, their students' and their own. They talked to me about the issues I wanted to raise in this book and kept me grounded in the realities of current public-school teaching.

Jan Larson is a teacher whose energy and talent for organization keep her classroom buzzing with activity. She's been teaching elementary and junior-high students for 18 years. The last 8 years, she's taught fourth graders at DeMiguel Elementary School in Flagstaff. Language arts has always been important to her, and she finds creative ways of working writing into almost everything she teaches. Her students come from a wide expanse of socioeconomic backgrounds: some from families living in brand new two-story homes in affluent neighborhoods, some from families living in mobile homes on unpaved streets. They are Anglo, Hispanic, and Native American. Jan is a member of several honorary organizations of teachers and is active in the community. Her professionalism helps us all.

Paula Nelson is a teacher with an infectious laugh who makes even the most mundane tasks seem fun. Currently she teaches third grade at Cromer Elementary School in Flagstaff. Her students live on the east side of town on ranches and in modest houses and mobile homes. A lot of them have horses. They are Navajo, Hispanic, and Anglo. For the most part, formal schooling is not high among their parents. Paula has been teaching for 16 years: 7th, 8th, 3rd, and 4th graders. Paula attended the NAWP Summer Institute in 1993; in 1995 and 1996, she taught classes for teaching assistants on the Navajo Reservation, helping them learn ways they can help their students learn to write.

Becky White is a teacher at Kinsey Elementary School in Flagstaff whose passion and commitment to teaching challenge all of us to do better. She has been teaching for 15 years: special education, learning disabled, secondary summer school, and sixth grade. For 7 years she worked with Upward Bound. Her students live on the south side of town and are Black, Hispanic, Anglo, and Native

American. University property borders the playground behind her classroom. She attended the NAWP Summer Institute in 1993, and in 1995 she began giving workshops to teachers. Sometimes she teaches model lessons in peer classrooms for teachers who invite her.

Bernadette Whistler is a second-grade teacher at DeMiguel Elementary School in Flagstaff. Her soft voice and gentle ways remind me how fragile we all are as writers. She has been teaching for 14 years, and this is her sixth year teaching second graders. Her students live on the west side of town. Some of them live in large houses with parents who have several degrees and are lawyers and teachers and successful entrepreneurs. Others of her students live just outside the city limits in mobile homes and more modest houses with parents who have less formal education. Her students are Anglo, Hispanic, Asian, and Native American. Several of them are in the gifted program. She attended the NAWP Summer Institute in 1991, and she writes about emergent writers in NAWP Publications.

Writing a book is an all-consuming task, and there are many other people who supported me in my work: my husband Greg Larkin, who patiently read endless drafts, did extra housework cheerfully, and cooked more than his fair share; Beth Yule, who transcribed dictation to get me started writing; Amy Welden and Jean Boreen, who helped me think through particularly difficult chapters; my daughter, Jane Hoskins, who didn't complain when I got too busy, and who shared her own writing with me; my editor Naomi Silverman, who talked through the ideas with me and gave me extensions when I couldn't meet deadlines; the reviewers Sharon Evans Brockman, California State University–Stanislaus, Judith A Doherty, Co-Director, Boston Writing Project and University of Massachusetts, and Janet Richards, the University of Southern Mississippi, who gave me new perspectives on my original ideas. Last, but certainly not least, I want to thank the students who helped me with this project: the elementary students who shared their writing with me and my university students who commented on drafts of chapters and helped me redraw confusing diagrams. Writing indeed happens in communities.

Notes to the College Instructor

The challenge of talking about modeling is to practice what we preach: to show showing rather than to tell showing. In other words, this book is about helping beginning teachers learn to write as they learn to teach writing. Of course, showing how to show has been my challenge throughout this whole book. So to take my showing one step further, let me show how I handle one section of this book with my students: the "Sharing Information" chapter.

As we begin, I say, "Now we're going to focus on learning to write exposition, or information-based writing."

Some of the students groan quietly.

"What is this kind of writing anyway?" I ask.

"Research papers," says Eric.

"Footnotes," says Melissa.

"Textbooks," says Jon.

"Yes," I say. "But it's more than that. Listen."

I read them several selections—the ones quoted in chapter 8, an essay about penmanship from *Country Living*, a passage from *The Weekend Refinisher* by Bruce Johnson—pieces of expository writing that I genuinely enjoy. Because most college students have had years of experience writing academic prose, I have to work hard to convince them that these pieces are really exposition. We spend one class period analyzing the passages, identifying audiences and purposes, listening for voices.

"Exposition is still writing," I say. "It's just writing that has as its goal to share information. It still uses the writing process! And the first step in the process is identifying a topic about which you have information to share."

I talk to them about the things I know how to do: quilting, gardening, teaching. I read them excerpts of writing I am doing: a set of directions for making a drunkard's path sampler quilt, the handout about forcing narcissus bulbs I began chapter 8 with, a chapter from a book I wrote about evaluating children's writing. We analyze my writing for audience, purpose, and voice.

"Because you're all going to be teachers," I say, "I want you to choose a topic you might teach one day. Give me some examples."

"Astronomy," says Jack from the back row.

"Yes," I say, " but pick a portion of astronomy—a one-lesson portion. I want this to be a handout, not a textbook."

"The planets in our solar system," says Elizabeth.

" Good," I say. "What are some other topics?"

"How to write a list poem."

"The lift on an airplane wing."

"'The Secret Life of Walter Mitty.'"

"Good," I say. "Now you must know your audience. And I'm going to choose it for you—students you might teach this material."

I hear some groans. "How do we know what they know?" asks Melissa.

I smile. "You'll need to find someone to interview. I have the names of some teachers who are happy to cooperate. Let me know what level student you need, and I'll put you in touch with a classroom of about the right age. If you have personal contacts, that's fine too. But you need to interview a student before you write. What will you ask?"

"What they already know."

"What they like about the topic."

"What they hate about the topic."

We laugh. "Good," I say. "What kind of voice will you need to use?"

"Reassuring," says Jack.

"Funny would work," says Eric.

"O.K." I say. "The important thing is to match your voice to your audience and your purpose."

"You're telling us to break all the rules," complains Melissa.

"What rules?" I ask.

"Rules like 'never use you,' 'footnote everything,' 'cover the whole topic.' Rules like that."

"Well," I say, "does Bruce Johnson follow those rules? Does Richard Wormser?"

"Not exactly," says Melissa.

"We're learning to write by following examples, not by following rules," I say. "As part of your prewriting, find a piece of exposition that has been published for the age group you are targeting. Study it. Follow its example. Interview a student: find out what she knows about your topic. Decide what she needs to know and why. Then write a rough draft. We'll give the final drafts to the teachers, who will give them to their students. You'll get letters telling you what the students thought."

Jon, a future drama teacher, wrote the essay in Fig. N.1.

The tenth graders who read Jon's essay wrote him back an enthusiastic letter: they had learned how to hang a light, and they had enjoyed reading his paper. Jon was ecstatic. His audience had responded positively!

As I wrote this book, I included applications after each chapter that can be used to help future teachers work on their own writing. If you like, you may include a writing strand in your class as well. You may evaluate this portion of the class by using a portfolio approach. All of the writings up through chapter 11 may be placed in a folder in draft form and graded on completion of the assignment (pass–fail–redo). For these assignments, instruct your students to follow the

Audience and Purpose: Ninth and tenth graders in a stagecraft class. They know very little about lighting except that they have seen the results. Because the course is a technical course, they need to know how to perform simple theatrical tasks.

Voice: I set this up like a textbook. I wanted to use an instructional, informative voice that made the procedures clear, relevant, and fun to read so my students would be motivated enough to read carefully.

Hanging a Light

The house is alive with the excited chattering of the audience members when the stage manager orders the crew to dim the house lights and open the curtain. The audience is silent with awe and anticipation as the first lights come up on the actor and the set.

This is what one expects when going to see a performance at a theatre. Now consider something a bit different. . .

The house is alive with the excited chattering of the audience members when the stage manager orders the crew to dim the house lights and open the curtain. An actor walks on stage in the dark and starts speaking his lines. Someone yells, "Lights! Lights!" Another laughs. Soon the audience is talking among themselves, and the actor walks backstage, dejected.

What was different between the two opening moments? Lighting is clearly the most important aspect of technical theatre because without lights no one and nothing on stage can be seen. The arrangement and coloring of these lighting instruments is usually done by the Lighting or Technical director, but it is the students who

FIG. N.1. John's informational piece.

put them in their correct places. You are the workers who have the important job of hanging these lights. Without you, the performance will have no chance of success. It is important that you learn how to do this safely and efficiently because it is a task that will be repeated many times by you if you choose to stay in this profession. O. K. then, how do you hang a lighting instrument? There are three important steps to remember in this process: safety, attaching the light to the beam, and focusing.

The most important aspect of technological theatre is the provision for safety. These lights weigh between 15 and 30 pounds and are positioned directly over the audience and over the actors on stage. One slip of these lights could easily kill a patron or a performer or at the very least cost the theatre between $500–$1000. For this reason, we use a device called a safety chain. This is a 2 foot piece of metal chain or wire rope that is used to secure the instrument to the batten or pipe in case the main grip provided by the C-clamp fails. It is wrapped through the yoke, the metal housing holder at the base of the light, and around the pipe 2 times and clipped to itself with a metal hook. I have seen a C-clamp fail before and the safety chain did its job and stopped the light from falling. The use of a safety chain is the first step in hanging a lighting instrument.

Once the safety chain is attached, your next job is to attach the light to a batten, one of the long metal pipes positioned over the stage. This is done by fastening the C-clamp directly to the batten. The C-Clamp is a thick metal hook that is shaped like a boxy "C." It can be found at the top of the yoke (the metal swinging arm that forms the base of the light). Place the C-clamp over

FIG. N.1. continued.

the batten and tighten the nut by hand. When it gets too hard to turn any farther with your fingers, give the nut a quick ¼ or ½ turn with an adjustable wrench to tighten ¼ or ½ more of a turn. Don't tighten any more than this or the next person will never be able to loosen the light! You should then check the C-clamp for a good tight fit and re-check the safety chain for good measure. Once you have completed these two steps, the light has been placed.

Your last step in hanging a lighting instrument is the aiming process. In theatre terms, this is called focusing. Often the light is focused at an angle above the actors to more closely simulate natural lighting. The instrument is focused vertically with a black circular plastic knob located on the left side of the yoke. You can loosen and tighten this knob by hand. When the desired vertical position or angle is reached, lock the knob down again and the light will stay like that. The horizontal control is a shiny oval metal knob located at the base of the C-clamp just to the right of the nut. When this knob is loosened, the lamp will freely swing to the sides if pushed. When the desired position is found, lock this knob down by hand as well and plug in the light. Remember not to overtighten because we may need to make some quick adjustments before the show.

Well, now you know the three steps in hanging a light. *The show will begin, the actors will be seen, and the audience will be entertained. You and your crew will have the satisfaction of knowing that none of it would be possible without your knowledge of how to hang a light.*

FIG. N.1. continued.

"prewriting" and "drafting" items in the particular chapter. Then have writing groups meet to listen and respond. Have students make notes of the comments they receive from their writing group and attach those notes to their draft. All prewritings, drafts, and group notes should be kept in the writing folder.

After you have finished chapter 11, have students choose one piece to finish (or two if you would rather). Ask students to choose their favorite piece from the folder; then ask them to return to that chapter and study the "revising" suggestions and do those things to their draft, incorporating the responses from their writing group to create the revised draft. Ask them to do several experiments from the self-critique in chapter 4 and then do a second revision. Create a rubric to use to grade this finished piece, share it with the class, and give them a chance to do one more draft based on the rubric. Ask them to edit that revised draft. Have a publishing party for the class when final drafts are complete, and be ready for a fascinating variety of topics! This year in my class Eric read a persuasive letter addressed to the County Board of Supervisors opposing a plan for a multi-million-dollar baseball park. Jill shared a cookbook of cookie recipes for her children. Travis shared a tall tale about a legendary skateboarder who dug the Grand Canyon as a ramp for skating. What fun we had listening to each new piece!

For the final grade in the class you will probably want to include some points for completing the writing folder (of drafts) and for the grade from the finished piece (from your rubric). This writing strand, then, will have modeled the method of writing the book proposes, and your students will have both used writing to learn the content of the text and practiced writing for communication.

PART I
THE LEARNING-TO-WRITE PROCESS

1

Learning To Write

When my daughter was three, we took a swimming class for parents and tots. The teacher was a young man in his late teens who had won lots of swimming meets. He was much too young to have had any instruction in the art of teaching, and if the letters he sent home to parents were any indication, he had had very little instruction in the art of writing. Yet it was from this teenager named Tim that I began to learn how to teach writing.

First, Tim had us get in the shallow end of the pool. We splashed each other gently and laughed a lot. Some of the children waded right in and were splashing hilariously in no time; others, like my daughter, hung back on the steps and had to be coaxed. Once everyone was happy in the pool, Tim played water games with the children. He threw a beach ball into the pool and had the children jump in after it. He showed them how to tiptoe deeper and deeper into the water until it was just under their chins. He played tea party on the bottom with them, opening his eyes to see if theirs were open too. In short, he got the children comfortable with the water, with him as their teacher, and with each other as companions. Before he began formal swimming lessons, Tim made sure his students felt safe in the water. He established comfort.

Once the children felt safe, Tim showed them how to float on their backs. The parents hopped in the pool and helped. Following Tim's directions, I held my daughter up, first with both hands, later with one, finally with none. I'll never forget the surprised look on her face when she realized she was floating by herself. After that she learned quickly to jump in the water and flip onto her back, sure that the water would hold her up. The first lesson Tim introduced was one at which he knew the children could all succeed. He built confidence.

When floating felt almost natural, Tim introduced the children to a swimming skill that would allow them to go places in the water—he showed them how to kick their legs to do the backstroke. Imagine 15 three-year-olds swimming madly all over the pool—on their backs! In a few lessons, Tim had made these small children safe enough in the water that they could be trusted to swim where they wanted to go in the pool, even in the deep end. He developed competence.

Perhaps these stages—comfort, confidence, and competence—are simply the stages of swimming lessons. Or perhaps not. Think about learning language. Think about how children learn to talk.

3

When babies are first born (sometimes even sooner), adults begin making them comfortable with language. We talk to children long before they can understand the words we use. Then when a child starts to talk, we respond with praise. Remember the first time a child you know said, "kuh-kuh"? What happened? Somebody said, "Oh, listen! She said *kitty*!" The child did not really say *kitty*; she did not even say anything very close. She only got the first sound, but the adult did not say, "Oh, that's not right! Say *Siamese cat*."

As children receive praise, they build confidence. They take risks with new sounds. Soon they actually say *kitty*. They become confident about their ability to talk.

As children get older, adults expect "proper English." And it develops—without drills and tests and tears. Adults teach children by repeating the construction correctly. If a child says, "I brung my books home," the adult says, "You brought your books home?" Usually the child says, "Yes, I brought my books home," and that is the end of it. Competence develops.

If we look farther afield into learning theory itself, we find support for a comfort–confidence–competence progression in Abraham Maslow's work (1970). Most of us have studied Maslow's hierarchy of needs as they explain motivation: physical needs must be met before safety needs become important; safety needs must be met before love and belongingness needs become important; love before esteem; esteem before cognitive; cognitive before aesthetic; aesthetic before self-actualization. In other words, before children can deal with the cognitive challenges of writing that develop their competence, they must feel safe, they must feel as though they are part of a community of writers, and they must feel respected: they must be comfortable and confident.

The work of social-cognitive theorists like Albert Bandura (1978) tells us that people learn by watching others and that the environment in which they learn makes a difference in how quickly and how effectively they learn. Furthermore, their work tells us that accomplished performance in any area requires more than learning and retaining information. Accomplished performance requires a conviction that one can accomplish the task undertaken and a self-regulatory system of goal setting and self-evaluation. In other words, Bandura's work suggests that for learners to become accomplished, they must feel confident and they must be in charge of their own work, where they are going and how well they are doing along the way.

The work of writing teachers like Donald Graves (1983, 1994), Lucy Calkins (1983, 1994), and Anne Dyson (1989, 1993) documents many of these general learning principles in children learning to write. In both *Writing: Teachers and Children at Work* (1983) and *A Fresh Look at Writing* (1984), Graves described classrooms as writing communities: comfortable, safe communities of children and teachers working together. In *A Fresh Look at Writing*, he described developing children's competence through mini-lessons, self-evaluation, and higher expectations. In *The Art of Teaching Writing* (1994), Calkins emphasized the importance of accepting children's individual learning and encouraging ownership of their writing through revision. In *Lessons from a Child* (1983), she commented on the natural confidence first graders have about their own writing. In *Multiple Worlds of Child Writers: Friends Learning to Write* (1989) and *Social Worlds of Children Learning to Write in an Urban Primary School* (1993), Dyson let us see the importance of the writing communities children build with each other.

From our observations of children and the work of learning theorists and writing researchers, we can posit a learning-to-write process that begins with children feeling *comfortable* in the writing classroom, feeling accepted no matter what their cultural and linguistic background might be, no matter what their current level of skill with writing might be, feeling a part of a community of writers that includes their peers as well as the teacher. From the foundation of comfort we can watch children begin to build *confidence*, knowing how to write, drawing on the strengths they already possess, hearing honest praise about the strengths they have as writers. Once we see children feeling safe and sure of themselves, we see them free to pursue *competence*, free to take ownership of their writing, free to learn to evaluate what they have written themselves and make their writing better, free to take risks that push the boundaries of what they have already learned about writing.

The process of learning to write is not a series of stages or steps. Comfort and confidence grow together; competence breeds confidence and comfort. As we look at these components of the writing process one at a time, perhaps we can avoid the temptation of thinking of this learning-to-write process as a series of stages by thinking of it as a wheel like the one in Fig. 1.1.

If we label the inner rim of the wheel *comfort*, the spokes become *confidence*, and the outer rim becomes *competence*. For the wheel to move, all three are required. Without the inner rim, the wheel won't stay together. Without the spokes only the rim can move—and it won't bear much weight! Without the outer rim, the

FIG. 1.1. Comfort–confidence–competence wheel.

ride is bumpy at best. But when the wheel begins to roll, the rims and spokes blur together. The wheel is just a wheel, moving as one entity. In the same way, when children are comfortable, confident, and competent, they begin to go places as writers.

IN THE CLASSROOM

Listen for a moment to third-grade teacher Paula Nelson talk about the learning-to-write process:

> Learning to write doesn't happen in just one year. As elementary teachers we have the job of bringing children to the writing process, but that is a process in itself. We just see a little chunk of this learning because we have our students for only one year. We never know what impact it makes later.

Listen to this story about one of Becky White's sixth graders:

> I had a student two years ago—he was a great student. He wasn't exactly scholarly, but he really got into the writing process. At open house this year he gave me a little booklet he had written for me over the summer. He asked me to wait to read it until I was alone, and what he wrote let me see a longer part of the learning process. He wrote:
>
> > I've got a problem. You see, all my life I have been the kind of kid that, like, do this, okay, you know, no questions asked. But you have made me think. You have made me ask myself why. You know, like, why am I doing this? What does this mean? You've made me ask and answer these questions I've never answered before. I used to be like a robot—what are my next instructions? You've made me write these pages. You've told me to tell me my problems or to write to you about my troubles. You have told me to trust you and I sure hope I can. I have decided to write a book about my life when I am older. I was taught not to ask questions but just do it and you yourself said to follow the Nike logo, but I know now it is okay to wonder. Now I know why and how.

That's what we do for kids with writing. It goes beyond the one year we have them in our class.

CHAPTER SUMMARY

As we teach children to write, we need to think about how they learn as well as about how people write. The work of Maslow and Bandura helps us understand learning as a progression of meeting needs and an interaction between social context and individual cognition. The work of Calkins and Graves helps us observe how real children in real classrooms learn to write. By synthesizing the work of these various researchers, we can think about learning to write as a process of comfort (overcoming fear), confidence (knowing what they do right), and competence (learning how to do new things or old things better). If we think of the learning-to-write process as a wheel with an inner rim of comfort, spokes of confidence, and an outer rim of competence, we can avoid the trap of thinking of this process as a linear set of stages.

APPLICATIONS

1. Think back to some skill or art or craft at which you have become proficient. Trace your learning of this art and comment on whether or not it falls into the comfort–confidence–competence model. If it does not, comment on what model it does fall under or why you think it varies. If it does, trace your comfort, confidence, and competence process for this art.
2. Think about something you have taught a child (like swimming). Try to map out how the child learned following the comfort, confidence, competence model. Comment on similarities or differences.
3. Read Calkins' *Lessons from a Child* and map out your own writing development (Part II) as a child. If you have a child of your own or know a child well, try to map out that child's writing development.
4. Think about your writing development beyond elementary school. Comment on your present levels of comfort, confidence, and competence with writing. Trace how your teachers helped (or did not help) your writing development.

2

Establishing Comfort

"Since the beginning of the year, I've changed my feelings about writing. It has been funner than I thought."

—*A sixth grader*

THE THEORY

Comfort is safety. It is feeling relaxed. It is feeling accepted. It is belonging. Maslow's hierarchy of needs is built on the foundation of physical well-being and safety. Our classrooms need to be as physically comfortable as we can make them. Children who are hot or cold or in some other way physically uncomfortable cannot learn to write. Maslow told us that once our physical bodies are taken care of, our social natures need tending: we need to feel love and a sense of belonging. Having someone to listen to us without judging establishes comfort. Being part of a group establishes comfort. Graves (1983) showed us a classroom community that included teachers and children. Dyson (1989) showed us conversations between children about learning to write. Daiute (1993) showed us teachers providing expert input and peers providing spontaneous support. In *Mind in Society*, Vygotskii (1978) suggested that what children can do with the help of others tells us more about their mental development than does what they can do alone (zone of proximal development).

THE PRACTICE

If, as writing teachers, we take the research seriously and want to create a comfortable atmosphere that will encourage children like the one quoted at the beginning of this chapter to change their feelings about writing, we must create a community of writers in our classrooms. This community includes us and will be a group of writers who accept one another and work together. As we build this community, we must find ways of accepting children's developmental levels and helping children to accept each other. We must be sensitive to the multilingual, multicultural nature of our classrooms, and accept children for where they have come from as well as for where they are. We must also show children how to write rather than just tell them how to write.

ACCEPTING CHILDREN WHERE THEY ARE

Development is highly individual. Parents who have more than one child often marvel at the differences in the developmental paths of their offspring. One child walks without bothering to crawl first, but he does not talk until he is almost two. Another child talks at 12 months, falls silent while she's learning to walk at 18 months, and then begins to talk again at 2 years. Some children learn to ride a bike before anyone has a chance to get the training wheels on; others keep the training wheels on long after they have learned to ride.

Once children get to school, we sometimes develop lock-step expectations for their academic development. Standardized tests, for example, often report results by *grade-level*, a mathematical average of what other children across the country happen to have done when they took the test, unconnected with what we think children "ought" to be able to do after a certain amount of school. We send children to pull-out programs because they read "below level." Curriculum guides dictate particular skills that are to be mastered at particular grade levels.

Far from starting out at the same place as writers, some children come to school writing the alphabet, others come writing letters to their grandparents, and yet others come never having held a pencil. Some children like to sit quietly and write; others would rather be throwing a ball. And as students progress through school, they encounter teachers who are more or less focused on writing, further emphasizing developmental differences.

The writing samples in Figs. 2.1 through 2.4 illustrate these differences. These samples were all written on the topic "My Favorite Place." See if you can guess what grade each writer was in.

If you guessed two third-grade writers and two sixth-grade writers, you were right. Figures 2.1 and 2.3 were written by third graders. Figures 2.2 and 2.4 were written by sixth graders. Surprised? As these samples illustrate, no matter what grade-level a teacher may find herself teaching, she will face a large range of developmental differences in writing. Accepting these differences in each child is an important step toward establishing comfort with writing among students.

But what does "accepting developmental differences" mean in a classroom of 20 to 30 children? One student writes several pages; another writes only a few

> When ever I am very bored I go to my fort. It is under a tree with branch's all around it. And it smell's like pine needle's and dust to. It keeps you very warm. Sometimes I climb the tree. The tree is very green. It is over my dog's tree house.

FIG. 2.1. Clayton's favorite place.

My Favorite spot

My favorite spot is the old rail road bridge. To get to my favort spot you have to follow Walnut Canyon. The bridg is about 30 ft high. There is a whole bunch of flowers, ponds and green grass. There are frogs in the pond. We drop them off the bridg. don't worry the frogs live thrue it. Some times we tie a whole bunch of ruber bands together and they go bungy jumbhing. There are vines that hang down from the rockes. Some times the is a little stream that runs thrue it. It would be my favort spot even if there wernt frogs. It is close to lake Merry. Thare are a whole bunch of lizards but dont worry we don't do anything to them. My name is roy. My house is about 2 miles from my favorite spot.

FIG. 2.2. Michael's favorite place.

paragraphs. "Revising" for the first student will mean working on metaphors; for the second it will mean adding concrete details. And that is okay. One student loves to write and will write two essays about two favorite places. Another student needs a lot of help and will copy his dictation over in his own handwriting. So "accepting developmental differences" may first mean helping children individualize their writing assignments.

Second, "accepting developmental differences" may mean watching for times in the day when you can give students who are struggling with writing a bit of extra help. This may mean allowing an "open" work period every day when students choose what they want to work on, and when you can form small groups of children who need to review a specific skill, paragraphing, for example. It may mean taking advantage of pull-out times (like band lessons) when you have fewer students in the room to work individually. It may mean occasionally working with children before or after school. In any case, it means being on the lookout for bits and pieces of time that are ordinarily lost and using those pieces of time to work with children who need your help. In short, it means looking at each child as a writer who is developing along a unique learning curve.

In the Classroom

Paula:

A couple of years ago I had a situation where I had a little boy who was going through some emotional difficulties because his father had committed suicide not long before.

Once I was at my grandma's and my grandpa's house. I was at the reservation with my grandma, grandpa and my cousin. I was playing with my cousin Ashley D. We were playing with my grandma's cats. Me, my cousin and brother have a special place. It is a hill, it has soft sand. At my grandma's and grandpa's house the sand is not soft and it hase rocks in it. We were walking with the cats. My cousin and I let the cats walk around. We didn't know the dogs where following us. The dog's names are Domino and Little Bear. I rolled down the hill. I didn't look and see if the dogs were down there. When I was almost to the bottom of the hill. The dogs saw me and I got scared they started to run and I got to the very bottom of the hill. Then the dogs jumped on me. They were licking my ears, on my face. So I tried to cover my ears. But they bit my hand. I tried to roll but the dogs ran after me. I ran back to my grandma's house. The dog's ran back too. I got away from my grandma's dogs. When I was inside, I was out of breath. So I got a drink.

THE END!

FIG. 2.3. Adrienne's favorite place.

This little boy also had a real block when it came to writing. Although he had wonderful stories, he hated to write. Part of the problem was that he had a difficult time holding his pencil because he had first learned to hold it incorrectly.

When it was time to write in the classroom, he would fight and pout and cry. Finally he would say, "I just hate writing. I won't do it. I don't want to do it!"

I would say, "Well, I really like to write. I'm going to write your story for you, but you will have to tell me what to write." And I began to transcribe his stories for him.

We started doing several projects like that. He liked the idea of seeing his stories on paper very much. He still didn't want to write them, but he enjoyed reading them to himself, and he enjoyed reading them aloud to the class because he usually got several laughs when he did so. This process went on for about 6 months. He finished the school year with me and went on to fourth grade.

In about November of his fourth-grade year, his teacher came to me and said, "Paula, you have to see this story that Tommy wrote! He wrote it all by himself, and it's pretty amazing!"

                          My favorite Place
                           My Grandma's
   My Grandma has a brick house in Flagstaff AZ.
She was born in Monrow Louisiana where she met my
Grandpa. This couples names are Ben and Leola.
They got married at a young age. I don't know how
young, but young. Then they became the Coleman's.
The moved to Flagstaff and then came along 7 kids
4 girls and 3 boys: Ricky, Diane, Frankie,
Annette, Shirley, Benjamin and Mary. They all live
in Flagstaff except Benjamin. He and his wilf
moved to Denver. Six of the kid had kid of there
own. 14 exactly. So you can tell I have a big
family like I said my uncle Ben lives in Denver
but he and his family came down a lot. That is
one of the reasons I like her house. Because there
is always someone to say hi to. There also are
two great grand kids. So I guess no mater were
this place is it will always be my favrite because
when my grandpa died friend and family came over
and prayed. It's like when I walk in the door all
I see is memories of my grandpa. Now lets get back
to the house. It is gray brick. It's really old,
with one story and 4 rooms. I remember my uncle
always told us it was going to be a preschool and
show us were stuff would have been. Like classrooms, bathrooms, and more. I love this place and
the people in it.

FIG. 2.4. April's favorite place.

Tears came to my eyes when I read it. It was obvious that he had found his voice. He was writing about his father, and how the two of them had planted a tree in the forest. The significance of the tree planting stood for the time he shared with his father. It was a short little story about half a page long, but in it he said everything he needed to say. It was tremendous that he was able to get to the point where he could write on his own.

This experience is one of my favorites to think about when I face difficulties among my students. Sometimes the children just need you to come to where they are. As the teacher, you have to be the one that provides all of the tools for them to be able to get past whatever they have to deal with—emotional problems or attention deficit disorder or learning disabilities. When I was transcribing Tommy's stories, the rest of the class wrote their own stories. Sometimes they would read their stories to each other. Sometimes they would talk about something that happened, and some of them just wrote by themselves. Everybody seemed comfortable with my transcribing Tommy's stories.

CREATING A COMMUNITY OF WRITERS

Another step toward establishing comfort with writing is creating a community of writers. Popular folklore tells us that writers are people who work alone: the poet shivers in a lonely attic, transcribing words his muse whispers in his ear. In reality, however, most writers work with other people. Even famous writers often work together. J. R. R. Tolkein, C. S. Lewis, and Dorothy Sayers were all part of a writing group they called "The Inklings." Tolstoy wrote *War and Peace* all day; his wife copied and corrected his manuscript all night. John Keats, Percy Shelley, and Mary Shelley shared their writing—different as it was. The Bronte sisters worked in the same household, but produced very different novels. Hemingway, Gertrude Stein, and the other members of the "Lost Generation" writers congregated across the ocean in Europe. Tracy Hickman and Margaret Weiss have written best-selling science fiction novels together. The list of writers who have worked with each other goes on and on. In fact, contemporary writing theorists talk about "discourse communities" when they talk about writing, groups of people who write to and with each other.

Beyond simply accepting children where they are, as teachers we need to actively foster a community of writers in our classrooms. This means encouraging students to give and receive peer feedback; it means encouraging students to use each other as real audiences; it means fostering conversation about writing in the classroom. (A community approach, by the way, can help offset some of the developmental differences. Strong writers can offer suggestions to weak writers; weak writers can be an audience for writers who produce at a rapid rate.)

A community atmosphere can be engendered in many ways. Some teachers convene a committee of the whole to talk about individual pieces of writing. In this method one writer volunteers to read. When he is finished, the teacher guides class response, asking questions like, "What are your favorite parts of this piece?" and "What questions do you still have?" Once class discussion is finished, the teacher summarizes revision suggestions for the writer.

Some teachers organize small groups and sit with the group to help students learn to give and receive comments. In this method the teacher takes three or four students to a corner of the room and acts as a group member. The teacher comments on his or her favorite part and asks a question or two. Often he or she gently prods students who are having a difficult time articulating their response. After group members learn to function on their own, the teacher withdraws.

Other teachers organize autonomous peer groups. Autonomous peer groups can be tricky, however. Children need to learn how to work together. So be patient! It may take practice before writing groups really jell.

Younger students often work well with writing partners. You might want to try the following:

Pair students and ask them to read each other's work. Rather than putting young children in groups of three or more, we can insure that all children have a chance to respond equally when we pair them with partners. These partners can rotate, giving children more opportunity for response.

Supply colored pens and pencils. Children can express themselves by choosing particular colors they like. You may want children to color code themselves as responders or simply allow them to use the colors as they want to.

Develop a visual response system: for example, stars for parts they really like and question marks for things they'd like to know more about. The class can develop the response system together, but an important point to remember is that there shouldn't be too many different kinds of marks!

Trade papers among sets of partners to get more feedback. If different students have used different colored pens, it is easy to tell how many peers read and responded.

For older students, who may be ready to function in more sophisticated groups, try the following:

Form Permanent Writing Groups

- Assign groups of three or four members. Smaller groups are too dependent on everyone being present all the time; larger groups take too much time.
- Create mixed groups of boys and girls. It is easier for groups to get off task if they are too comfortable with each other.
- Choose group members who are neither best friends nor worst enemies. You want the group to focus on writing, not on relationships.
- Mix writing abilities in the group. If children can depend on each other for different input, the group will work better and the writing will be of higher quality.

Teach Students How to Work in Groups

- Model a writing group for your class—with other adults, with older students you had last year, with a videotape.
- Give each student a job in the group: facilitator, time-keeper, recorder.
- Rotate jobs each time the group meets.
- Ask for feedback from members of the group about the success or failure of group procedure.

Organize Group Sessions Around Reading Student Writing Aloud

Ask groups to focus on the ideas being communicated in the writing. To keep them from getting sidetracked by questions of spelling or punctuation, ask each writer to read the latest draft aloud. Ask listeners to respond to the meaning of what was read.

Give Groups a Focus

Give students instructions about how to respond to each other's writing. A good starting place is to ask listeners to tell the writer two things they liked and ask the writer two questions about things they would like to know more about. Very young children may need an adult present in the group to facilitate focus. As the year progresses and students become more adept at responding to each other's writing, you can introduce other focuses such as a writer's notebook or a grading rubric (see chap. 13).

Provide Group Members With a Writer's Notebook

The notebook can be a construction-paper folder or a more elaborate, purchased folder. It might contain a typed list of group guidelines, already-formatted response sheets, paper to write on, a section to keep drafts in, and any reference sheets you might have given in class (commonly confused words, rules for end punctuation, etc.).

Make Groups Accountable for Their Work Together

Give points for group work—the same number of points to each group member. In other words, if the group gets 10 points for its meeting, give each member of the group 10 points. Have the recorder fill out a group report form like the one in Fig. 2.5. Older students may not need a form. Recorders can simply take notes on group members' responses to each other.

Whether your students are young or older, be realistic about what writing groups can accomplish. Allow them to develop over time. Sometimes teachers get frustrated with the superficial feedback some members of writing groups give to each other. They try writing groups once or twice and then give up. Give your writing groups time to develop: children need to practice giving feedback. However, whether or not children ever learn to give insightful critiques of each other's work, writing groups are a community-building tool. They give children an audience; they give children the support of peers who have a common goal. Simply having someone to read aloud to (and hearing other people's writing) builds a community of writers. Writing groups are only secondarily revision or editing tools. No matter what the quality of the feedback, the time spent in writing groups is well worth it!

In the Classroom

Becky:

In order for kids to get more comfortable with each other before we move into writing groups, we play a get-to-know-you bingo game. There are twelve squares and instead

Writer's Name	+s	?s	Responder's Name

FIG. 2.5. Peer group report form.

of numbers each square has a question such as "What's your favorite food?" or "What's your favorite TV show?" I give them a couple of minutes to fill in their own answers. When they are ready, we put the timer on and everyone scurries around the room with only 15 minutes to find another student with the same answer as they have. No student can write their name twice on any paper. It's a slight madhouse, but the students are enjoying themselves. The bonus, of course, is that they all get more comfortable to find out they have many things in common. Putting those students in writing groups now becomes a much easier and more trusting task.

THE MULTILINGUAL, MULTICULTURAL CLASSROOM

Establishing comfort in a classroom, however, is more than a matter of accepting developmental differences among students and forming writing groups. In a multilingual, multicultural classroom, the feeling of belonging to the growing community is sometimes elusive for children who have grown up speaking a language other than English. Sometimes it is even an elusive feeling for teachers facing groups of children who speak languages the teachers do not know. In a multicultural classroom, the teacher needs to take time to observe and listen to the children. Peregoy and Boyle (1993) reminded us that this process of observation and interpretation is a gradual one for the teacher, just as the process of acquiring a second language is a gradual one for the students. Because the process of second-language acquisition is gradual, teachers also work with children who have varying degrees of fluency in English: some will be just beginning; others will be at an intermediate level; others will be so advanced that their English rivals that of their native-speaker classmates. Given this diversity, we may sometimes feel hesitant to teach writing. Hudelson (in Rigg & Enright, 1986), however, assured us that children just learning to speak English can write in English even before they become fluent speakers. Synthesizing five key findings, she told us that children's writing development in a second language often parallels writing development in a first language.

With this reassurance that writing development in a second language is not qualitatively different from writing development in a first language, let's take a look at activities we can use to encourage children who are learning English to be comfortable with writing.

Encourage Writing Accompanied by Artwork

Pictures can extend the meaning children can create with the words they write. When teachers encourage children to explain their pictures, the children can expand what they have written. Igoa (1995), Franklin (1989), and Peregoy and Boyle (1993) all commented on the importance of encouraging children who are just learning English to use pictures with their writing.

Use Dialogue Journals Between ESL Students and Native Speakers

In dialog journals children write back and forth to each other. Encouraging children to communicate with writing increases fluency and helps build community. Igoa, Franklin (cited in Rigg & Allen), and Peregoy and Boyle all suggested journals that more than one child keeps.

Take Dictation from ESL Students and Write More Complex English for Them

Because child second-language learners are often able to speak more English than they can write, dictation helps bridge the gap between spoken and written language. Igoa encouraged teachers to use language experience stories from second-language learners to help with the transition from spoken to written English.

Encourage Knowledge in the Classroom to Be a Function of the Community Rather than "Owned" by Individuals

When we set up our classrooms in ways that encourage students to learn together and help each other, a lack of facility with English is not as troublesome for individual learners. Carole Edelsky (1989) suggested that teachers design long-term projects that several students contribute to in different ways. Igoa reminded us that immigrant children have often been uprooted from their homes and need the psychological support of other children. Group work provides that support.

Language considerations are not the only sources of discomfort for students of different backgrounds. Sometimes cultural expectations confuse the way we communicate with each other. As an example, let's take an Anglo teacher working with Navajo students. Let's look at a few "normal" teacher expectations that can cause discomfort for Navajo children.

The teacher expects students to look at her to show respect.
Navajo culture teaches children to lower their eyes to show respect.

The teacher expects students to ask questions when they need help.
Navajo culture teaches children not to ask questions.

The teacher expects students to compete to answer questions correctly.
Navajo culture teaches children never to outdo a clan member.

The teacher expects students to work individually.
Navajo culture teaches teamwork.

The teacher expects students to write about topics she assigns.
Navajo culture teaches that certain subjects are taboo at certain times of the year.

When we compare the conflicts between the expectations of the teacher and the students, it is easy to imagine an uncomfortable classroom—both for the students and for the teacher! And unfortunately, most of these expectations are assumptions, unspoken rules that govern behavior. To establish a comfortable classroom for children from different traditions, teachers can do the following:

- *Consciously include models from different cultures.* Children feel comfortable when they know the teacher values variety. For example, when you study famous Americans, include *The Real McCoy: the Life of an African-American Inventor,* by Wendy Towle (1993). When you study American folktales and legends, include models like *Antelope Woman: An Apache Folktale,* by Michael Lacapa (1992). When you study rural life, include models like *Eskimo Boy: Life in an Inupiaque Eskimo Village,* by Russ Kendall (1992).
- *Watch for signs of discomfort.* Children who are comfortable are relaxed. Children who are uncomfortable are tense. Tense children may mean that something feels wrong.
- *Watch kids when they are relaxed.* Notice how students of one culture interact with each other. Pay attention when adults come into the room. Notice how children interact with adults.
- *Ask about behaviors they find confusing.* Adults and children alike are usually eager to talk about their traditions and explain the reasoning behind them.
- *Take time to get to know individual students.* Comfort can almost always be established when we get to know each other as people. When trust has been established, cultural differences seem less threatening.
- *Encourage students to tell their stories to each other.* Stories draw us together by emphasizing our similarities and acknowledging our differences. Dyson and Genishi (1994) collected essays that look at the power of stories to create classroom communities that include children from diverse backgrounds.
- *Talk about the challenges children face relating to each other.* As more and more children face the challenges of our multicultural society, writers have begun to address this issue head-on. Share some of these books with your students. *Less than Half, More than Whole,* by Kathleen and Michael Lacapa (1994), for example, tells the story of a young boy who is both Anglo and Native American.

In the Classroom

Becky:

I have one student who is an enigma to me. Three years ago he came from Mexico, and he spoke no English. It has been tremendous the strides he has taken, but he has absolutely no confidence in himself. It is really hard to break through the defense mask that he has on. He has yet to read at a publishing party.

What I have done to try to get him comfortable is work with him after school. I am there every day until 5, and I tell parents that I am there and kids can stay after school if they want to. So he stays after school and I will type his writing for him. He will write the first draft and almost every single word is misspelled because he's still learning English. But he writes it, even though it's hard for him.

A couple of weeks ago he stayed after school on his own. He had written two pages on his favorite place. He told me what he wanted me to type, and I would stop different places and say, "I'm confused by what you mean here." Then other times I would say, "If this is where you love going, can you tell me more about it?" He was very resistant, but I know he was very happy that he had his paper finished on time, but he would never admit it.

When we publish our writing in the classroom, I've suggested to this student that he pick five classmates and go outside the room to read his finished product. He declined at the first publishing party but ever since he has done what I suggested. It was successful and the class was supportive and willing to change the usual venue. He came so close to presenting to the whole class at the very last publishing party. At the last minute he balked, yet was willing to have more students listen out of the room than before. Now that's progress!

SHOW (DON'T JUST TELL)

Sometimes it is easy to forget that teachers should belong to their own classroom communities of writers. In fact, we can concentrate so hard on making our students comfortable working together, we may forget to join the group we have created! Graves (1983) and Calkins (1994) gave us portraits of classrooms in which the teachers are members of their own classroom communities. As writing teachers we can show students how to write rather than simply give them good instructions. When teachers come from behind their desks and write with their classes, they become guides in the unfamiliar territory of writing. Children become more comfortable. Let me give an example.

A couple of summers ago I went on a river trip through the Grand Canyon with my husband and a group of teachers. None of us had been down the Colorado River, and only a couple of us had ever been on a river trip. We gathered on the river bank excited, but also nervous. We had heard that there were rapids ahead, and the river was full. We looked at the big inflatable raft and at the churning water, and one person suggested that we consider going home.

Finally our guide appeared, a Hualapai Indian who had spent his entire life living and working on the Colorado River. At first we felt awkward and strained with our guide who, after all, wasn't very much like us and who knew so much more about the river than we did. However, at his invitation, we climbed into the raft together, riders on the sides and in the middle, our guide at the rudder. At first the river was calm and smooth, and our guide showed us how to balance in the raft and how to handle the oars. When we did encounter the rapids, he shouted "Watch me!" as he worked hard to keep the boat from capsizing. Once we were through the rapids, he pointed out different geological features we were seeing and told us some of the history of settlements in the Canyon. By the middle of the trip our guide had become one of us, and we were asking him questions. He was still more experienced in the ways of the river than we were, but he had brought us a long way from our novice status by both showing and telling us what to do.

The same thing can happen in a writing classroom when the teacher shows students how to write rather than just tells them. When the teacher climbs into the same rubber raft that students occupy (in other words, when the teacher writes with the students), the comfort level in the classroom goes up. Children learn to talk by imitating what they hear; they learn to walk by imitating what they see; they learn any number of things by imitating adults, so learning by imitating is comfortable for children.

Teachers have many options for showing how to write.

- *On the overhead.* Some teachers write on the overhead to show students how they themselves write. They take the same assignment the students are working on and write. Students can see a writer at work, and give input. Once students have seen how the teacher thinks of ideas and puts those ideas into sentences and paragraphs, they feel more comfortable writing themselves.
- *By writing their own assignments with the class.* Some teachers write their own assignments before they make them. At each step along the way, they share their writing with their students. Figure 2.6 is Becky White's favorite-place model she shared with her class to show them what kind of writing she wanted them to do.
- *By sharing samples of writing from previous students.* Another way teachers show students how to write is by saving good examples to use the next year. Children like to hear what their peers have written, and they often get good ideas for their own writing. If you want to use this kind of showing, however, be certain to get written permission to use student work this way—both from the student writer and the parent. A simple letter home explaining that you want to keep student writing and how you plan to use it with a place for a signature will usually be sufficient.
- *By reading published writing.* A fourth way to show children how to write is to read them examples from published writers. By reading samples from Nez (1995), for example, the teacher can illustrate voices in which she herself could never write, but that might spark enthusiasm in students.
- *By combination.* Because a classroom is a community of individuals, some combination of the different types of showing is probably the best. Different children respond to different models: some will respond to your writing, some to other children's writing, some to famous authors' writing. Whatever forms of showing you choose, examples of real writing will help children get comfortable with writing. The old saying, "One picture is worth a thousand words," is just as true about teaching writing as it is a book. Once students have a clear picture of what they are trying to do, they feel comfortable doing it themselves.

In the Classroom

Becky:

Sometimes I model storytelling with a silly game. We all sit in a circle and I start a story. I just give a character in a place doing something. Then I call on someone else in the circle to add a little bit. Then that student adds a little and calls on someone else. Sometimes it gets really funny. For example, if I start a story about a boy playing basketball on his driveway, the first student may say that the basketball flew over

THE FALLS WITH NO NAME

By the fall of 1971 I had been in school two and a half years and had changed my major four times. I quit college yet continued to work. My father encouraged me to do more than work, "Travel," he said "Go see Ruth in Australia." Ruth Dunne was an exchange student who'd lived with us when I was in high school. I did what my father suggested and several months later off I flew, destination, Australia.

After nine months of seeing many beautiful sights of Australia and New Zealand, I cashed my ticket home and joined the many young travelers trekking through Asia. Many exotic countries, incredible sights and landmarks were before me. One place in particular I have never forgotten and my trip took place over twenty years ago.

Located in the middle of Laos is a major city, Luang Prabang, bustling with activities and people. Laos, a country, is located on the continent of Asia. It's north of Thailand and west of Vietnam. While there, a Laotian guide offered to drive me and three other travelers to a nearby falls just outside the city limits. At first we were leery because the communist known as Phatet Lao had control and we feared attack. Curiosity got the better of us and away we went. I'm so glad we threw caution to the wind because this trip was never to be forgotten.

When we arrived and got out of the car we could hear the roaring water but not yet see it due to the dense jungles. Working our way forward, the roaring became thunderous to the point no one could hear the other talking. The sight that greeted our expectant eyes took our breath away. The waterfall was over one hundred feet high with three tiers crashing down furiously, drops of

FIG. 2.6. Becky's favorite place.

water racing each other to the bottom. The falls were twice as wide as their height. White, frothing water cascaded to a large pool made inviting by its crystal coolness.

To the right of the falls, a small trail leading to the top beckoned. We ventured forth and carefully climbed to the first tier as the ground was wet and slippery. That first tier opened to a wide shelf and housed a large cavern behind the falls. Since the trail could be seen on the other side we walked into the cavern. The water speeding down created a spectacular wall especially when looking out to the jungle. Now on the left of the falls, I had to work hard not to get dizzy because of how high we were and the narrow precarious trail.

The hike took about forty minutes, the deafening noise still making it impossible to speak. As we crested the top the thunderous roars immediately stopped. I felt like part of the Twilight Zone as though we had passed from one world to another. Only soft sounds of moving water, soft breezes, and workers in a distant rice paddy could be heard. The stream looked so small, so peaceful, it was hard to believe it created the waterfall not more than ten feet away from us. The jungle that had surrounded us on our hike opened here to reveal hills layered with rice paddies, their brilliant green made brighter by the sun.

Standing rooted for many minutes, my mind snapped the photo that has remained as clear as the day I was there. When I think of places that comfort and inspire me, this one tops the list. To be in a spot so perfected by God's hands where serenity and peace flow like the mighty water within these falls, there is no better place.

FIG. 2.6. continued.

the roof of the garage, and the next student may say it went into the deep dark woods behind the house, and before you know it bigfoot is playing basketball! It's fun and it gets my students over being afraid of making up their own stories.

CHAPTER SUMMARY

To help our students feel comfortable with writing we need to accept that they are individual writers at very different places in the learning-to-write process rather than expecting them to all reach some "grade-level" expectation. We also need to remember that learning a second language or coming from a different cultural background can cause discomfort. We can observe and listen to our students to begin to understand how to help them join the community of writers we are creating. We can also help our students feel comfortable by encouraging children to give and receive feedback on their writing and by showing them what writing is rather than simply describing it to them. We can model writing with our own work, with work from past students, or with published work. These attitudes and strategies can make our classrooms into comfortable places for writing: places where children are relaxed and ready to write.

APPLICATIONS

1. Remember back to a year when you did a lot of writing in school. Who in your class was the best writer? Who was the worst? Where did you fit in? Describe the differences in the writing abilities in that class.
2. What do you know about cooperative learning? Have you ever experienced it as a student? Connect what you know about cooperative learning with the concept of a classroom community of writers.
3. Remember back to a time when you found yourself in an uncomfortable culture: whether it was a family you didn't fit into, a new part of the United States, a trip abroad, or—some other situation. Comment on behaviors you found strange in the other people. Comment on how you eventually got comfortable (if you did).
4. On pages 5–6, of *Writing*, Graves (1983) said, "The teaching of writing demands the control of two crafts, teaching and writing. They can neither be avoided, nor separated. The writer who knows the craft of writing can't walk into a room and work with students unless there is some understanding of the craft of teaching. Neither can teachers who have not wrestled with writing, effectively teach the writer's craft." Do you agree? Why or why not?
5. Form a writing group with two or four of your peers. Bring a sample of a piece of writing you really like (your own or a published author's) to share with your group.

3

Building Confidence

Last year I thought writing was too hard for me, so I didn't write. This year I found out I can write. I'm not scared of it anymore.

—*A sixth grader with learning disabilities*

THE THEORY

Confidence is the feeling that says, "I can do this!" It is the feeling that says, "I may not be perfect, but I'm good enough!" It is self-esteem and the esteem of others. Training wheels on a bicycle build confidence; past successes build confidence; a professional blueprint builds confidence.

Maslow (1970) told us that learners must fill their needs for self-esteem and self-respect as well as for the esteem and respect of others before they go on to cognitive learning. Bandura (1978) told us that learners must feel self-reliant in order to learn complex concepts and perform sophisticated tasks. In *Lessons from a Child*, Calkins (1983) observed confident first graders who felt free to express themselves with written words, and third graders who had lost their confidence and learned to write with few risks.

THE PRACTICE

As a writing teacher, I must build my students' confidence before I expect competent writing. *Confidence*, however, is one of those words that is hard to define. The student quoted at the beginning of this chapter might define confidence as getting over being scared or as finding out writing was not as hard as he thought it was. As teachers, then, we need to look for ways to assure our students that writing is not scary or too hard for them.

A series of successes builds confidence. Experienced tightrope walkers, for example, head out across the rope confident they will reach the other side because they have done it many times. However, even new tightrope walkers can head confidently across the rope if there is a net below waiting to catch them if they

24

fall. As teachers, we can build confidence for beginning writers by equipping them with a writing safety net—the writing process. In 1982, Hairston observed and recorded a "paradigm shift" from product to process in teaching writing. After 15 years, the writing process is still an effective way to help students learn to write. By helping children focus on how to write rather than on simply what to write, the writing process gives children a place to start, a plan of attack.

Building on knowledge and abilities we already possess also builds confidence. Gardner's (1983) theory of multiple intelligences provides us with a roadmap for drawing on seven ways of knowing about the world to teach writing. Using this theory, we can build the confidence of students who may not be particularly adept at verbal–linguistic interactions but who are adept at other ways of knowing about the world. We help our students build on knowledge and skills they already possess to learn something new, namely how to write.

A third way of building confidence is by letting students know what they are good at, what they are doing right. Confident pianists know how to pick music to perform that shows off the skills they possess. If they can do arpeggios, they pick music full of arpeggios. If they can play counterpoint, they pick music built on counterpoint. Teachers can build this confidence in their student writers by honestly praising the good qualities of their students' writing.

TEACHING THE WRITING PROCESS

Briefly put, the writing process is a structure for how to write, a procedure to follow, a map across the wasteland of an empty piece of paper. It builds confidence in students because it gives them a place to start and suggestions about what to do along the way. It lets them know when they are finished writing. In reality, of course, there is no "writing process." The writing process is not a concrete noun like *elephant* or *table*. Each writer has his or her own writing process, and each piece of writing dictates its own process.

A quick survey of books about writing shows us many models of the writing process. Proett and Gill (1983) organized the writing process as groups of actions that happen "before students write," "while students write," and "after students write" (p. 3). Tompkins (1990) defined the writing process as a series of five stages: "prewriting," "drafting," "revising," "editing," and "publishing" (p. 10). Nelson (1995) called the writing process a "river of writing and being" (p. 35) that begins with feelings and experiences, progresses through personal journals, and finally arrives at public communication. Murray (1987) compared the writing process to the electron pathways in our brains. Root (1994) called the writing process "wordsmithery," made up of "commitment," "string-saving," "starting," "drafting," "revising," and "going public" (pp. 1–15).

Perhaps Dillard (1990) described the writing process best:

> When you write, you lay out a line of words. The line of words is a miner's pick, a woodcarver's gouge, a surgeon's probe. You wield it, and it digs a path you follow. ...You make the path boldly and follow it fearfully. You go where the path leads. At

the end of the path you find a box canyon. You hammer out reports, dispatch bulletins. The writing has changed, in your hands, and in a twinkling, from an expression of your notions to an epistemological tool. The new place interests you because it is not clear. You attend. In your humility, you lay down the words carefully, watching all the angles. Now the earlier writing looks soft and careless. Process is nothing; erase your tracks. The path is not the work. (p. 1)

If Dillard is right, if the path is not the work, if process is nothing, why do we teach children writing process at all? The answer is that the writing process is a beginning place for beginning writers. It is a safety net that builds confidence as a new writer sets out across the tightrope that is good writing.

If our survey of writing process models is accurate, if there is no one model of the writing process, what do we teach? The answer is as individual as teachers' own preferences: a particular teacher teaches whichever version of the writing process is most comfortable for both the teacher and the students. Over the years students will learn many approaches to the writing process, eventually creating their own. For our purposes, let's take a look at a common model made popular by National Writing Project sites across the country—the prewriting, drafting, revising, editing, publishing model.

Prewriting

Prewriting is intellectual work that happens before a writer begins to draft sentences and paragraphs. Accomplished writers tell us that more than half of the clock hours they spend on a piece of writing happen before they ever start writing sentences. Prewriting usually targets the following three large areas.

Choosing a Topic to Which the Writer Is Committed. At best the writing process is a lot of hard work, so it is important that writers have a topic about which they feel strongly. Helping students find topics they care about is sometimes difficult. Sometimes teachers even have to convince students that they have something they care about! But when student writers choose topics they care about, the rest of the writing process becomes a tool, a means to an end, a way to communicate important ideas.

Considering Communication Context. Before they ever write, effective writers ask themselves who would be interested in reading about their topic and why that person would be interested, in other words, who the target reader is and why that reader is reading. Sometimes student writers have only the teacher as a reader and only a grade as a purpose, so they write as if no one cares about their ideas. When students know *who* and *why*, they can choose *how*: formal or chatty, angry or conciliatory, humorous or serious, and so forth.

Collecting Ideas. Before they write, effective writers brainstorm, list, cluster, map, and draw diagrams and flow charts. They research, interview, and begin a folder of ideas. Effective writers gather an abundance of material—some from inside their heads, some from outside, that they sift through and add to as they write. (For more details about prewriting, see chaps. 7–10.)

Drafting

Drafting is the process of putting words in sentences and in paragraphs. Effective writers go through many drafts, anywhere from 2 to 200. Some writers refer to the very first attempt at sentences and paragraphs as the "zero" draft and the next drafts as rough drafts and revisions.

The Zero Draft.   Drafting usually begins with freewriting, a method of writing that focuses on speed and quantity rather than on quality. Good writers may spend several hours freewriting and wind up throwing away many of the pages and paragraphs they generate. (To freewrite, write your topic at the top of a blank sheet of paper. Then set a timer for 3–5 minutes and write continuously, never stopping or picking up your pencil. If you can't think of anything to write, simply write your name over and over until something new comes to mind. Practice freewriting, gradually increasing the time to about 15 minutes.) Somewhere in the process of the zero draft, something more interesting develops than the first idea: the topic takes a new turn, the audience changes, a new purpose emerges. So the zero draft goes in the trash, and the first draft begins.

The Rough Draft.   The rough draft is the "keeper" draft, the one that heads in the right direction, the one that is satisfying enough to the writer to stand up under the scrutiny of revision. Sometimes student writers become impatient with drafting because the rough draft seems like everything they have to say. That's when we challenge them with revising.

Revising

For good writers, revising always merges with drafting. Revising is the process that leads to drafts that are different in content or structure from one another. It is the ability to step back from a draft and ask how the ideas could be better—not just a little better, but a great deal better. It is an attitude of experimentation. When effective writers revise, they experiment with structure. They ask themselves if there is a better order to use, a better place to begin, a different place to end. They even ask if an essay might work better as a pamphlet or as a short story. They revisit communication context. They ask what might offend, confuse, or intrigue the reader. They ask if there might be another reader who would like the piece more. They look at completeness. They ask what details might be added, what ideas belong in another paper, what ideas have been left out. (For a more detailed explanation of revision, see chap. 4.)

Editing

For good writers, editing is an important task preceding publishing or sharing. Once the writer is satisfied with the ideas and structure, it is time to edit. Editing prepares the manuscript for someone else to read. When writers edit, they look at mechanics: spelling, punctuation, capitalization, paragraphing, and so on. They work to make interesting sentences, leaving out extra words, adding descriptive words, creating sentence variety. (For a more detailed explanation of editing, see chap. 5.)

Publishing and Sharing

Sharing is the whole reason for writing. Without it the writing process is nothing more than a dull school exercise. Sharing lets someone important read or hear what the writer has written. It is a time for celebrating the completion of important intellectual work. Teachers sometimes provide ways for their students to share through publishing parties, complete with treats. Sometimes student writers invite their parents to hear them read at school. Sometimes they mail their writing to outside readers. Sometimes they publish in school newspapers or even city newspapers. Some businesses display student work. Some school districts have contests for writing. Some classes make books for their school library. Always they give the writing to the chosen reader.

The Recursive Process

Even though we have looked at the parts of the writing process as though they were a linear series of steps, in reality the writing process is recursive: it goes forward and then back, skipping a step here and there, returning to where it began, leaping forward beyond where it ought to be, looping back on itself. A diagram of this model of the writing process might look like Fig. 3.1. Or it might look more like the stew pot in Fig. 3.2.

Whatever kind of diagram we choose to draw, it is important to remember that the writing process is not a series of rigid steps. Good writers don't prewrite on Monday, draft on Tuesday, revise on Wednesday, edit on Thursday, and share on Friday. Instead they engage in all the activities of writing at appropriate times.

FIG. 3.1. A model of the writing process.

FIG. 3.2. Another model of the writing process.

Sometimes they revise prewrites; sometimes they prewrite revisions; sometimes they share drafts; sometimes they revise finished pieces.

Furthermore, the writing process does not look the same in every context. The expository process is different from the literary process. The writing process in second grade is different than it is in sixth grade or in college. In the primary grades, the writing process begins with oral language, telling stories to each other before writing or retelling other peoples' stories—folktales or books—before making up personal stories. The whole class may listen to a story and then retell it together. After listening to 20 or more stories, students may choose a favorite to retell. This oral component of the writing process may last a month or more. In different contexts, different ingredients of the process may be more or less important. Emergent writers, for example, may focus on drafting, while developing writers may focus first on prewriting, then on revision. As we look closely at reasons to write, we look at adapted versions of the writing process.

In the Classroom

Bernadette (2nd grade teacher):

> I prepare for writing with my children by telling them stories. At first the stories are all oral. I like to start by having them listen because it helps develop their imagination.

Sensory pictures are brought to their minds through oral imagery. TV and even books with pictures tend to take away our imagination. Telling the stories orally causes children to imagine and remember every detail. Gradually we work into reading. I like to do author studies for writing models, so we may read a lot of books by Tommy dePaula. For writer models I use dePaula because he *retells* stories and legends that were told orally to him. Grimm fairy tales are stories retold by the Grimm brothers. Then I have the children pick their favorite story and retell it orally first and then in writing.

I used to have a chart on my wall with all the stages of the writing process, but I don't do that anymore. Now we just write. For prewriting I tell them, "I'm in the mood to write and I'd like to help you get into the mood to write." After we prepare, I tell them, "That was called prewriting."

Becky (6th grade teacher):

The writing process is just a starting point. Sometimes a student will do all of the parts of the writing process and then everything changes. When we were doing our favorite place assignment, I had one student who wrote her whole paper on a trip to California. She did her prewriting and her drafts and her revising. Then we had Thanksgiving. We were going to edit, do our final drafts, and publish after we came back. This student's parents took her to Hawaii for Thanksgiving, and when she came back she did her final draft on Hawaii because she had a new favorite place! And that's fine. The writing process is just to get you started writing. I accepted her prewriting and drafts on California and told the children that that happens to writers all the time. If children start something and then want to change, that's okay.

Paula (3rd grade teacher):

When we finish a paper, we have a publishing party. The children read their stories, and then their peers write a little "love note" to tell what they liked in the stories they heard. The delight on their faces shows how it makes them feel to share their writing with an audience that is respectful. This year, I nervously anticipated our first publishing party because I have a class that chatters constantly. I worried that they wouldn't be respectful listeners. But it was absolutely heartwarming. For 2½ hours they were quiet and respectful. They listened to each other's stories. The children learn to feel good about their writing when they realize that their peers are interested in hearing their stories.

BUILDING CONFIDENCE BY USING MULTIPLE INTELLIGENCES

Students are all different. Even though abilities with schoolwork differ, everybody is good at something! In the 1980s, a Harvard researcher named Howard Gardner wrote a book called *Frames of Mind* (1983) that offered some insight into how and why we are all different. Gardner described *intelligence* not as a single ability but as a constellation of seven abilities: capacities that all people possess unless they have suffered brain damage. His work tells us that although all people have these seven capacities, individuals develop one or more of these intelligences to varying degrees depending on talent, personal motivation, and environmental nurturing. He went on to tell us that unless we have suffered brain damage, all of us can learn to use all of the intelligences competently. Through his experiments, he isolated seven intelligences: verbal/linguistic, musical/rhythmical, logical/mathe-matical, body/kinesthetic, visual/spatial, interpersonal, and intrapersonal. Accord-ing to Gardner, these intelligences work together, and many tasks that we do depend on more than one intelligence. Riding a bicycle to the store for a soda, for example, depends on body/kinesthetic intelligence for balance, on visual/spatial intelligence for finding the way, on verbal/linguistic, logical/mathematical, and interpersonal for purchasing the soda.

Although Gardner was a researcher and theorist, educators like Armstrong (1994) have seen ways that Multiple Intelligence (MI) theory applies to the classroom. Because our students come to us with these intelligences developed to varying degrees, we can draw on their strengths to aid new learning. We can also help them develop intelligences they have not used much by encouraging them to participate in new activities. When we draw on multiple intelligences to teach writing, we allow our students to build on their already developed intelligences to learn: some students in one lesson, others in another. Thus, we put all our students on sure ground at some time or another, building their confidence in writing by connecting it to capacities they already feel good about. At the same time, by offering a variety of ways of learning, we help our students develop intelligences they may not have had nurtured before. Of course, different intelli-gences support different kinds of learning more or less easily. The idea is not to include every intelligence in every lesson, but to draw on a variety of intelligences throughout the learning process.

Verbal/Linguistic Intelligence

This intelligence is the capacity for language. Children who have been talked to, listened to, read to, and encouraged to write will have developed this intelligence. Children who are confident with their verbal/linguistic abilities will be avid readers, writers, and talkers. They love to tell jokes and play word games. Because writing is a verbal ability, it depends heavily on verbal/linguistic intelligence. Most of our traditional ways of teaching draw on verbal/linguistic intelligence. We can extend traditional ways of teaching writing through verbal/linguistic intelligence by

- doing oral activities before writing—storytelling, discussing, interviewing;
- reading aloud—both models and student writing;
- reading to get ideas for writing;
- drawing literature study and writing together.

Musical/Rhythmical Intelligence

This intelligence is the capacity to enjoy and create music. It includes perception of melody, beat, and tone. Children who have developed this intelligence will tap their feet to music, make up their own tunes, and possibly be able to play a musical instrument. We can draw on musical/rhythmical intelligence to teach writing by

- reciting poetry aloud and clapping to accentuate the rhythm of the words;
- singing folk songs and having students write new verses;
- creating readers' theater with writing;
- listening to raps and having students write their own.

Logical/Mathematical Intelligence

This intelligence is the capacity to use numbers and to reason well. Children who have developed this intelligence ask questions constantly. They want to know *why*. They like number games, and they enjoy problem solving. Lists and outlines appeal to them. We can draw on this intelligence to teach writing by

- teaching outlining;
- looking at the writing process as a logical progression of tasks;
- offering cause-effect scenarios as prompts for writing;
- teaching grammar rules and sentence diagramming.

Body/Kinesthetic Intelligence

This intelligence is the capacity to use the body effectively. It includes athletic, expressive, and manipulative abilities. Children who have developed this intelligence enjoy sports. They may be good with tools, and they may express themselves eloquently through gestures and facial expressions. We can draw on this intelligence to teach writing by

- acting out stories before writing them;
- writing plays that include stage directions;
- playing charades with vocabulary words;
- encouraging students to do projects to accompany their writing.

Visual/Spatial Intelligence

This intelligence is the capacity to perceive the visual–spatial world accurately and change that world in some way. It includes the ability to guide and hunt as well as the ability to design and build. Children who have developed this intelligence are sensitive to color and line. They may be able to draw and orient themselves in space quite accurately. They can often visualize actions in their heads. We can draw on this intelligence to teach writing by

- using diagrams to teach writing concepts: triangles, clusters, webs, maps;
- using pictures as prompts for writing;
- encouraging students to include drawings and pictures with their writing;
- using color coding for mechanical errors;
- doing imagination exercises before writing.

Interpersonal Intelligence

This intelligence is the capacity for interacting with other people. It includes the ability to perceive another person's moods and motivations. It includes responding to other people's feelings and reading body language. Children who have developed this intelligence are leaders. They often enjoy working in groups and joining clubs. They are the ones who notice when someone is not feeling well and try to help. We can draw on this intelligence to teach writing by

- doing collaborative writing projects;
- using peer groups for brainstorming, revising, and editing;
- connecting writing activities to the community outside of school;
- inviting guests to the classroom to tell stories or to talk about writing.

Intrapersonal Intelligence

This intelligence is the capacity to know oneself. It includes the ability to know one's own strengths and weaknesses as well as awareness of one's own moods and internal states. It includes self-discipline and self-esteem. Children who have developed this intelligence are sometimes introspective. They enjoy time alone and are often quite goal-oriented. We can draw on intrapersonal intelligence to teach writing by

- having students keep personal journals;
- having students choose their best pieces for portfolios;
- allowing time for self-reflection about writing;
- using life maps and personal topics as springboards for writing.

When we teach writing by drawing on all the intelligences, our instruction becomes richer and more varied, just as the writing our students generate becomes richer and more varied. Furthermore, we include all students in learning to write, not just the students who have already developed their verbal/linguistic intelligence.

In the Classroom

Paula:

> I often use music in my classroom. I have a sister who writes melodies for songs, and sometimes we write words for these melodies. We listen to a lot of songs and learn to sing them as a class. We pick a favorite song and make up our own verses to it. Then we talk about the meanings of the words and write a song of our own together.

Becky:

> I usually start out writing with an activity that has a lot of prewriting emphasis: something where we just make stuff, something the students can manipulate with

their hands. It's sort of like playing with toys. That gives them lots of ideas and they can start with some journal activities and write something short. Then they share it, and I tell them it's good. Because it is. Another way I start sometimes is with poetry—poetry is a great medium because it is short and there are patterns they can follow, rhythms they can hear. Children like to share their poetry, and it is quick. They write good poems and they tell each other they're good. They start to feel good about their writing.

BUILDING CONFIDENCE THROUGH HONEST PRAISE

Sometimes mistakes seem to leap out at us as teachers. There is a billboard I pass on my way to school every morning that has an apostrophe in the wrong place. I see that misplaced apostrophe every day, but I couldn't tell you what the billboard is advertising. Even my training as a teacher pushes me to see mistakes in student writing. Years ago when I was first a teaching assistant in graduate school, I was told that "five grammatical errors equals an *F*." Whenever papers were handed in, I would first count the errors; then I'd go back and read the paper if there were fewer than five errors. Although this example may seem extreme, I think the mentality that fostered it lingers. In order to build confidence in our students, we must stop focusing on errors and start pointing out the positives, the things children are doing *right*. However, because of the way many of us were taught to write, finding the good points may be trickier than it sounds. We may have to train ourselves to overlook errors for a while and concentrate on what is going right: an interesting idea, a clear voice, a vivid description, effective paragraphing. And then, of course, we must let the students know we noticed!

Sometimes we fight the error mentality by praising everything that children write. But confidence is built on accurate self-knowledge: knowing where your strengths actually lie. As teachers, we need to train ourselves to see the truly good things about our students' writing. One student may have interesting ideas; another may have a clear sense of audience; a third may use logical organization; another may have clear handwriting; another may have the courage to try an assignment that seems beyond him or her. Honest praise is affirmation and response. It lets the student know his or her writing did what he or she intended. If a student meant to make me laugh and I laugh, that is honest praise.

To build students' confidence with honest praise:

- *Train yourself to know what makes good writing.* In order to know what students are doing right, we must know what goes into a piece of writing—what students must do besides spell words correctly. Knowing what makes a good piece of writing may take years to really learn. As you go through this book, look at the information two ways: as information you might be learning for yourself and as characteristics of good writing you might be able to spot in your students' work. (Take process, for example. Some students are good at gathering ideas for prewriting; others are good at responding to other people's writing; others are good at other things.)

- *Train yourself to see the good things first.* Often because of the way we were taught, we see the errors first. One way to break this habit is to work with it instead of against it. Let yourself see the errors and shake your head sadly, but do not write them down. With the mourning for the errors out of the way, concentrate on what is right about the piece of writing. Then record those things. Eventually you will learn to see the good things first.
- *Train yourself to tell students when you see them doing something right.* As you work with your students, looking over their shoulders, reading their drafts, helping them collect ideas, teach yourself to verbalize praise when you see something going right. Too often we focus on helping children do something better. That is an important part of teaching, but it does not build confidence. So as you work to build your students' confidence, give them immediate positive feedback.
- *Train yourself to allow your students to write what they have to say.* As adults it is sometimes hard not to rewrite children's pieces for them. Sometimes when we read a child's draft, we get an idea of a piece we would like to see written; however, that may be the piece we would write rather than the piece the student is writing. It does not build confidence to take the piece away and make it our own. Children must write their own pieces. (For more information about student ownership of writing, see chap. 4.)

In the Classroom

Becky:

> It's important that children feel they have control of their own writing, not that it's dictated to them what to write and how to write it. When they feel like it's their own they will make more of an effort to create something that is worthwhile and that they can be proud of. I bite my tongue. I try not to guide their writing. I try not to direct it from my standpoint as a teacher. Instead I ask continuous questions and accept their answers.

CHILDREN BUILDING CONFIDENCE WITH WRITING

Take a look at Figs. 3.3 through 3.7. They show a sixth grader using the writing process to write a pourquoi tale, a story intended to explain some natural phenomenon. The story began by the class reading several pourquoi tales together. Next the teacher asked her students to choose an animal they knew a lot about and write a pourquoi tale about some characteristic of that animal. Patricia chose a pig. She filled out the prewriting frame, wrote a draft, and then read her draft to her writing group for their comments. She wrote a second draft, which the teacher edited; last she wrote her final draft.

When the teacher made positive comments to Patricia they included: "Good setting: I feel like I've been to the farm!"; "Good description of Bibly"; "I laughed at the joke just like Bibly did!"

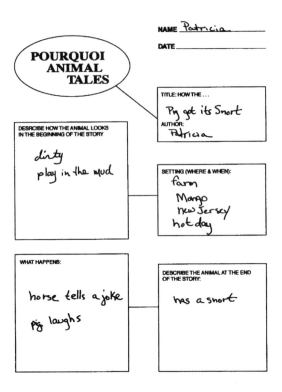

FIG. 3.3. Prewriting for pourquoi tale.

How the pig got its snort

One hot summer day there was this farm in New Jersey. The farm was in this little town called Mongo. On the farm their was all different kinds of animals. My favorite animal was the baby chicks. But we got to talk about the pig. The pig's name was bibly. bibly was short fat and stubby and the most of all dirty. Bibly loved to play in the mud, we had to give him buttermilk baths almost everyday. One time the pig was taking a mud bath when this horse came up to him and asked why he didn't talk. the pig just shook his head. The horse said why don't you say neigh like me. bibly tried it but didn't like that noise. So the pig started laughing and accidently put a snort in his laugh. the pig said hey I like that noise so the pig snorted again and that's how the pigs snort came to be.

FIG. 3.4. Rough draft.

REVISION NOTES AND COMMENTS   **NAME** Patricia

SUBJECT OF PAPER: Pourquoi tale

WRITE TWO SPECIFIC REASONS YOU LIKED THIS PAPER:

I like the name Bibly.
I like the horse.

WRITE TWO QUESTIONS ABOUT THIS PAPER:

Why did the pig laugh?
Did the pig want a noise?

NAME OF PERSON REVISING: Group 2

DATE:

FIG. 3.5. Revision group comments.

COMFORT AND CONFIDENCE: THE WHEEL BEGINS TO ROLL

Of course, comfort and confidence are not mutually exclusive categories. Writers who are comfortable with writing become more confident. And writers who are confident relax, becoming comfortable. Knowing a writing process helps students feel comfortable; peer groups build confidence. Knowing that the teacher notices what they are doing right makes students feel comfortable; being accepted makes them confident. As comfort and confidence grow together, the writing wheel begins to roll.

CHAPTER SUMMARY

To write well, students need to have confidence in their abilities as writers. As teachers we can build that confidence by giving them a safety net, a writing process that shows them how to write—where to begin, what to do next, and so forth. A second way to build confidence is to help children learn to write by drawing on

```
            How the pig got its Snort
  One hot summer day there was this farm in New
Jersey. The farm was in this little town called
Mongo. On the farm there were all different kinds
of animals. My favorite was the baby chicks. But
we got to talk about the pig. The pig's name was
Bibly. Bibly was a short, fat, and stubby. Most
of all dirty. Bibly loved to play in the mud. You
had to give him buttermilk bath's everyday.
  One time the pig was taking a mud bath when this
horse came up to him and the horse said, "what's
wrong," the pig replied, "well you see I want to
make a certain noise like you do." The horse said,
"try neigh." The pig said "I don't like that
noise." The horse said "oh Bibly while you think
of a noise can I tell you a joke." "Okay" said
Bibly. "Okay" said the horse then he said "knock
knock" Bibly said "who's there?" The horse said
"pig," Bibly said "pig who," the horse said "pig
up your feet or you'll trip." The pig just started
to laugh and laugh and the pig accidently snorted
when he laughed. Bibly said "hey I like that
noise." So thats how the pig got his snort.
```

FIG. 3.6. Revised draft.

other strengths they have developed—multiple intelligences. As teachers, when we encourage students to draw on other ways of knowing about the world than simply verbal/linguistic ways, we tie writing into other intelligences students have developed. Third, confidence is built on knowing what we are doing right. As teachers we can help students build confidence by training ourselves to spot the things that are going right with writing and then telling our students about those things. Honest praise builds confidence.

APPLICATIONS

1. Compare your own writing process to the writing process model discussed in this chapter. Think back to the last important piece of writing you did. Did you prewrite? If so, when? How did you draft? Did you revise? If so, how? Of what did your publishing consist?

How the Pig Got Its Snort

One hot summer day there was a farm in New Jersey. The farm was in a little town called Mongo. On the farm there were all different kinds of animals. My favorite were the baby chicks. But we got to talk about the pig. The pig's name was Bibly. Bibly was short, fat, and stubby and most of all dirty. Bibly loved to play in the mud. You had to give him buttermilk bath's everyday.

One time the pig was taking a mud bath when this horse came up to him and the horse said, "what's wrong?" The pig replied, "well, you see I want to make a certain noise like you do." The horse said, "try neigh." The pig said "I don't like that noise." The horse said "Oh Bibly. While you think of a noise can I tell you a joke?" "Okay," said Bibly. "Okay," said the horse. Then he said, "Knock, knock." Bibly said, "Who's there?" The horse said, "Pig up your feet or you'll trip." The pig just started to laugh and laugh and the pig accidentally snorted when he laughed. Bibly said, "hey I like that noise." So that's how the pig got his snort.

FIG. 3.7. Final draft.

2. Write your own "My Favorite Place" (chap. 2). Follow the writing process discussed in this chapter.
3. Look back at the four "My Favorite Place" samples in the previous chapter. Pick the one you think is the worst. Find three positive things you could say about that piece.
4. Take the informal multiple intelligences self-assessment below. Comment on how your most well-developed intelligences can be used to support your writing. Comment on which intelligences you would find it easiest to teach with. Comment on which intelligences you might need to develop more in order to help your students.

Howard Gardner's Multiple Intelligences
An Informal Self-Assessment

Following are 10 descriptors for each of Howard Gardner's seven intelligences. Circle the number that best matches how you react to each descriptor. When you

have finished all 10 descriptors for one intelligence, add up your total points in
that category. Then go on to the next intelligence.

Verbal/Linguistic Intelligence

	not at all		some		very much
I enjoy working crossword puzzles.	1	2	3	4	5
I like puns.	1	2	3	4	5
I'm good at telling stories.	1	2	3	4	5
I love to write.	1	2	3	4	5
I love to read.	1	2	3	4	5
I would like to be an editor.	1	2	3	4	5
I would like to be a reporter.	1	2	3	4	5
I would like to be a poet.	1	2	3	4	5
I would like to be a TV interviewer.	1	2	3	4	5
I would like to be a civic leader.	1	2	3	4	5

TOTAL POINTS FOR VERBAL/LINGUISTIC INTELLIGENCE =

Visual/Spatial Intelligence

I love to draw.	1	2	3	4	5
I think in pictures.	1	2	3	4	5
I love to read maps.	1	2	3	4	5
I doodle.	1	2	3	4	5
I daydream.	1	2	3	4	5
I would like to be a painter.	1	2	3	4	5
I would like to be a surgeon.	1	2	3	4	5
I would like to be an interior designer.	1	2	3	4	5
I would like to be an engineer.	1	2	3	4	5
I would like to be an architect.	1	2	3	4	5

TOTAL POINTS FOR VISUAL/SPATIAL INTELLIGENCE =

Logical/Mathematical Intelligence

I like to solve problems.	1	2	3	4	5
I love computers.	1	2	3	4	5
I ask lots of questions.	1	2	3	4	5
I enjoy making calculations.	1	2	3	4	5
I want things to be orderly.	1	2	3	4	5
I would like to be a researcher.	1	2	3	4	5
I would like to be an accountant.	1	2	3	4	5
I would like to be an efficiency expert.	1	2	3	4	5
I would like to be a computer programmer.	1	2	3	4	5
I would like to be an auditor.	1	2	3	4	5

TOTAL POINTS FOR LOGICAL/MATHEMATICAL INTELLIGENCE =

	not at all		some		very much

Musical/Rhythmical Intelligence

	not at all		some		very much
I love to sing.	1	2	3	4	5
I play an instrument.	1	2	3	4	5
I make up my own tunes.	1	2	3	4	5
I pay attention to background music.	1	2	3	4	5
I hear the rhythm in language.	1	2	3	4	5
I would like to be a singer.	1	2	3	4	5
I would like to be a dancer.	1	2	3	4	5
I would like to be a music critic.	1	2	3	4	5
I would like to be a storyteller.	1	2	3	4	5
I would like to be a disc jockey.	1	2	3	4	5

TOTAL POINTS FOR MUSICAL/RHYTHMICAL INTELLIGENCE =

Body/Kinesthetic Intelligence

	not at all		some		very much
I like to play sports.	1	2	3	4	5
I am good with tools.	1	2	3	4	5
I can mimic what I see.	1	2	3	4	5
I invent my own tools.	1	2	3	4	5
I do crafts.	1	2	3	4	5
I would like to be a dancer.	1	2	3	4	5
I would like to be a mime.	1	2	3	4	5
I would like to be a professional athlete.	1	2	3	4	5
I would like to be a builder.	1	2	3	4	5
I would like to be an actor.	1	2	3	4	5

TOTAL POINTS FOR BODY/KINESTHETIC INTELLIGENCE =

Interpersonal Intelligence

	not at all		some		very much
I like to collaborate on projects.	1	2	3	4	5
I have a lot of empathy for others.	1	2	3	4	5
I am a good listener.	1	2	3	4	5
I am a good leader.	1	2	3	4	5
I am a good arbitrator.	1	2	3	4	5
I would like to be a counselor.	1	2	3	4	5
I would like to be a salesperson.	1	2	3	4	5
I would like to be a social worker.	1	2	3	4	5
I would like to be a family doctor.	1	2	3	4	5
I would like to be a teacher.	1	2	3	4	5

TOTAL POINTS FOR INTERPERSONAL INTELLIGENCE =

Intrapersonal Intelligence

	not at all		some		very much
I have a lot of self-insight.	1	2	3	4	5
I like to work alone.	1	2	3	4	5

	not at all		some		very much
I have high expectations for myself.	1	2	3	4	5
I daydream.	1	2	3	4	5
I am goal oriented.	1	2	3	4	5
I would like to be an author.	1	2	3	4	5
I would like to be a researcher.	1	2	3	4	5
I would like to be a psychologist.	1	2	3	4	5
I would like to be a philosopher.	1	2	3	4	5
I would like to be an explorer.	1	2	3	4	5

TOTAL POINTS FOR INTRAPERSONAL INTELLIGENCE =

A Personal Profile

Look back at your total points in each intelligence. List your two highest scores; list your two lowest scores.

The two intelligences I have developed the most are (highest scores):

The two intelligences I have developed the least are (lowest scores):

4

Developing Competence

When I first came to Mrs. White's class I thought it was really weird with all the
writing going on. But now I really care about what I write.

—A sixth grader

THE THEORY

Competence, says the *American Heritage Dictionary* (Morris, 1976), is "the state or
quality of being capable, adequate for the purpose, or sufficient." Competent
drivers are people who can safely and efficiently use cars to go where they want
to go. Competent cooks are people who can combine a variety of ingredients to
create appealing, nutritious meals. Competent animal trainers are people who can
teach animals to behave in appropriate ways. Competent writers are people who
use writing as a tool to communicate the meaning they intend.

Competence, then, is a goal of learning. Maslow (1970) talked about
self-actualization (the development of human potential) as the goal of learning.
For Maslow, self-actualization is the process of people exploring who they are
as individuals and developing their unique potentials. Bandura (1978) talked
about complex performance as the goal of learning, and he told us that a
requirement for accomplished performance is a self-regulatory system that
includes goal setting and self-evaluation. Graves (1994) talked about giving
child writers responsibilty for their own writing. McGilly (1994) talked about
active, self-directed, intentional learners. Calkins (1994) talked about "living
the writerly life" (p. 21).

Whatever we call *competence*, for writing it means children feeling ownership of
their own work. It means children writing for their own purposes to readers they
choose. It means children being able to evaluate their own writing and improve
it themselves. Competence, then, is not being able to check off a list of behaviors
a child has accomplished; rather it is a constantly growing set of abilities that
enables appropriate communication through writing to grow as the child writer
grows. Competence is children caring about what they write.

THE PRACTICE

Competence builds on the foundations of comfort and confidence. Student writers take ownership of their writing when they feel sure enough of themselves to begin to use writing to meet their own individual goals. As teachers we can help our students become competent writers by setting up instructional situations that allow children to make decisions about what they want to write, to whom they want to write, why they want to write, and how they want to write. In other words, we encourage children to think of writing as a personal communication tool rather than as an isolated skill they must acquire in school.

When children make the choices of personal communication, they can begin to evaluate what they have written themselves. They can learn to ask themselves whether what they have written will communicate what they intended, or if it requires further revision. As competence develops, children learn new ways of revising their writing to bring it ever closer to their intentions. They can learn to evaluate their own work against their own standards or the standards of others. They can stretch the meaning of *writing community* beyond support and encouragement to teaching each other.

MAKING COMMUNICATION CHOICES

Writers own their work when writing is a tool they use to communicate a message they consider important to a reader they consider important. To begin thinking about student ownership of writing, then, we need to think about the communication triangle. We might draw it as shown in Fig. 4.1. Communication, then, is the interaction among a speaker, the purpose, and the listener. We can draw a writing triangle in the same way. It might look like Fig. 4.2. When children choose their own topics, readers, and purposes, they begin to use writing as a tool, as a means to an end. They begin to own their writing. They begin to become competent.

Let's take as an example: the much maligned "My Summer Vacation" topic. Traditionally this topic has been assigned by teachers to ask students to summarize what happened to them over the 3-month absence from school. If we draw a writing triangle for this traditional piece of writing, it will look like Fig. 4.3. In this communication context, the teacher owns the writing: the teacher assigns the

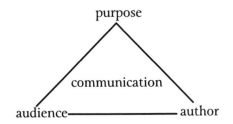

FIG. 4.1. Communication triangle.

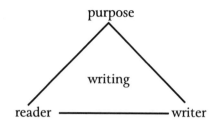

FIG. 4.2. Writing/communication triangle.

topic for his or her purpose and tells the students what content should be included (a summary of a particular 3-month period).

However, the problem is not in the topic itself. It is in the ownership of the writing. Traditionally teachers have owned this topic. Let's look at what happens to the topic when students own their writing. In this situation, the teacher encourages students to adapt the topic to their own interests. Adaptations might include *The Best Part of My Summer Vacation*, *My Dream Vacation*, *The Best Summer Vacation I Ever Had*, even a satire or spoof of the topic. Once students have found some way of interacting with the topic that is important or fun to them, they can choose real readers and real purposes. For Ashanique, *The Best Part of My Summer Vacation* becomes a thank-you note to her friends in California. For David, *My Dream Vacation* becomes a wish-letter to his grandparents for a future visit to their farm. For Roberto, *The Best Summer Vacation I Ever Had* becomes a memory piece to share with his older brother. For Mikki, *My Summer Vacation* becomes a horror story spoof to read to her best friend for a good laugh.

Whatever the specific choices they make, students take ownership of the piece of writing by adapting each corner of the triangle for themselves as in Fig. 4.4. The piece of writing becomes a tool for communication with someone important. Competence begins to develop.

REVISION: THE SELF-CRITIQUE

Once children begin to care about what they write, revision becomes necessary to their work. However, revision is very likely the most difficult part of writing,

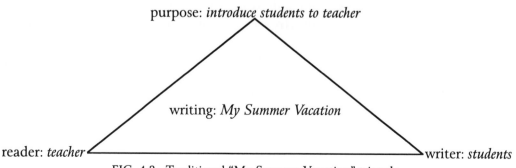

FIG. 4.3. Traditional "My Summer Vacation" triangle.

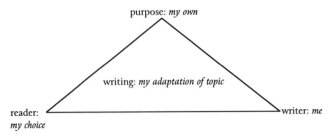

FIG. 4.4. Student ownership triangle.

for it calls writers to "re-see" their work. It calls us to another *vision* of the first attempts we have made at communication. Revision requires higher-order thinking skills like synthesis, evaluation, and application. It requires stepping back from the excitement of discovering we have something to say, to an objective look at how we have said it. In his book *After THE END*, writer Barry Lane (1993) contended that revision is more than a single stage of writing: "From my work as a writer I know that revision is more than a stage in a four-, five-, or seven-step process; it is the source of the entire process" (p. 5). In fact, he joked that his seven-step writing process looks like this: "1. Revise 2. Revise 3. Revise 4. Revise 5. Revise 6. Revise 7. Revise" (p. 2). When writers are ready for this objective look, they can get input from three sources: an expert editor, peer response, or self-critique.

In writing classrooms, teachers function as the expert editor. We can usually look at a student draft and make concrete suggestions for revision. But if writing competence is grounded in student ownership of writing, expert editor input is tricky, requiring the teacher to see an individual student's writing through that child's eyes rather than through his or her own. Teachers who have developed this skill ask their students questions that help students clarify their own thoughts and ideas rather than make suggestions for "improvement." By the same token, peer response for revision can be tricky in an elementary classroom. Too often, peer editors become overly enthusiastic about another child's writing, overwhelming the original idea with a new one of their own. (For this reason, I see peer response in the elementary classroom as largely a tool that builds community and comfort rather than a tool for revision. See chap. 3.) The self-critique, then, becomes a very important tool for helping beginning writers develop competence with their writing.

Sometimes we shy away from self-critique for young students because "do-overs" seem tedious and boring. (In fact, revision may not be appropriate for emergent writers, for whom competence means enthusiasm for learning to write.) Developing writers, however, can be challenged by the self-critique when we help them think of it as a series of experiments that might make their writing more effective. (For an in-depth look at revision as experiment, see *Deep Revision* by Meredith Sue Willis [1993].) When we help children think of themselves as scientists who need a first draft to experiment on, we help them begin to develop objectivity about their own writing. They find out that whether they like the first draft or not does not matter. Scientists do not worry about whether they like the object they are experimenting with; they are simply curious. They ask questions and try new things. Student writers can adapt this scientific curiosity to help them revise.

Seven experiments you can use to help children develop curiosity about their own writing follow. Introduce them one at a time but help students see that eventually they might consider their drafts from all of these angles.

Experiment #1 Put Yourself in Your Reader's Shoes

No matter how hard we try to write for a target reader, the real person we usually write for at the beginning is ourselves or our teacher.

Ask Questions

1. Who is a real person who might want to read what you are writing? _____. (Your teacher is not a valid response because he or she gets paid to read your writing. Think of someone else.)
2. How would _____ feel after reading this writing: Excited, angry, bored, sad, …?
3. What questions do you think _____ would ask you?
4. Which part would _____ like best? like least?

Take Action!

1. Answer the foregoing questions, filling in the blanks with your reader's name.
2. Make a list of changes you could make that would make your reader like your writing more.
3. Try a new reader. Who is someone else who might want to read this piece? What changes would you make for that reader?

Experiment #2 Take Control of Your Writing

When you've got a name for your reader, it is easier to decide what your purpose is—why you want to write this piece in the first place.

Ask Questions

1. Do you want _____ to laugh? to cry? to think? to …?
2. Are you trying to teach _____ something? If so, what?
3. Are you just trying to share something about your life with _____? If so, why?
4. Do you want to convince _____ to think or do something differently? If so, why?

Take Action!

1. Reread your draft, imagining that you are _____. Will this writing do what you want it to? If so, how? If not, why not? Is it doing something else? Is that okay?

2. Make a list of changes you might want to make.

Experiment #3 Listen to Your Writing Voice

The words we use give a certain mood to our writing, a written voice. The voice carries part of the meaning.

Ask Questions

1. What voice can you hear in your writing now? Is it funny, sarcastic, angry, comforting, brave, curious, …?
2. Does the voice support or clash with your purpose?
3. How will the voice make your reader _____ feel?
4. Is this the voice you want?

Take Action!

1. Read your writing aloud to someone else. Ask your listener what mood he or she gets from your writing.
2. Decide on how you want to tell this piece of writing. Is the mood you are setting the one you want to keep? Think of another mood that might work.
3. Circle words that cause the mood or voice of your writing. Make a list of words you want to change.

Experiment #4 Check Out the Details

When writers go back and look at what they've written, they often remember things they forgot or find paragraphs where they got off the subject.

Ask Questions

1. Are you bringing up the things you want to say in the best order? Or would there be a better order?
2. Is your piece too short? Do you need more details or examples to explain what you're talking about to _____ (your reader)?
3. Is your piece too long? Have you given unnecessary details that might bore _____?
4. Is there a better place to start than where you've started? Is there a better place to end?

Take Action!

1. Make a list of the subjects of each of your paragraphs. Number the subjects in the order they are in your writing.
2. Try a different order. (For example, make # 3, #2 or #4.) Read your writing aloud in the new order.
3. Make a list of four or five things you could add to your writing.

4. Make a list of two or three things you could leave out.
5. Try a new starting place. Try a new ending place. Read your writing aloud with the new beginning and ending places.

Experiment #5 Go Multi-Media!

Changing from writing to some other art form often gives writers new ideas when they go back to writing.

Change the medium

1. Ask someone to read your piece aloud to you.
2. Go to an art exhibit.
3. Watch a movie.
4. Listen to music.
5. Act out a scene.
6. Draw pictures to go with your writing.
7. Talk to someone who was part of your subject.
8. Go to the place about which you are writing.

Take Action!

1. Go back to your writing, and look at it from a new angle. Ask yourself what you could draw on from outside of writing that might give it more energy.
2. Write a few brand new paragraphs.

Experiment #6 Break the Mold!

Try the dot puzzle in Fig. 4.5. Connect all the dots with four straight lines. Don't pick up your pencil or draw over your own lines. [Hint: It is impossible if you stay inside the imaginary lines of the invisible box.]

Ask Questions

1. What are the imaginary lines you have drawn to box in your writing (reader, purpose, voice, even form)?
2. How else could you use this piece of writing (a poem, a song, a pamphlet, a poster ...)?

.   .   .

.   .   .

.   .   .

FIG. 4.5. Dot puzzle.

Take Action!

1. Write a few paragraphs of your piece to a different reader (someone older or younger, for example). Try a new voice. (If you change to writing to your grandmother, change your words so she'll approve.)
2. Change your purpose. (If you were funny, be serious. If serious, try silly, etc.)
3. Write a few paragraphs of your piece of writing as something else. (For example, make an essay into a story, a story into a song, a poem into a picture.)

Experiment #7 Put Your Writing Together a New Way

The purpose of revision is to put the writing back together in the very best way possible. (Re-vision means "see again.") Look at your writing in new way.

Ask Questions

1. Go back through your experiments. Which ones worked best?
2. Which ones showed you that your first idea was better?

Take Action!

1. Use scissors and tape to put your writing together in a new way. Cut out sections you want to leave out.
2. Tape in new details. Tape in new ideas you got from your experiments.
3. Write a new piece, following your cut-and-paste revision.

Of course, sometimes experiments work and sometimes they do not. Some of these revision experiments will work to produce a better piece of writing on one draft but fail on another. In the long run, success or failure of a particular experiment does not matter. What matters is taking the step back from the draft and experimenting with it to see which way is better. As children become adept at self-critique, they learn which experiments to try in a given context. As competence develops, revision becomes less a series of experiments and more an attitude of curiosity about drafts.

SELF-EVALUATION

Closely related to self-critique is self-evaluation. In fact the only real difference is that self-evaluation occurs when writing is finished. Writers who can step back from a finished piece of their own work and evaluate where it worked and where it did not learn what to do differently next time. Writing classrooms offer many opportunities for children to evaluate their own work.

Evaluating Against Their Own Whos, Whys, and Hows. When children choose their own communication contexts in which to write, self-evaluation about the success of their writing within its context is natural. Children can give their writing to the reader they chose and then judge for themselves how successful the writing was in accomplishing its purpose. For example, if Ethan wrote a Halloween memory for his younger brother to make his brother laugh, he can give his brother the piece and watch to see whether it made his brother laugh or not. He can then evaluate for himself which parts worked the best and which parts didn't work as well.

Evaluating for Portfolio Choices.   In classrooms where teacher evaluation re-volves around portfolios, children can choose which pieces of their writing they wish to include in their portfolios by evaluating for themselves which pieces show their best work. The teacher can provide guidelines for what should go in the portfolio, but children can choose for themselves which pieces meet the teacher's guidelines. Teachers can ask self-reflection questions which help children evaluate their own choices. A few examples of questions designed to help children evaluate their choices follow.

- Which piece shows that you understand changing your writing for different readers? How does this piece show your changes?
- Which piece shows that you understand prewriting? Include your prewrites with your piece.
- Which piece shows that you understand revision? Explain what experiments you did and how your piece changed from your first draft to your finished draft.

Evaluating Against a Class-Designed Rubric.   When teachers evaluate writ-ing with rubrics (see chap. 13), students can help design the criteria for the rubric. Using small groups or a whole-class discussion, the teacher can help students generate what characteristics make a good example of the particular assignment the class is working on. Once the characteristics have been listed and prioritized, children can evaluate their own work against the class rubric.

Evaluating Against a Personal Rubric.   When students are working inde-pendently on various writing projects, part of their assignment can be to generate their own list of good characteristics for their own project. Once they are finished writing, they can evaluate their own work against their personal rubrics.

Setting New Goals for Learning to Write.   Once children get good at evaluat-ing their own writing, they can explore what they want to learn next about writing. When children set their own goals, they take charge of the learning-to-write process, moving beyond the limits of a single classroom and a single year.

PEER TEACHING

As teachers, we know the magic of teaching: the best way to learn something ourselves is to teach it to someone else. We can help our students use this magic by creating opportunities for them to teach what they have learned to someone else.

Teaching Younger Children.   Cross-age peer tutoring can be fun and rewarding for both groups of children. When second graders lead kindergartners into the mysteries of writing down their own stories, both groups learn more than they knew at the start of the lesson. When fifth graders help third graders edit their writing for spelling errors, spelling becomes less of a burden for both groups. When sixth graders write stories for second graders, both groups learn about writing for a real audience.

Sharing Techniques with Peers.   In a comfortable community of writers, children can share individual expertise with their peers. The key to a supportive rather than competitive experience is preparation. When the teacher analyzes the children's writing sufficiently to provide everyone in the classroom an opportunity to be a peer teacher at least once during the sharing time, peer teaching can be fun and rewarding for everyone. (Children who are always on the receiving end of peer teaching can lose confidence in their writing rather than gaining competence.)

In the Classroom

Becky:

> When I first started teaching writing all I knew about was teacher-owned writing. The revision that was done was teacher owned, and the editing was teacher instigated. Now my most important teaching goal is to give my students ownership of their writing. Ownership is a springboard to motivate students to really re-look at their papers, to do their own revision. Writing becomes just like anything else they own—they take it out, play with it, look at it over and over again. Once they have ownership of their writing, they feel pride and when you have pride in something of course that is when you look at it.

Paula:

> When I first started teaching, we did a lot of writing in my classroom. The children wrote books, poems, and stories. The problem was that they were teacher-owned rather than student-owned. Looking back, I find that I really guided my students' writing too much. As I took classes in graduate school, I began to hear about the writing process, which emphasized "prewriting." In my classroom, we began to do more prewriting through activities, cooking, and brainstorming descriptive words and ideas. But I was still directing my students' writing too much and influencing what they wrote.

> When the children came to me with writing blocks, I helped them write because I didn't understand yet that a writing teacher could actually allow students to "own" their own writing and at the same time maintain control of the classroom. After I attended the Writing Project Summer Institute, I found that the pieces of the jigsaw

puzzle that I already had began to fit together in a new way. From that point on, I began to encourage my students to write for themselves, not for me.

Giving students' ownership of their writing has made a world of difference in the products I see. Some students progress by leaps and bounds, and others just inch along. But now their progress is their own and not mine. When we finish the year, some students love writing and others don't. But however they feel, during the school year they have given something to themselves because their writing has been their own.

CHILDREN DEVELOPING COMPETENCE

Remember the "My Favorite Place" assignment in chapter 2? One sixth grader got so involved with the piece that he wrote seven typed pages, or about 1600 words, about his trip to Disneyland. Without being told to do so, this student divided his narrative into four chapters and worked very hard to include concrete details as well as his own thoughts about what happened. He chose for his reader the student teacher, who he liked and had learned to make laugh. His purpose was to share his trip and feelings about the trip with her, so his writing was much more than a description of his favorite place. The chapters were called "Act 1: Getting Ready," "Act 2: On the Road," "Act 3: I'm Going to Disneyland," and "Act 4: Return to Disneyland." The excerpt in Fig. 4.6 is from Act 1. Notice the personal voice and the details.

My 1992 Disneyland Trip
ACT I
Getting Ready

Disneyland has always been my favorite place to be in the world. Disneyland is like a magical cure for adults and kids alike with a virus called stress.

In the beginning of summer in 1991, I had the evil virus of stress. I had no friends to play with when my best friend and I had just had a nasty fight with each other. We've had this fight countless times. Always about his brother doing every known thing with the two of us. He would defend his brother and I would go against him. My

---

FIG. 4.6. Joseph's favorite place: Act I.

mind became absolutely focused to saving money when my parents announced that we were going to Disneyland next spring because my dad's side of the family was going to have a reunion. The first one in years. I was short of money, and I promised to myself that I was going to change that. Summer was suddenly over and I went to a new built elementary school called Porter Elementary.

In no time at all I became less excited about the trip. I guess because I had school, homework, chores, and friends to play with. Then came Christmas and then New Years Day. January breezed by, then February. The spring break came and I packed all of my clothes except five pairs for school. It came to a point where I couldn't get my Mon to wash the five pairs and I had to start living off my traveling bag. Then came one week till the trip. I made a small calendar that had sort of a missile launch that a number counter from greatest to least and at the last day there was a picture of Disneyland and fireworks all around it. When the day came that I put a huge "X" on Disneyland, I nearly had a heart attack. My whole family had a heart attack. Everyone getting ready for the trip. My Mom was just having the best time. For my Mom's side of the family, Disneyland has been the most perfect place for a reunion. Thanks to my grandparents on my Dad's side, this whole reunion possible. It was the first time my whole Dad's side of the family had reunion in many years.

As we were packing, our parents gave me and my two brothers new traveling bags. But I was nervous, even scared that we may be attacked by someone because it was a month since the violent Los Angeles riots. My parents told me time and time again that there was nothing to be afraid of. The police have the problem under control.

FIG. 4.6. continued.

> The next day we would be in the state of California and in a new city. I tried to get some sleep that night. but it was the hardest and most difficult task in the world. I thought is was silly and if someone saw me I would be so embarrassed. I even tried counting sheep and I can't remember which number I got to, but it was very high. I decided that counting sheep was just keeping me awake. After about 30 minutes, I went to sleep.

FIG. 4.6. continued.

COMFORT, CONFIDENCE, AND COMPETENCE: THE WHEEL ROLLS SMOOTHLY

When a bicycle rolls down the street, the inner rim, the spokes, and the tire blur into a single bicycle wheel. When children learn to write, comfort makes them confident, competence makes them comfortable. Writing becomes a tool, like a bicycle wheel, that can take them where they want to go.

CHAPTER SUMMARY

Developing competence in writing is a lifelong pursuit that begins with viewing writing as a tool for personal communication. When children own their writing and use it to communicate something they consider important to someone they consider important for a real reason, they begin to develop competence. As they take more and more ownership of their writing, children begin to see revision as an opportunity to experiment with their writing to get a new look at how well the draft they have written works for the purpose they have in mind. At the same time they begin to evaluate their own work to set new goals for their own learning. As competence develops, children are able to teach younger students or their peers things that they have learned to do well when they write.

APPLICATIONS

1. Go back to the "My Favorite Place" piece you wrote for application #2 in chapter 3. Draw a communication triangle for it. Choose a real person you know who might like to read about your favorite place. Choose a reason for this person to read your piece. Ask yourself how you could write your piece to accomplish the purpose you have in mind.

2. Experiment with your "My Favorite Place." Do at least four of the experiments in this chapter by writing two or three new paragraphs for each of the experiments. Revise your earlier draft. Explain how you changed your draft and why.
3. Create a personal rubric for your "My Favorite Place" by listing the characteristics you think make a good personal essay. Evaluate your piece against your rubric. Choose one characteristic you would like to learn more about for your own writing.
4. In your class, pair off into "peer teaching partners." Explain how you did one thing you did well in your "My Favorite Place" to your partner. Have your partner explain to you how he or she did one thing well.

5

The Conventions of Writing

THE THEORY

Just as competence means making choices about communication purposes, it also means following the conventions of writing, getting surface errors out of the way so readers can reach the meaning easily. How to handle helping children learn the conventions of writing is one of the prickliest problems writing teachers face. On the one hand, we know that a large body of research (Braddock, 1963; Hillocks, 1986) tells us that formal grammar study does not improve children's writing. On the other hand, we know that the ability to use the conventions of writing is part of competence and correct style. (See Noguchi, 1991, for an excellent discussion of this issue.) Most textbooks and many curriculum guides list grammar skills students are expected to acquire, and parents often ask hotly why we are not teaching more grammar. When we step back from individual classrooms and look at broad instructional trends, we find textbooks used in fourth grade covering the same topics as textbooks used in sixth or even eighth grade (parts of speech, parts of the sentence, the four kinds of sentences, capitalization, punctuation, subject/verb agreement, homophones, homographs, roots, prefixes and suffixes, etc). In spite of this repetition of instruction, eighth graders often make the same errors fourth graders make, and college students often make the same errors eighth graders make. Year after year the same parents complain to teachers about the conventions of writing. To try to understand this situation better, let's analyze a *conventions instruction* triangle (Fig. 5.1).

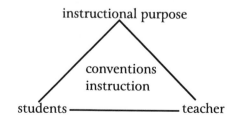

FIG. 5.1. Conventions instruction triangle.

Students

Because students are our instructional audience, let us begin with the student corner of the triangle. According to Vygotskii (1978), development and learning interact to form a zone of proximal development: tasks that children cannot do alone but that they can do with the help of others—teachers and peers. He went on to say that the initial mastery of concepts builds a foundation for the later development of complex processes in thinking. To apply Vygotskii's theories about learning to grammar instruction, then, we may say that for young children following the conventions of writing is best accomplished as a group activity. Further, we can say that this activity of working together toward correctness lays the foundation for future individual competence with conventions.

Teachers

As teachers, most of us have had very little formal training in grammar. Even English majors, unless they studied linguistics, have had very little training in grammar, and almost none in grammar as it applies to writing. In this age of rapid change, most teacher training programs no longer include a "grammar for teachers" course. Those courses have been replaced by courses in rhetoric, multicultural education, and computer technology. Recently graduated teachers may remember the difference between a noun and a verb from tenth-grade English, but they are at a loss to explain to students where to put commas beyond saying something overly simplistic like, "Put a comma where you breathe." (For a review of some basic editing rules, see the Appendix.)

Thus we come to one of the central conflicts in grammar instruction for writing—the difference between *grammar* and *editing*. Grammar is the formal study of the structure of language. In fact, there is not a single heuristic for grammar today; instead there are multiple ways of examing language: traditional, structural, transformational, the list goes on. Grammar, then, is a pursuit of linguistics. Editing, on the other hand, is the study of how educated folk communicate by means of written words. Editing, of course, is the more important concern for writing teachers and their students.

Instructional Purpose

When we ask ourselves why we need to teach grammar as part of writing instruction, we answer "to help the reader." Writers usually know what they mean, even considering invented spelling or idiosyncratic punctuation. Readers, on the other hand, expect writing that conforms to a standard written code. The instructional purpose we have for teaching writing conventions to students, then, is to teach them to edit for their chosen readers.

As teachers, we can prioritize mechanical concerns for our students by asking which deviations from the written code will be the most troublesome to the reader for whom the writing is intended. In the primary grades, mechanics is not much of a concern. Emergent writers usually write to parents and peers—sympathetic readers, to say the least. Invented spelling is acceptable, even encouraged, because it allows emergent writers to use more words than they could otherwise.

In the intermediate grades, however, student writers begin to widen their audiences, and thus their mechanical priorities. Top priority might go to capitalizing the first word of each sentence and spelling frequently used words following accepted practice. Second priority might go to placing periods at the end of sentences. A lower priority might be showing verb tense and keeping singular and plural consistent throughout a particular sentence. Once priority concerns have been addressed, editing concerns like sentence variety, comma placement, and spelling of homophones can be taken up. At any grade level with any particular group of students, a teacher can prioritize mechanical concerns according to the priorities of the readers.

There are, of course, various levels of reader demand for standard use of mechanics. On one end of the spectrum are documents that are written strictly for the self for informal purposes: grocery lists, for example. If the list is for myself, I can spell items I need to pick up with private abbreviations. If the list is for my husband, I may need to use more complete spellings. On the other end of the spectrum are formal written documents that I will be judged by others, such as resumes. The level of "correctness," then, is dictated by the audience and purpose of the piece of writing.

An Example

Armed with this theory, let's turn to a real example of student writing and analyze what kind of grammar and mechanics effort is needed in various communication contexts. To illustrate, take a look at the "Division Mystery" in chapter 11 (Fig. 11.8, p. 140). In a context in which the author will read her story aloud so her classmates can do the calculations and find the answer, writing conventions are irrelevant. In a communication context in which the class will trade stories with another class, writing conventions begin to matter. In this second context, the author needs to copy her paper over and correct spelling errors like *happing, donutes, axiously, comming, rember,* and so forth, spellings that will look wrong to other fifth-grade readers, shifting their attention away from the puzzle of the story to particular words. In a third context in which the class is intending to make a book of math stories to put in the class library to be kept from year to year, the author needs to go even further. For this communication context she needs to type her story and change paragraphs wherever the speaker changes, and make her spelling conventional. Her readers in this context will be students and possibly a few parents. Because the book will be kept from year to year, it needs to to look like a book (typed). In book format the failure to shift paragraphs in dialog will look wrong. However, even in this situation the tense shifts ("I walked to my bedroom and shut the door. Something is going on and I have to find out what!") are unimportant. Most parents who might look at the book over the years will not even notice the tense shifts, and those who do will be willing to overlook this rather sophisticated error from a fifth grader. However, should the teacher decide to make a book of math writing activities for other teachers and include this story as an example, even the tense shifts should be corrected. Teachers would notice.

THE NEED FOR CONVENTIONS

How much time and effort a writer spends on making his or her piece "correct" depends on what is going to happen to the writing. It depends, in fact, on who the reader is, what the purpose is, and how it will be shared. Mechanical errors are a problem when they shift the focus of the reader to mechanics and away from meaning. As teachers we can help our students (and ourselves) determine how much time and energy to spend on conventions by analyzing who is going to read the piece and what will bother that reader.

Of course, in some classroom situations every piece that children write goes home. Does that mean, then, that every piece has a parent as a secondary reader and therefore needs to be brought up to parental standards? The answer to that question of course depends on the individual school–parent contract, but my own answer is "No." One teacher I know deals with this problem with a rubber stamp. This stamp says, "UNDER CONSTRUCTION," and she uses it on all papers that will go home that have not been thoroughly edited. Another teacher I know sends home a letter at the beginning of the year explaining to parents how she plans to deal with the conventions of writing and why. Whenever questions come up, the letter is a starting point for the conversation. A third teacher I know uses Back-to-School night to explain her philosophy on accuracy writing conventions. The list could go on. Because parents are a secondary instructional audience for us as teachers, we must acknowledge their expectations without letting those expectations drive our instruction in writing.

In this context of reader expectations and purposes of writing, we can address the conventions of writing with our students. Perhaps looking at this instruction through the lens of the 3 Cs we've been using will help us decide where and how to begin.

ESTABLISHING COMFORT WITH CONVENTIONS

Make a distinction between grammar and editing with your students: teach editing. Teaching verb complements is probably a waste of time for writing instruction. Teaching students to capitalize the first word of every sentence is probably a good use of time. However, a theoretical understanding of how English works may be important, so if you wish to teach a separate grammar unit, go ahead, but don't expect that instruction to carry over into your students' writing.

Prioritize editing rules your students need to learn: teach the rules one at a time. Begin with the most glaring error most of your students are making. Overlook errors you haven't taught. Work with students individually on idiosyncratic problems.

Too often our zealous wish to make writing conventional results in overwhelming our students. Develop comfort and confidence with editing before tackling competence.

BUILDING CONFIDENCE WITH CONVENTIONS

Teach editing rules in a series of minilessons sprinkled across a long block of time. In each minilesson focus on one definition, one concept, or one rule. Provide an explanation and a chance to practice. Effective minilessons can be structured as follows:

- The rule;
- Correct examples of the rule;
- A chance for students to practice the rule;
- An activity that applies the rule to real student writing.

Because effective minilessons usually last only 15 minutes or so, it is important to keep them tightly focused. Although a grammar book may list "using end marks on sentences" as one rule, the concepts imbedded in the rule would probably dictate three minilessons: one on periods, one on question marks, and one on exclamation points.

Use Multiple Intelligences to teach editing.

- Color code mechanical concerns. For example, mark spelling errors with yellow, capital letter errors with green, period errors with purple.
- Play games that allow students to move around. For example, give different students name tags that identify them as words or punctuation marks (one student is "did"; another is "capital letter"; another "batman"; another "lost" or "lose"; another "his"; another "cape"; two others are a "period" and a "question mark"). Have them arrange themselves in a question, putting the captial letter where it goes and the question mark. Have them rearrange into another sentence that is a statement. Put students on teams and have a race.
- Have students clap syllables to words that are particularly difficult to spell.
- Have students help one another learn editing rules. Give group grades for good editing among the group. Identify error experts. Give each person in the group the responsibility for one error.

DEVELOPING COMPETENCE WITH CONVENTIONS

Make writing conventions concrete by tying them to real writing and the expectations of real readers. Rather than going into an exhaustive explanation of proper nouns, tell your students that the adults who will read their stories posted on the wall at Back to School Night expect to see names capitalized. Explain that they expect to see paragraphs and margins. Show them examples from books they are reading.

- Ask children to identify their target reader.
- Ask children to decide how much they think that reader will notice errors.
- Guide children in making a list of errors they want to be sure to correct as they edit.

Help students take responsibility for conventional spelling. Oddly spelled words seem to leap out at us as readers, so conventional spelling is an important editing concern. However, the ability to spell conventionally seems to be a function of visual memory. In other words, good spellers "see" written words in their heads and writing out the word in question often helps—a misspelled word looks wrong. In any classroom, then, students with strong visual memories will just naturally be better spellers than students who rely on auditory cues to spell. Nonetheless, conventional spelling is important to almost every reader. If we cannot expect every student to spell completely conventionally, we can teach them to take the responsibility for the spelling in their work.

- Offer spelling lessons in the context of real writing for real audiences and real purposes.
- Offer dictionary lessons in the context of real writing for real audiences and real purposes.
- In classrooms where computers are available, teach students to use spell checkers, reminding them that spell checkers cannot catch homophone substitutions.
- Allow students to ask other people how to spell words they know they are having trouble with. At a time when questions will not disrupt other people's work, students can ask peers who are good spellers. Parents can also be spelling resources.

Devise a system of accountability for editing. Keep track of what minilessons have been taught and give editing points for avoiding those errors, but keep the number of points in a reasonable balance. Don't overlook the other things that go into a piece of writing: topic choice, audience awareness, prewriting, content building, drafting, peer response, organization.

Keep track of editing patterns for individual students. Develop an editing checklist based on your series of minilessons. Have students record personal errors on a personal checklist. Ask students to review their personal checklists whenever they edit. When a pattern of errors emerges for individual students, ask them to

- write out a rule that is consistently causing them trouble;
- locate and correct sentences from their own writing that illustrate the rule;
- write several new sentences illustrating correct usage of the rule;
- make up a personal plan for remembering the rule when they write.

Reward this work by giving points to raising the grade on the paper.

A NOTE ON PROOFREADING

Sometimes we expect students in the intermediate grades to be able to proofread their own papers. In fact, proofreading is a traditional part of writing. All writers are supposed to know how to proofread, whether or not they have been taught how to do it. However, proofreading is a specialized skill used by editors at publishing companies to make a living. It is far more complicated than just reading the paper over. In fact, modern reading theory (Goodman, 1976; Smith, 1982; Rumelhart, 1977) tells us that when readers know a lot about what they are reading (when they have detailed background knowledge), they do not look at every letter or every mark of punctuation or even every word of print to comprehend. When a writer is reading his or her own writing, the background knowledge is complete. In fact, the writer actually knows more about what he or she has written than is on the paper. In a proofreading situation, then (when the reader is the writer), the reader needs very little print to construct meaning; therefore, it is unlikely he or she will notice something as small as a letter reversal (spelling) or a missing punctuation mark. His or her brain knows what he or she meant to write and sometimes sees what was meant, even when it is not on the paper (see Bratcher, 1994b, for a more thorough explanation of this theory).

In spite of all the explanations of why proofreading often does not work, it is still an important first step to effective editing: if a writer cannot find his or her errors, knowing all the editing rules in the world won't help a bit! As teachers, then, we must find workable solutions for this dilemma. The suggestions that follow may help:

- *Separate proofreading and editing from revising in the writing process.* One peer group can be formed to give content feedback; a second group should be formed to help with proofreading and editing.
- *Teach students how to proofread.* Explain to them that they are doing more than "reading." In fact, they are not really reading at all; they are looking at each letter and each mark of punctuation. Give them practice finding errors on worksheets before they look for errors in their own work.
- *If possible, have students proofread a typed copy.* Errors leap off a printed page more than they do off a handwritten page. Word processors make this suggestion workable.
- *Whenever possible, have students proofread for each other.* It is much easier to see errors in someone else's work.
- *Have students read each other's work aloud.* Stumbles and false readings often pinpoint errors.
- *When students must proofread their own work, let significant time pass before they try to proofread.* The more time that passes, the more writers forget what they meant to say, and the more they can look at what they actually put on the paper.
- *When students must do their own proofreading, teach them to disrupt the flow of meaning in their writing and break it down into separate sentences.* The best way I know to accomplish disruption of meaning is to have students read their

writing sentence by sentence, beginning with the last sentence. Reading backwards destroys the logical connections of sentences to each other and makes them stand out as grammatical units.

- *Be tolerant (although not completely permissive). Keep a sense of humor about proofreading.* Done carefully, proofreading is a tedious process. Emphasize how silly most errors are. Demonstrate humorous interpretations the reader might put on mechanical slips. Do not expect children to do things professional writers have help with.

WRITING CONVENTIONS AND SECOND-LANGUAGE WRITERS

Grammar is an important field of study in and of itself, completely separate from editing writing. Because native speakers of any language possess an unarticulated knowledge of the structure of their language, formal study of the grammatical principles that underlie editing rules is usually not necessary for native speakers when they write. In other words, children who have grown up speaking English do not need to study the principles of English grammar to learn how to spell or where to put punctuation marks. (They might need to study the principles of grammar for other reasons, but that's a different story.) Students who are native speakers of another language, of course, possess a different set of unspoken grammatical rules than children who are native speakers of English. But even among children speaking American English, there is variation among the grammatical rules they learned from their parents when they were learning to talk. The issue of grammar, then, is a larger one than I have discussed. I would argue, however, that it is not the place of the writing teacher to try to change the grammatical principles of spoken language. Instead, it is the role of the writing teacher to pass along the standard code system that will be accepted by an educated reader.

As I mentioned at the beginning of this chapter, editing is an audience concern. For example, the rules of African American Vernacular English (AAVE) dictate a different use of *to be* in first-person, present tense (I be here) than does standard written English (I am here). Depending on who the audience is and what the purpose is, one or the other is correct. If I am a native speaker of AAVE writing to another native speaker of AAVE for an informal purpose, *I be here* is the correct construction. However, if I am a native speaker of AAVE writing to an audience for a formal purpose (my high-school principal or my boss, for example), *I am here* is the correct construction. It is all a matter of context. The issue, then, is not to take various grammars away from children; it is instead to give them another one that will help them communicate in writing to particular audiences.

Most of our classrooms include students, then, who know a variety of grammars other than standard written English grammar. These students face an extra challenge when they begin to edit their work for convention-demanding readers. Briefly put, these children make most of the same errors their native-speaker peers make plus errors that occur from moving between language systems. If as teachers we fail to take this added challenge seriously, we run the risk of overwhelming second-language writers (who even at the third-grade level are doing something most Americans cannot do).

Take a concrete example: a third grader who has grown up speaking Navajo at home and who is learning to write in English. In this student's writing we will probably see unconventional spellings similar to the ones we would expect to see from almost any third grader. We will also see unconventional punctuation, also common among third graders. In addition, we may see missing plural *s* markers. These last errors are a direct result of the student working to translate from Navajo to English. In Navajo, for example, there is no plural marker equivalent to our *s* marker. If I translate Navajo literally I will say, "I have one new cow, but my neighbor has four new cow." But what if the teacher (like me) doesn't know Navajo?

To further complicate matters, each language is different, and in classrooms with students coming from a variety of language backgrounds, it is very unlikely that teachers will have sufficient background knowledge of all the languages represented to be able to spot translation errors. So, how do we handle the second-language writer when it comes time to look at writing conventions?

The work of Mina Shaugnessy (1977) suggests an answer. In her work with basic writers at City College of New York, Shaugnessy observed that most grammatical errors in writing are not random but are based on logic. She found that by analyzing the errors in an individual student's writing she was able to find patterns in the errors. Once she found the patterns, she was able to analyze the logic that drove those errors and thus reteach the logic that drives standard writing conventions. Even if we do not know the logic of the first language the student has internalized, we can use Shaugnessy's method to find patterns of errors and thus find which English conventions the student needs extra help learning.

In practical terms this means keeping a record of unconventional constructions from writing to writing. The student can keep the record, an aide can keep the record, or the teacher can keep it. A record could be as elaborate as a grid chart with conventional constructions down one side and writing assignments across the top, or it could be as simple as a handwritten list with slash marks accumulating from one assignment to the next. In any case, once several pieces of writing have been completed, a pattern of unconventional constructions that can be analyzed will emerge. Using the pattern as a diagnosis, the teacher can "prescribe" particular English rules for individual students. This method, of course, can be used for first-language speakers as well. Keeping their own records and doing their own pattern analysis develops competence with conventions for all writers, not just second-language writers.

Once the patterns are clear, the teacher can help second-language writers prioritize conventions on which to work. As one convention, say the plural marker *s*, becomes a habit, another one can move to top priority. This way second-language writers can take control of their own translation and learn English conventions at a comfortable rate rather than feeling overwhelmed by the magnitude of the task before them.

In the Classroom

Becky:

> I send letters home at the beginning of the year explaining the writing process and how we do it in my classroom. That letter moves naturally into our first publishing party and what it is. I invite the parents to come in for it. Once in a while they do. But whether they come or not, I think they understand how I'm teaching writing.

Paula:

> I always try to plan an event at the end of the year. For example, I might have multimedia presentation with slides that I have taken or pictures that the children have drawn. Each child will read a piece or two, and then we'll sing a song that we have written. Usually about 4/5 of the class will have a parent in the audience. We have our program in the music room. I have had several parents come back in later years to thank me for what their child has learned to write. I feel that my writing program is successful—and that's as important for me as it is for the children.

CHAPTER SUMMARY

Following the conventions of writing is part of communicating with readers: particular readers expect particular conventions to be followed. Grammar is important to writing, not as understanding the structure of language, but as written usage—editing and proofreading. Editing rules should be taught in a series of minilessons focused on priorities that develop from reader expectations and student errors. Teaching students to proofread and edit for each other is the most effective way of correcting student writing. Providing a system of accountability helps students form new writing habits and avoid old patterns.

APPLICATIONS

1. Find a list of the grammar concepts you are expected to teach (appropriate to grade level). From this list identify the ones that apply to writing. Prioritize those rules as you think the parents of your students would.
2. Choose one of your top three rules from question number 1 and design a minilesson following the principles outlined in this chapter.
3. Take the self-diagnosis provided in the Appendix. Work through a minilesson for yourself from those provided. Use one of the pieces of writing you have done for an earlier chapter to apply that rule to your own writing.

PART II
REASONS TO WRITE

6

To Communicate

We write for many reasons: to gather our thoughts, to discover what we know or how we feel, to communicate with other people, or just for fun. Sometimes we write for ourselves; sometimes we write for others.

When we write for others, we write to communicate. Rhetoricians—people who study communication—use many methods to categorize the kind of writing we use to communicate with others. Some methods divide writing into two categories: fiction and nonfiction, creative and standard, personal and impersonal, American and world. Some methods categorize writing by logical structure: comparison/contrast, cause/effect, most important to least important, chronological order. Some methods categorize by genre: short story, drama, poem, novel, essay. Some methods categorize by time: contemporary, modern, 16th century. (See "Modes of Discourse" by Frank D'Angelo [1976] for a thorough discussion of the development of rhetorical thought on the forms of discourse.)

In the late 1960s a rhetorician named James Kinneavy adapted the standard communication triangle we looked at in chap. 4 to propose a new classification system of written products. In an article called "The Basic Aims of Discourse" (1969), he suggested that if we substitute *content* for *purpose* in the communication triangle and *writing* for *content*, we can draw a triangle that helps us classify writing according to its purpose. If we adapt Kinneavy's triangle for use in schools, we draw a "reasons to write" triangle like the one in Fig. 6.1 (see Bratcher, 1986). Using this new triangle, we can categorize any piece of writing we teach as a communication situation created by the interaction of the demands of content, reader, writer, and the writing itself. Let's look at these components one at a time.

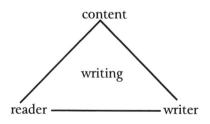

FIG. 6.1. Reasons-to-write triangle.

Content. Any piece of writing contains information of some sort. Short pieces usually focus on a narrow subject; longer pieces focus on broader subjects. Even poems include some kind of information, perhaps about a particular place or feeling.

Reader. When a writer sits down to write, he imagines himself writing to a particular person, someone he believes will be interested in what he has to say. Often, of course, other people become readers because they too are interested.

Writer. When writers compose content for a particular reader, they give it personality by how they write: the words they choose and the sentences they write. For example, a writer might write about her garden to her mother in a funny way to make her mother laugh, or she might write about the same garden to her daughter in a serious way to teach her daughter something. The writer gives her writing a personality that matches her reader and her purpose.

Writing. Each piece of writing has its own form. A letter is a different kind of writing than a poem or a textbook, for example. Each form has its own conventions or expectations. Readers expect a poem to look a certain way on a page; they expect to see dialogue in fiction and footnotes in a research article.

Any piece of writing, then, can be looked at as the interaction of these four components. Depending on the *main* reason a writer is writing, we find a particular component of the triangle emphasized more heavily than the other three components. Using these emphases, we can look at writing from four different angles, which can help us develop rough categories along the lines that Kinneavy proposed. The triangle reminds us that we are writing to communicate, and it opens up easy ways of discussing the varieties of writing without overwhelming either the teacher or the students. As we nudge our students from comfort and confidence with writing toward real competence, we can expand their understanding of writing by looking at the main reasons we write.

REASON #1: TO TELL OUR OWN STORIES
(EMPHASIS ON THE *WRITER*)

When writers write to tell their own stories, they emphasize the *writer* corner of the triangle (Fig. 6.2), creating personal writing. In personal writing the compo-

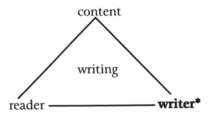

FIG. 6.2. Personal triangle.

nents of the communication triangle are defined by *writer* concerns. The *writer* speaks with his or her "I" voice. *Content* is experiences and feelings the writer has had. The *readers* are people who care about the writer as a person. Likewise, the *writing* forms are personal: diaries, journals, letters, personal narratives, and memoires.

The Moon and I by Betsy Byars (1991) is an example of personal writing. Look at the following excerpt:

> Louisa and I were going to the Charleston Museum one afternoon. The museum was about five blocks away. It was a big, roomy old museum that featured, surprisingly, a lot of Egyptian artifacts and a live reptile room.
>
> Louisa and I were halfway to the museum when we realized Bubba was following. "Leave us alone," Louisa turned to say.
>
> "I'm not bothering you. Am I bothering you?" Bubba lifted his hands innocently to show he was blameless.
>
> As far as I was concerned, the museum trip, which I had looked forward to—I especially loved the mummy and the reptile rooms—was ruined.
>
> At the end of the block we turned again. Bubba was still there. (p.19)

Children can analyze the reasons-to-write triangle for this piece as in Fig. 6.3. Because everything in the triangle relates back to Byars, it is easy to see that Byars' main reason for writing this piece was to tell her own story.

REASON #2: TO SHARE INFORMATION
(EMPHASIS ON *CONTENT*)

When writers write to share facts about the world, they emphasize the *content* corner of the triangle (Fig. 6.4), creating informational writing. In informational writing the components of the communication triangle are defined by *content* concerns. *Content* is facts about the world, information that readers can use in whatever way they choose. The *readers* are people who need or want the particular information being discussed. The *writer* speaks with an impersonal third person voice—discussing the "it" of the information being offered. Likewise, the *writing* forms are content forms: reports, brochures, informative essays, procedures,

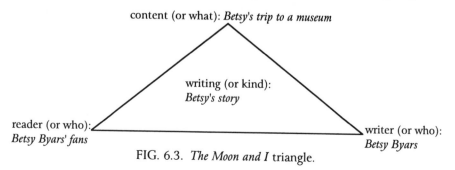

content (or what): *Betsy's trip to a museum*

writing (or kind): *Betsy's story*

reader (or who): *Betsy Byars' fans*

writer (or who): *Betsy Byars*

FIG. 6.3. *The Moon and I* triangle.

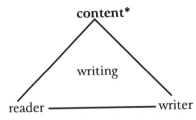

FIG. 6.4. Informational triangle.

how-to explanations, classifications, descriptions. Graphics are often an important part of informational forms.

Rocks and Fossils by Ray Oliver (1993) is an example of informational writing. The book is a how-to hobby book with many pictures and diagrams. Look at the following excerpt:

> When lava escapes from a volcano it loses its heat quickly and solidifies. There isn't much time for any crystals to grow in the cooling lava flow. You can recognize lavas because they often look glassy with few, if any, obvious crystals. The crystals are there but they are very small. Sometimes the lava will have lots of holes in it where gases bubbled out of the molten rock. One of the most common lavas cools to form the rock basalt, which is often black. You may need to use a hand lens to find any crystals in basalt. (p.16)

Children can analyze the reasons-to-write triangle for this piece as in Fig. 6.5. Because everything in the triangle relates to rocks, we can see that Oliver's main reason for writing was to share information.

REASON #3: TO TRY TO CHANGE THINGS
(EMPHASIS ON THE *READER*)

When writers write to try to change something, they must concentrate on writing to a reader who has the power to make the change they want. They emphasize the *reader* corner of the communication triangle (Fig. 6.6), creating persuasive writing.

In persuasive writing, the components of the communication triangle are defined by the *reader* corner. *Readers* are people the writer wants to motivate to

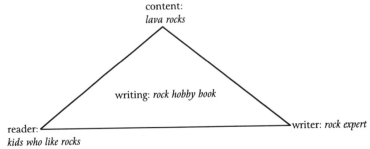

FIG. 6.5. *Rocks and Fossils* triangle.

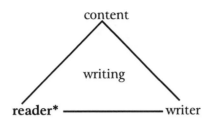

FIG. 6.6. Persuasive triangle.

do something differently. The *content* is drawn from readers' beliefs or actions and focuses on changing those beliefs or actions. Persuasive writers use different kinds of content to change their readers: facts, feelings, quotations from persons the readers respect. The *writer* speaks directly to the reader, usually with a second person voice—asking "you" questions, giving commands, and so on. Likewise, the *writing* forms focus on the reader: letters, pamphlets, persuasive essays, political brochures, advertisements, editorials, religious writings.

A "Just Say No" poster is an example of persuasive writing. A recent one I saw showed kids embracing each other with big smiles on their faces. The caption read, "Don't do drugs. Do hugs!" Children can analyze the reasons-to-write triangle for a "Just Say No" poster as in Fig. 6.7. Because this triangle revolves around opposing drugs, we can see that the main reason the writer made the poster was to try to change attitudes of people.

REASON #4: FOR THE LOVE OF WRITING
(EMPHASIS ON *WRITING*)

When writers write because they love to write, they emphasize particular forms of writing (Fig. 6.8), producing *literary* writing. In literary writing, the components of the communication triangle are defined by the demands of the particular form of the *writing*: creative nonfiction, poetry, fiction, drama, folktales, tall tales, humor. Because art can be about any topic, *content* may be drawn from anywhere: the author's life or imagination, the audience's experiences or beliefs, even factual data. The *writer* speaks with whatever voice the form requires: his or her own, a borrowed voice, an imagined voice. The *readers* are people who love the particular form: lovers of poetry read poems; lovers of novels read novels, for example.

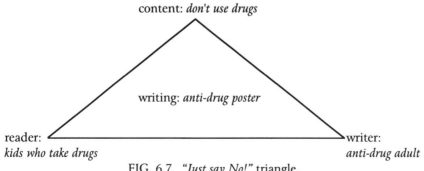

FIG. 6.7. *"Just say No!"* triangle.

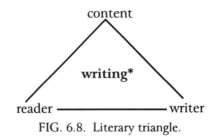

FIG. 6.8. Literary triangle.

The Wind in the Willows by Kenneth Grahame (1985) is an example of literary writing. Look at this excerpt:

> Mole had been working very hard all morning, spring-cleaning. First with brooms and dusters, then standing on a little table with a brush and a pot of paint, slap-slap, up-and-down, until he was aching all over.
>
> Suddenly he flung down his brush, said, "Bother!" and "Hang spring-cleaning!" and bolted out of the house into the fields outside.
>
> "This is fine," he said to himself. "This is better than painting the house!" (p. 1)

Children can analyze the reasons-to-write triangle for *The Wind in the Willows* as in Fig. 6.9. Because everything in the triangle relates to the story, we can see that the writer's main reason to write was that he loved writing stories. This is an example of literary writing.

LOTS OF REASONS TO WRITE

Of course, most writers have more than one reason to write. Melville's main reason for writing *Moby Dick* was to create art, or write a novel, but sharing information about whaling was another reason. *Moby Dick*, then, is a hybrid of literary and informational writing. Docudramas (like *All the President's Men*) are other examples of this hybrid, their writers writing both drama and history. Testimonials aimed at getting an audience to give up drugs or adopt a new lifestyle illustrate another common hybrid: personal writing used to persuade. Social protest novels like those of H. G. Wells or Charles Dickens cross boundaries of both literary and persuasive writing. The list could go on.

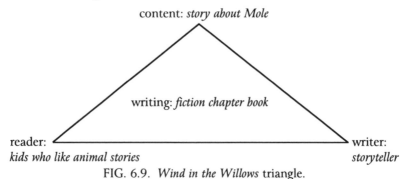

FIG. 6.9. *Wind in the Willows* triangle.

Within any single piece of writing, a writer is committed to all the components of the communication triangle. As I write this text, for example, I am writing to share information about teaching I have learned over the years (*content* and *writer*): the content grows out of what I've taught and would be very different if I had been a biology teacher rather than an English teacher. Occasionally I use personal examples to illustrate content. I am also committed to particular readers (elementary school teachers), so my examples are drawn from elementary classrooms rather than from college classrooms. The form that interests my publisher (the textbook) dictates certain writing conventions: subheadings, chapter summaries, questions for the reader at the ends of each chapter, appendices for information that might not apply to every reader, and so on. Various parts of the book fall more or less into different categories. The opening of chapter 14, for example, is largely personal writing, though I use literary techniques occasionally. The four chapters that follow this one are largely informational, though I use personal techniques occasionally. The teacher evaluation chapter is largely persuasive, though I use informational techniques occasionally.

As we look together at these four categories (personal, informational, persuasive, and literary) in the next chapters, remember that they are teaching tools, advance organizers for the complexities of human communication through writing. As students become more sophisticated about writing, share hybrid writing with them. A series of historical novels like *Walker of Time* by Vick (1993) can illustrate writing that has two purposes: to tell a story and to teach history. A biography like *The Real McCoy* by Towle (1993) can illustrate how information can be used to persuade society to expand its definitions of itself. Show children how the communication triangle spins on any one corner until it blurs like a top released from its string.

REASONS TO WRITE IN THE CLASSROOM

Sometimes published examples of a particular genre seem completely removed from everyday writing. To bring reasons for writing closer to home and to reassure your students that you too write like this, help them analyze an example of your writing. To illustrate, look back at Mrs. White's "The Falls with No Name" in chapter 2. If we analyze this essay using our reasons-to-write triangle, we find something like Fig. 6.10. Because everything in the triangle relates back to Mrs. White, it is easy to see that her main reason to write was to tell her own story.

Student Writing

To connect the reasons to write with their own writing, analyze pieces of student writing (perhaps from students not in the class). Of course, the first year you teach writing, you won't have student examples to model with unless other teachers you know have some they are willing to share. However, every year after that you will have your own. Simply save copies of the best pieces your students write. (Don't forget permission slips!)

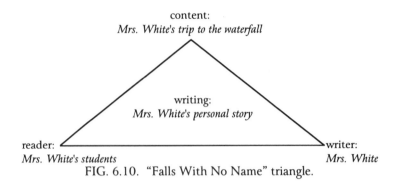

FIG. 6.10. "Falls With No Name" triangle.

To illustrate, look back at "How the Pig Got Its Snort" in chapter 3. A reasons-to-write triangle for this piece might look like Fig. 6.11. Because everything in this triangle relates back to the pourquoi tale, it is easy to see that the writer's main reason to write was to tell a story. This is an example of literary writing.

Students' Own Writing

To give ownership of the reasons-to-write triangle to your own students, ask them to analyze examples of their own writing, either on their own or in small groups. As a class, brainstorm examples of writing they might do that illustrate different reasons to write. Have them draw reasons-to-write triangles for some of their ideas.

A WRITING ROAD

As students begin to analyze their own communication in different writing settings, the wheel of comfort, confidence, and competence begins to go somewhere. Writers begin to see that different writing roads lead to different destinations (Fig. 6.12), and they begin to be able to make choices about where they want to travel and which road to take to get there. Writing begins to be a vehicle for communication. Students find they have reasons to write.

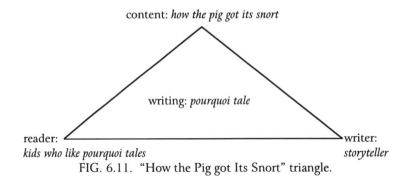

FIG. 6.11. "How the Pig got Its Snort" triangle.

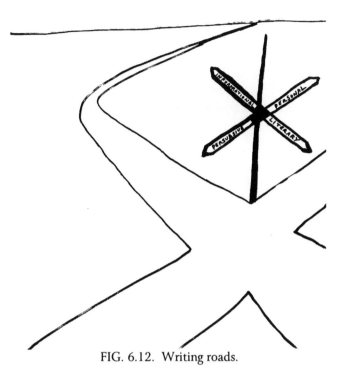

FIG. 6.12. Writing roads.

CHAPTER SUMMARY

If we adapt the standard communication triangle to make a "reasons to write" triangle, we draw one like Fig. 6.1. Writers who emphasize the *writer* corner of the triangle write to tell their own stories. Writers who emphasize the *content* corner write to share information. Writers who emphasize the *reader* corner write to try to change things. Writers who emphasize a particular kind of writing write for the love of writing. However, it is important to keep in mind that the reasons-to-write triangle and these four categories are simply teaching tools. In real-world contexts, writers usually have many reasons to write.

APPLICATIONS

1. Choose a topic you know a lot about: a hobby or skill, a special interest, a job you've had, an obstacle you've overcome in your life, something you feel strongly about. Choose a reason to write about your topic (to tell your own story, to share information you know, to try to change something, to create literature from your experiences). Make a writing triangle for your topic based on the reason you chose. Write a draft of the piece to the reader you chose in the form you chose.

2. Using the topic you wrote about in #1, choose a different reason you might write about that same topic. Make another reasons-to-write triangle based on your second reason.
3. Think about the last few letters you have written in your daily life.
   (a) List the reasons you wrote those letters. Did any of the letters have more than one reason? Which reason was the most important?
   (b) Choose one letter. Brainstorm other forms you might use to write about the topic of that letter. Draw several reasons-to-write triangles for the new pieces you could write.

7

Telling Our Own Stories

Dear Katie,

Your mom tells me you're collecting family stories from before you were born for a school project. I've got one for you that happened when I was five years old—30 years before you were born!

That summer my family moved from Kentucky to Texas. I was small for my age, like you are, and I looked more like a boy than a girl with my brown hair chopped off straight like yours was last year, but I already felt like I had a lot of responsibility for the family. You see, my mother, your Grandmother Bratcher, was pregnant.

There were already five of us in my family—my Grandmother Bratcher (your great-grandmother), who lived with us, my father (Granddaddy), who was busy at the church most of the time, my mother (Grams), who was busy unpacking boxes from our move, my two-and-a-half-year old brother Richard William (your father), and me. The new baby would make six. Our green house on the corner was small, too small for six people since it only had two bedrooms. But I loved it anyway. It was built on a hill that was made of fossils, just like the ones in your rock collection. On hot afternoons, which was almost every day in Texas, I walked down the hill that made our driveway and counted the fossils in the retaining wall that kept the front yard from washing away when it rained.

But in spite of the fact that none of us was sure just where the new baby would sleep, I was excited about her arrival. I was excited because I was anxious for a sister. I imagined that the baby would be a warm, living doll that I could dress up in ribbons and bows and play house with. Grams warned me that there would be diapers too, but I didn't care. For weeks we thought up names for this new sister. I suggested Elizabeth. Granddaddy suggested Elaine. Great-grandmother Bratcher suggested Mildred. But it was Grams who suggested the name we all finally agreed on—Linda Diane.

The day of Linda Diane's birth drew nearer and nearer. I got more and more excited. I went through the old baby clothes Grams had kept from when I was a baby and picked the best ones to give to my sister. I practiced folding diapers. I hung around the crib your daddy had just grown out of and imagined a sister with golden curls. (Why I thought she would have blonde hair, I'll never know—no one in our whole family has blonde hair—do they?)

And then it happened. One afternoon when the thermometer said 101 degrees, Grams went to the hospital. For two whole days I sweated in that little green house,

79

waiting for the moment when Grams and Linda Diane would come home from the hospital.

Finally that happened too. The old faded green car chugged its way to the front of the house. I ran out the door and up to Grams. Tugging on her skirt I said, "Let me see her, Mother! Let me see her!"

Grams looked at me a little strangely, but I didn't notice. All I had eyes for was Linda Diane. She was beautiful. She had the bluest eyes you ever saw. But instead of gold curls, she had black curls. But I didn't care. My little sister was home at last.

When we reached the porch, Grams sat down on the steps. I stood on the ground and leaned against Grams' knees.

"Be very gentle with him," said Grams.

I stared at my mother. "Him?" I cried. "How can Linda Diane be a him?"

"Linda Diane isn't Linda Diane," said Grams. "Linda Diane is Michael Edward, a wonderful little brother for you."

I guess I don't need to tell you I was crushed. I knew Michael would never wear the pretty baby clothes I had picked out for him. I knew he would never wear bows in his beautiful curls. I doubted if my mother would let me play dolls with him. I struggled with my disappointment for a while and then sat down on the step beside Grams. I held out my arms for the new baby.

Michael Edward lay in my lap and looked up at me with the most beautiful blue eyes you've ever seen. (Have you ever noticed Uncle Mike's blue eyes?) It took me a few weeks to adjust to the loss of my sister, but eventually I came to love my new brother, who grew up to be your uncle. I've never told him the story of Linda Diane and what an unwelcome surprise he was, and I guess I never will. Don't you tell either!

Love, Aunt Suzanne

When writers write to tell their own stories, they draw on their own memories and emotions. When I wrote this story of the birth of my brother for my niece, I started with memories that were over 40 years old! At first my memory was sketchy, so I began to search for details I had lost. I asked my mother to share her memories with me. I looked at faded black and white photographs in a yellowing family album. I began to write. As the memories flooded back, I was able to fill in the details I thought my niece would find interesting, particularly the surprise we all had when my hoped-for sister turned out to be a brother! It is this delving into our own pasts that makes personal writing so much fun.

Once writers have filled in the details of their memories, they must think about their readers. They ask questions like "Who wants to hear this story?" "Why do I want to tell this reader this story?" "What do I want this reader to do when he or she finishes reading my story?" "What should I emphasize?" "What will I have to explain?" "What should I leave out?" As I drafted and revised, I changed the names I called my family to the names Katie knows them. "Mother" became "Grandmother Bratcher" or "Grams"; "Richard William" became "your father." I decided that I wanted to share the surprise I felt when I first saw my brother with

Katie, so I hid the fact that the story was about Uncle Mike's birth until the very end. Because Katie was 7 years old at the time, I chose simple words to tell my story. Because Katie was collecting stories for her class, I wrote the story with a beginning, middle, and end. Because she lived 1,500 miles from me, I framed the story in a letter.

Personal writing, then, focuses on remembering and sharing those memories with people who will care about them. When writers write about themselves they write in letters, journals, diaries, and memoirs. They use an "I" voice and describe events from their own perspective. Sometimes they write only for themselves.

Take a look at this entry from a diary by Elizabeth Yates (1981):

January 7, 1918

Christmas ended last night with the burning of the tree but I think it was the best Christmas ever.

As soon as Jinny got back from college we started learning our lines and rehearsing the play she had written. It's our present to Mother and Father. We gave it on Christmas Eve in a corner of the living room.

Before we began, Mother lit the big candle that has such a lovely waxy fragrance. "It must always be the first light in the house," she said, and the only reason she gave was that her mother did it and her mother's mother before her. "It's a tradition, an Irish custom that goes far back into the past." When Mother touched a match to the wick she said, "Wish or pray." I wished, but I think she prayed. (p. 13)

Yates began her diary when she was a young girl. When she wrote it, it was just for herself, a record of her life, a way of making meaning from her experiences. She treasured her diary and kept it into her adult life. Only after she had become a well-known writer did she share her childhood diary by allowing it to be published.

Sometimes writers write personal writing not just for themselves, but also for family members or close friends, like I did. When writers write for close audiences, they use journals, letters, and informal narratives. Sometimes writers write personally for less intimate, even anonymous, readers. We find this kind of personal writing in published forms: autobiographies, essays, personal narratives. *War Boy* by Michael Foreman (1989) is an example of personal writing written for a large impersonal audience. Foreman's readers are children, and the purpose of this unusual picture book is to show what it's like to be a child in wartime. Read the following excerpt:

Mother grabbed me from the bed. The night sky was filled with lights. Searchlights, anti-aircraft fire, stars and a bombers' moon. The sky bounced as my mother ran. Just as we reached our dug-out across the street, the sky flared red as the church exploded....

We were safe. And we were together. We were three brothers and Mum. Ivan, Bernard (known only to us as Pud) and myself. (Our father had died one month before I was born.) Also with us was Aunt Louie.

In the morning we returned home. Mum went to the loo, which was outside in the yard, and found a hole in the roof and a bomb, unexploded, in the floor. Pud pulled it out and carried it to 'Pal' the policeman in the police box on the corner. (pp. 11–14)

Although this book is personal writing, Foreman wrote it for an audience who did not know him or his story. In fact, he wrote his story so his readers might get a feeling for a piece of recent history about which they were too young to know anything.

Personal writing, then, grows out of the lives of its authors. Even if they do not keep diaries or write personal narratives, children are familiar with self-expression. They know it from stories their parents and grandparents tell. They know it from answering standard prompts like "What did you do in school today?" or "Tell me about Jon's birthday party." They know it from notes and letters written to them, either on paper or over the internet, and from letters and notes they write back. As teachers, then, we simply need to encourage students to tell their own stories and write those stories down for someone to read.

ESTABLISHING COMFORT WITH PERSONAL WRITING

Children, like all of us, find themselves intensely interesting. We begin life self-absorbed. Tiny infants have no conception of other people, except as deliverers of goods and services. As toddlers develop, "sharing" is a challenge. As children mature, we teach them to think about other people, but one of the cornerstones of a healthy personality is a positive sense of self—a good self-image and the ability to take care of the self. Because sharing our "selves" is the subject of personal writing, this kind of writing often comes naturally to children, making it a good place to begin writing instruction. To get children started telling their own personal stories, try the following activities:

- Have students tell personal stories verbally to peers or younger students in the school before they write.
- Allow students freedom to choose what experiences they wish to share. (In other words, don't dictate a class theme.) In some Native American cultures, for example, there are taboos children must avoid when they tell stories about themselves. Certain ceremonies, for example, are not to be shared with people from other cultures.
- Allow students to write their memories to themselves first without worrying about choosing a reader.
- Give time for students to read journal entries aloud to a partner they choose before they begin writing.
- Respond with content comments to pieces of writing that are about intensely personal issues. For example, avoid giving a grade to a piece of writing about the death of a favorite pet.

INVITING ALL CHILDREN TO TELL THEIR OWN STORIES

Sometimes we inhibit children from telling their own stories because the models we offer are too homogenous. Children listen to the stories we tell and think, "My life hasn't been anything like that. I don't have any stories to tell." Although it is not possible to model a story for every child in the classroom, we can offer enough variety in our models that children feel comfortable telling their own stories. *Working Cotton* (Williams, 1992) is a first-person narration of what it is like to pick cotton. *A Chair for my Mother* (Williams, 1982) is a first-person story about saving money to buy a comfortable chair. Look at this excerpt from "Darkness at Noon: Solar Eclipse" by Shonto Begay (1995), for example. It tells a personal story that happened on the Navajo Reservation.

> I was ten years old when the stars came out at noon. After penning the sheep and goats in the corral for their noon rest, I felt a strange sense of uneasiness. The chirping of birds was absent, the buzzing of insects stopped, even the breeze died down.

> My toes felt the sand still warm through the holes in my sneakers. The landscape fell under a shadow on this cloudless day. As I hurried through the tumbleweed and the rabbitbrush, it got darker. I looked up and saw twinkling stars far above. The dogs were lying in the doorway.

> I ran into the darkened hogan. Immediately I was told to sit down and remain quiet. I couldn't even eat or drink. My aunt said the sun had died. (p. 18)

Sharing stories from many places invites children to tell their stories, even if the stories come from other places than middle America.

BUILDING CONFIDENCE WITH PERSONAL WRITING

When writers write to tell their own stories, the writing process focuses on the writer more than it does in other kinds of writing. Prewriting consists of delving into personal memories and identifying people who would care about these memories. Drafting consists of telling the story with an "I" voice. Revising and editing consist of telling the story so someone else can understand and enjoy it. Publishing happens when writers share their personal stories with readers who care about them. Activities children might do to write personal stories include the following:

Prewriting

- gathering memories
- talking to family members about those memories
- asking who wants to hear this story
- asking why the reader wants/needs to hear it
- asking how to tell the story

Drafting

- writing the memory as a story
- choosing a personal form
- making sure the story has a beginning, middle, and end

Revising

- sharing drafts with each other
- answering questions peer group members ask
- rethinking reader concerns

Editing

- adding pictures
- cleaning up grammar and spelling as appropriate for target reader

Publishing

- sharing the final piece with classmates
- sharing the final piece with its intended reader

To help children draw on their multiple intelligences to tell their own stories, try the following:

Intrapersonal intelligence. Ask children to make a list of favorite gifts, favorite possessions, favorite people, favorite things to do, favorite places to go. Ask them to remember stories about these favorite things.

Verbal/linguistic and Interpersonal intelligences. Tell personal stories aloud in class before children write. Provide ways for everyone to get to tell a story.

Visual/spatial intelligence. Ask children to draw pictures to go with their stories. Ask them to make a collage about their story or bring photographs from home.

Body/kinesthetic intelligence. Ask children to pantomime their stories for the class. Play charades to guess what the stories are about.

Logical/mathematical intelligence. Ask children to tell their stories in chronological order. Ask them to tell you what the most important parts of the story are and what the least important parts are. Help them give more details about important parts and less about unimportant parts.

Musical intelligence. Teach children to sing "My Favorite Things" from *The Sound of Music*. Ask them to share their favorite songs with you. Ask them what stories they could tell about their songs.

DEVELOPING COMPETENCE WITH PERSONAL WRITING

Because children are naturally egocentric, personal writing often feels natural to them and they take automatic ownership of their stories. However, imagining their readers' needs does not feel so natural. Competence with personal writing, then, often focuses on learning to tailor the stories for someone else. Readers, purposes, and forms are often more difficult for children to identify in personal writing than in other types of writing because children tend to remember their lives from their own individual perspectives. However, once children begin to think of readers, personal writing can be immensely rewarding because it builds bridges to other people that children sometimes do not build for themselves.

Identifying Memories to Share

The first challenge of the personal writer is to find a story someone else might want to hear. It is all well and good to say that personal topics come from our memories and our emotions, but what does that really mean? First, as teachers we must help our students think of themselves as authors with stories to tell. Sometimes we say to our students, "I want you to tell a story about yourself," and they reply, "I can't think of anything interesting." So our first task is to help children think of an interesting personal story to tell. Activities that will help follow.

- Life maps. These maps begin at birth and end at the present day. When children draw life maps, they focus on important events like moving, adopting a pet, making a new friend.
- Place maps. These maps depict physical spaces in which a person has lived. For example, if a child has lived in the same house all of her life, then she could draw the street she lives on, where her friends live, where the school is. Or the place map could be a floor plan: where the important parts of the house are, where my bedroom is versus where the living room is, what happens in the living room versus what happens in the back yard.
- Body maps. Another form of life map is a body life map. Ask children to draw an outline of their body. Ask them to place scars on knees, elbows, ankles. (There can be scars on the heart as well.)
- Photographs. Pictures can help generate stories as well. When students look at old photos of themselves as younger children or pictures of friends that may have moved or are growing up too, they remember incidents that might make interesting personal narratives. Pictures of family members that live far away may generate personal letters. Post cards from places children have been or would like to go may generate personal writing as well.
- Family stories. Most of us know stories about ourselves that we do not remember. These family stories make great starting places for personal writing.
- Favorite songs. Music can start memories flowing. Ask students to listen to or sing a song that was a favorite when they were younger. Remind them of different categories: play songs, lullabies, church songs, learning songs, songs they sang themselves, song that were sung to them. Then ask what memories the songs bring up.

- Favorite possessions. Toys, clothing, books, souvenirs—all of the possessions we have a hard time parting with carry stories with them. A child may remember a favorite dress her grandmother made and with that memory may come a memory of a particular birthday. Another child may look at an old dog collar and remember stories about a puppy that has since grown up.

Identifying Readers

Once students identify a personal topic they would like to write about, the next challenge is identifying a reader who would like to read the story once it is written. Sometimes writers come up with stories they want to tell, but they cannot think of anyone who would want to read it. You might suggest the following readers:

- Parents and other family members. Most parents enjoy reading memories from their children's perspectives. And most children enjoy revisiting experiences with their parents and family members. The home reader is a natural for personal writing.
- Peers in the classroom. Most children are comfortable telling their stories to someone else in the class. However, unless student writers choose a particular person in the class to write to, the sense of readers becomes abstract and often results in "generic" writing. Sometimes a child in another classroom can be the reader. Sharing personal stories with a new person can be fun, especially when the new person shares stories back.
- Pen pals. The traditional pen pal letter exchange can take on new energy if letters are focused on particular stories children want to tell. Sometimes pen pal letters are boring to write (and to read) because they stay so abstract. But when children exchange letters that focus on pet stories, for example, barriers come down quickly! Pen pals can be students in another country or they can be students of another teacher you know in a different city or school in your town.
- Younger children. Younger children can also provide good readers for an elementary writer. For example, sixth graders might tell memories from third grade to third graders. Or third graders might write stories about their first day at school to a group of new first graders.
- Older folks. Nursing homes are full of people who enjoy interacting with children, even on paper. A pen pal exchange between school children and housebound older adults can be rewarding for both groups.
- Characters from stories. Sometimes books and stories elicit memories from children. *The Island of the Blue Dolphins* (O'Dell, 1960), for example, may call up memories of the beach or memories of Sea World. Student writers can write to characters, sharing how their lives have been the same or different from the characters' experiences.
- Past/future children. Children from history and future children can provide interesting readers, too. When students imagine what the past was like or what they think the future might hold, they see their own experiences differently.

Identifying Why and How

When writers know what story they want to tell and who they want to read that story, the next challenge is to discover why that person should read it and how to tell the story so that the purpose is fulfilled. A writer, for example, might want to tell a particular story about himself to make his reader laugh, to make his reader think, to share a surprise with a reader, to share a memory with a reader who was there. The list of reasons for telling the story could go on and on. For student writers, "why and how" emerge when they answer the question, "What do I want my reader to do when he or she reads my story?"

- Have students rewrite a piece for the same readers but with a different purpose. If they first wrote to amuse, suggest that they write now to tell how the experience affected them later on. Let them pick which one to send.
- Have them rewrite a piece with the same purpose but for a different reader. If they wrote for a sibling, have them write for a grandparent. Let them pick which one to send.
- Provide opportunities for students to write to outside readers. Help them analyze what common ground they have with an outsider. Show them how to build writing bridges between themselves an outsider.

Choosing a Form

Personal writing comes in many forms: autobiography, letters, diaries, journals, personal experience narratives, travelogues. Whatever the form, however, the first-person "I" voice makes personal writing instantly recognizable. The content is drawn from the writer's life and the sentences use descriptive language to allow the reader to see, hear, taste, feel, and smell what the writer experienced. Personal writing usually follows a past-to-present chronological order.

- Introduce students to a variety of personal forms.
- Provide them with models they can follow.
- Encourage them to use all their senses to tell their stories.
- Work on sequencing their stories.

CHILDREN TELLING THEIR OWN STORIES

Personal stories, of course, take many forms. Figure 7.1 is a story about when the writer was a baby, written by a third grader. Figure 7.2 is a story about winning a contest, written by a second grader. Figure 7.3 is an excerpt from Joseph's story about his trip to Disneyland (Fig. 4.6). This excerpt is "Act 3."

My Baby story

A long time ago when I was one year old. I was wearing red swet pants and a red shirt. I was with my brother Ben who 11. We were taking the pulp out of my pumpkin and Ben had just finished cutting the top off my pumpkin. My littler brother Paul said to stand on the stool and put my head in the pumpkin. So I stood up on the stool and put my head in the pumpkin. Some of the seeds got stuck in my hair and on my clothes it was October 29th and my brother had gone to get a drink. I had to have a bath.

ThE END

FIG. 7.1. Joe's baby story.

IN THE CLASSROOM

Paula:

As a primary teacher I am teaching the emergent writer. My students have been reading for a few years now, and they are just starting to really learn how to write. One of my main emphases is to get them to enjoy telling their stories. We'll talk through a lot of stories in the beginning of the year. I want them to enjoy telling each other their stories—just for the fun of it.

I like to start with baby stories. Children always like to tell stories about themselves to each other. They are still young enough that they really associate with small children and babies. I ask them to go home and find out something funny that they did when they were little, and then we come back to school and share the stories. We tell the stories orally, and we laugh and laugh. We say, 'Did you do *that*?' and we laugh some more. We spend a lot of time sharing and enjoying the stories. Each child tries to come up with a better story than the others—to make us all laugh.

After we've had lots of fun, I have them write their stories. Then we share them as they are writing. In third grade they love to share their writing. They just can't get enough of sharing. When we're done writing the stories, they take their stories home and share them with their parents. And their parents laugh too. Everybody loves to hear baby stories, so this makes a great place to start writing in the fall. The children have something they want to write about, they have a purpose, and they have readers who enjoy their stories as much as they do.

DREAMS DO COME TRUE

In 1995 I went to down to Phoenix for the AZ State Cinderella finals, for the Cinderella Scholarship Program. I spent a full week in Phoenix. On Monday we did interviews with the judges, Tuesday we did sportswear, Wednesday was party dress, Thursday was Tot Personality. Friday everyone did a group dance for the parents. Friday night was finals night and I was called up for top 10. Then the MC Raph, sang a song called "Thank God for Children" to all 10 of us. Then the top 5 girls doing everything again.

Then we went up on stage again and the MC called out 4th thru 1st alternate and I was left on stage without a trophy. Then I was named the new AZ State Cinderella Tot. The first ever for Flag-staff!

My number for the pageant was 26 which is now my lucky number. I received a "round crown", flowers, a 3 ft. trophy, a septor and a robe I get to wear all year long at all the pageants.

This happened the 3rd year I competed at state. The first year I was last alternate, the 2nd year I was top 10 and State Tot Personality. I always dreamed that I would win and I did. This proves that the Cinderella sayings "that dreams do come true" and "winners never quit and quitters never win" are the truth.

THE END

FIG. 7.2. Danielle's contest story.

THE PERSONAL WRITING ROAD

When children tell their own stories in writing they set out on a writing road that runs from important personal experiences to people who care about them. This road is a friendly road and a good place to start learning to write. Comfort and confidence are almost built-in with personal writing. Once a writer feels comfortable and confident on one road, the next road is not quite as daunting.

ACT 3
I'm Going to Disneyland

When I woke up I was blinded by a very bright light from the bathroom. It was about 6:45 AM and I laid in my sleeping bag thinking in one hour I will be in Disneyland. I laid there with no movement but inside I was jumping for joy. After I got out of the shower and got fully dressed, my Mom, sister and brothers went to the dinning area of the inn, with me right behind them. My Dad was just getting out of the shower and told us to go ahead without him. I still remember what I had for breakfast: two blueberry beagles and a cup of fruit punch. It was a hard task to keep the food down because I was so nervous that I just couldn't eat. I finally managed and in no time at all, we went to Disneyland. I saw that huge sign that said "welcome" to us. We paid a man in a toll booth money to park and we got to enter. We waited for my grand parents. My Aunt Nedra was there with her family to. My grandparents cam and we entered the park. I couldn't believe how many Oriental people were there.

One of the first rides we went on was Splash Mountain; it was the first time I had ever gone on it. The last time we came to Disneyland it was under construction. It was a fun ride and the two story drop was great. I screamed my lungs out and when we hit the bottom of the drop, I got a second shower that day. After we got off Splash Mountain, some of my cousins and my family got on the Haunted House right next to Splash Mountain. It was the most ire place I've been in years. Doors were moving, ghosts were flying and dancing around, and at the end of the ride there was a ho-bow ghost that was hitch-hiking. When I looked in the mirror in front of me I saw the ghost sitting between my cousin and I. When we got off the cart,

FIG. 7.3. Joseph's Disneyland story.

we headed for a new line. I knew I went to far,
but when I went back my family was gone. My cousins
were gone also. It's been kind of a tradition in
my family that every time we go to Disneyland, I
get lost. I was going to make the best of it
though. So I went on countless rides and went into
shops and I even bought some stuff. After two
hours, maybe even more, I found my parent and
brothers at the spot were to meet in case you get
lost.

That night we saw the new Fantasmic show that
had just started. It was cool but most of the time
I couldn't even see. After the show we said goodbye
to my grandparents and relatives and went to the
hotel. I was really tired and wanted to go right
to sleep. After changing my clothes I went to bed.
Tomorrow, Wednesday we would go to Universal
Studios. On Thursday we would go back to Disneyland, but after that we would go home.

FIG. 7.3. continued.

CHAPTER SUMMARY

Personal writing focuses on sharing life experiences. Beginning writers often need
to be encouraged to think of stories to tell that a reader might find interesting.
Readers for personal writing care about the writer as a person, and children can
be encouraged to think of people who would like to know more about their lives.
Children can usually find stories to tell to younger students or relatives. Personal
writing is told in the first-person "I" voice and it uses descriptive language to tell
the story.

APPLICATIONS

1. Make your own life map. What episodes from your childhood could you
   share with your students? Why would they find these episodes interesting
   or entertaining?
2. Make a list of favorite family stories told about you. Which of these stories
   might your students like to hear? Why would they enjoy those stories?

3. Make a list of your favorite possessions when you were growing up. Are there stories attached to any of these possessions that your students might like to hear?

4. Make a communication triangle (chap. 4) for one of the episodes you identified as interesting to your students in 1–3, using your students (present or future) as the reader corner. Why do you want to tell them this story? How will you tell the story? Write a personal piece based on this communication triangle.

5. Choose a different reader for the story you told in #4. Why might you want to tell this story to this new reader? How would you tell the story differently to accomplish this new purpose for this new reader? Write a few paragraphs of the new version. Compare the two versions. How did your story change? Why did it change in these ways?

8

Sharing Information

Hyacinths for Christmas: A Fall Girl Scout Badge

To have frilly pink, white, and blue hyacinths blooming at Christmas time, buy your bulbs now (late September or early October). You can get them at a nursery like Warner's or at a variety store like K-mart.

- **Keep the bulbs in a cool, dark place** (like a shed outside or even in a dark container in the refrigerator) until early November (about six weeks before you want them to bloom).
- **Bring them into the house**, and if you want to watch the roots grow, pot the hyacinth in a glass container. You can use a special "hyacinth glass," or you can use a large ordinary drinking glass filled with marbles or styrofoam packing peanuts.
- **Set the bulb (pointed end up) on top of the marbles** or in the top of the hyacinth glass. Fill the glass with water, being careful that the water doesn't actually touch the bulb. (If the bulb sits in water, it will rot.) The roots will grow down to the water if it's close but not touching.
- **Put the glass in a dark, cool place**. (Probably not out in the shed because you don't want the water to freeze.) A cupboard under the sink or a box out in the garage is a good place. Leave the glass there for three or four weeks—until you see a green shoot about two inches tall growing from the top of the bulb. Be sure to check the water once a week to make sure the roots can reach it.
- **Take the glass out of the dark** and put it in a bright window. The warm, sunny window is like spring to your hyacinth, and the shoot will grow taller and taller and finally bloom into a frilly hyacinth! Once the flower has bloomed, move it out of the direct sun so it will last longer.
- **On Christmas day** put your hyacinth under the tree or on the table. Or give it as a gift to someone who might enjoy a flower in the snow.

When writers write to share information, they begin with a topic they know about and readers who want or need the information the writer knows. When I wrote the instructions for the Christmas Scout badge, I chose to write about forcing hyacinths because I force bulbs almost every winter. I knew how to force bulbs, but my daughter and her friends did not.

In this example, I had become an expert on forcing hyacinths by reading books, talking to other gardeners, and doing it myself. However, writers of informational pieces can become experts in other ways too. Sometimes informational writers have become experts by going to school or by reading other people's writing. Sometimes they have become experts by watching other people. Sometimes they learn about their topics by teaching the topic. Sometimes they learn by living through a particular set of circumstances. No matter how they have learned, writers of informational writing know a great deal about their topics!

Once informational writers have become experts on something, they think about their readers. They ask questions like, "Why do these readers want to know this information?" "How much do they already know about the topic?" "What concepts are going to be easy for them?" "What concepts are going to be difficult?" Because the girls in my daughter's Girl Scout troop were not gardeners, as I wrote I had to explain vocabulary terms, list supplies, and suggest places where they could purchase their supplies. Because they wanted to learn how to force bulbs to use as Christmas gifts, I had to time my instructions for the fall. I force my bulbs in a small greenhouse, but only one of the girls in the troop had access to a greenhouse, so I had to adapt the instructions so they could be followed in an ordinary kitchen. Because the girls were not gardeners and not likely to be interested in extra information, I chose a brief instruction sheet as my form rather than an essay with paragraphs that would take longer to read and be harder to refer to.

Informational writing is all around us. It is in textbooks, how-to books, newspapers, magazines, pamphlets, brochures, encyclopedias, and reference books of all sorts. We receive brochures about products ranging from medication to bicycle helmets. We read biographies, self-help books, and histories. We use textbooks and professional journals in schools. Companies send us assembly instructions for bookshelves and basketball hoops. Our computers come with manuals and disks filled with information. In magazines we find book and movie reviews, reports of current events, and explanations of the latest scientific theories.

Even children's publications are filled with informational writing. Look with a critical eye at the next issue of *Highlights for Children* or *Jack and Jill*. You will probably find more informational pieces than stories.

Let's look at two examples of informational writing that are very different from mine. The first is from *Rattlesnakes* (1989), a Zoobook.

> Rattlesnakes have wonderful senses that help them to hunt. Using their senses, they can find prey at any time of the day or night. They can even locate warm-blooded animals *in complete darkness*! When we humans want to find something, we use our eyes and ears the most. Rattlesnakes have eyes and ears, and they sometimes use them to find prey. But they mostly use their *sense of smell* and their *sense of heat* to hunt. (p. 8)

The writers of this book worked for the San Diego Zoo, and they had had much experience working directly with rattlesnakes. They were true experts, but they were also writing to children. They tell us why they wanted to share what they knew about rattlesnakes with children on the first page:

> Rattlesnakes have a bad reputation. Many people think of them as dangerous snakes that can kill a person with a single bite from their poisonous fangs. For this reason,

they are feared—and perhaps even hated. There is no doubt that rattlesnakes can be dangerous to people. In fact that is one reason why you should read this book—to find out more about the danger, and to learn how to avoid it. But more than that, you will find out that rattlesnakes are one of the most fascinating groups of animals on earth. (p. 1)

Because these writers were writing to both interest children and help them be safe, the book is full of pictures and interesting facts. It also contains tips about how to treat rattlesnakes to avoid being bitten. However, the writers do not try to tell their readers everything they know about rattlesnakes!

Let's look at another different example of informational writing, a passage from *The Iron Horse* by Richard Wormser (1993):

At high noon, the horse and one-ton steam locomotive lined up side by side, the locomotive on its tracks, the horse and carriage on the ground alongside. The crowd grew quiet as the starter raised his gun, counted to three, and fired. They were off and running, the locomotive spewing black smoke and glowing sparks, the horse panting and snorting. (p. 1)

The writer of this book did not become an expert by being present at this event; in fact his book is about events that happened many years before he was even born! He became an expert on this topic by reading and doing research. He lets us know that is how he learned by appending a bibliography of 17 sources at the end of his book. Occasionally throughout the text he quotes from his sources to support a conclusion he has drawn for himself. The following passage illustrates:

Most railroads were not held responsible for accidents, and their executives seldom felt guilty about them, even if there was gross negligence on the railroad's part. One newspaper, outraged by this, published an angry editorial:

A train thunders down a curve ... a rail snaps ...two cars are hurled off a bank, six or seven corpses and a score of injured victims taken from the ruins, and nobody is to blame. Nobody ever is ... Boilers are bursting all over the country, railroad bridges breaking, rails slipping, human life is squandered ... but nobody is to blame. (Wormser, 1993, p. 160)

Wormser, then, studied books and other people's writing to teach himself the information he wanted to share, but by the time he sat down to write, the information was his own. He draws the conclusion that people eventually became outraged at the it's-nobody's-fault attitude and uses the quotation from an outside source to support his belief. He wrote his book because he had become an expert on his topic, and he wanted to share what he had learned with children who were interested in trains.

Informational writing, then, grows out of a writer's knowledge. How it is written depends on who is going to read it and why they want to read it. As teachers, our first challenge with this kind of writing is to help our students locate topics they are either already experts on or are interested in studying enough to become experts on. Our second challenge is helping children identify readers who are genuinely interested in the information the children know.

ESTABLISHING COMFORT WITH INFORMATIONAL WRITING

Students often feel uncomfortable with informational writing. They assume it is "boring" or "too hard." Modeling informational assignments helps establish comfort. As an example, let's look at how Paula Nelson introduces informational writing to her third graders.

It is 9:00, time for Language Arts. Ms. Nelson begins with expert stories (from *Invitations* by Regie Routman, 1991). She says, "Who knows what an expert is?"

A stocky little boy with curly blonde hair raises his hand and shouts out, "I do."

"Okay, Tommy," says Ms. Nelson. "Tell us."

"Someone who knows a lot."

"That's right," says Ms. Nelson. "Did you know that everyone is an expert at something? I'm an expert at lots of things. I'm an expert at singing in the car. If you ever see me driving down the street with my windows rolled up and my mouth open, you'll know I'm singing at the top of my lungs. I'm also an expert at making chocolate sundaes. I know just how much ice cream my bowl will hold and I know just how much chocolate syrup it takes to make the ice cream taste perfect. When winter comes I'm an expert snowman-maker. I always give my snowman rocks for eyes so he can watch the cars that come down my street. What are you expert at?"

"I'm an expert pizza-eater," says one little boy.

"Me too," says another.

"I'm expert at taking care of cats," says Brandie.

"Skateboarding!"

"Horseback riding."

"Good," says Ms. Nelson. "What we're going to do is write about something we're expert at. We're going to write expert stories. You want to hear mine?"

"Sure!" shouts Tommy.

"All right," says Ms. Nelson. "Listen and see if it gives you any ideas for your expert story. My story is about killing spiders."

"Gross," says a girl on the front row.

"I know," says Ms. Nelson. "I hate spiders. That's why I'm such an expert at killing them. I suppose I ought to catch them and take them outside, but I don't. So if you want to learn how to kill spiders, my story will tell you." She begins to read:

Killing Spiders

Even though I'm not crazy about admitting this, I am an expert at killing spiders! Living on the edge of the forest, as I do, I have what seems like more than my share of spiders coming into my house. And, although I know they are helpers because of the way they kill insect pests, I just don't like them in my house. When I see them on the wall or the floor, they make my skin crawl!

I have developed a near sure-fire method of taking care of spiders over the years. Newspapers seem to be the best weapons. I roll a newspaper tightly and get a good grip on it. Then I slowly and quietly walk over to the spider. Spiders do have eight eyes, after all, and are able to catch many movements within a room. It is easy to send them scurrying for shelter. When I come within range, I take aim with the newspaper and hit the spider hard! (If it is not hit hard enough, it will suffer and run away, injured.) Finally, after everything is said and done, it is necessary to clean up the damage.

So, even though spiders are often helpful, they are simply doomed if they come into my house!

"I can do that," says Brandie. "I can write about how to take care of cats."

"Good," says Ms. Nelson. "I bet all of you can do this."

Teachers who model expository writing for their students establish comfort because they show children real expository writing, taking it out of the exclusive realm of textbooks and encyclopedias. Comfort comes when children identify topics about which they have information to share.

Helping Children Identify Topics

- Have students brainstorm topics about which they are experts. Topics might include places they have lived, occupations their parents pursue, particular pets, hobbies, care of younger siblings, favorite authors.
- Ask students to bring informational books they like from home. Have them share mini book reports. Suggest that they might want to write on the same topic the book is about.
- As a class, make a list of topics about which students would like to know more. Ask children to identify topics they might be able to write about from this list.

BUILDING CONFIDENCE WITH INFORMATIONAL WRITING

When writers write to share information, the writing process focuses on content about which the writer has become expert. Prewriting may focus on becoming expert by gathering facts or data from a variety of sources, including personal experiences, other people, and books from the library. Or it may focus on identifying facts the writer already knows from past experience. Drafting often consists of experimenting with a variety of formats: a pamphlet, a set of instructions, a diagram. Revising often focuses on organizing with subheadings and adding graphics. Editing often includes adding references from outside sources. Publishing consists of sharing the final draft, often with a reader outside of the classroom. Activities children can do to share information follow. (Emergent writers can do these activities in small groups or as a whole class.)

Prewriting

- surveying what the writer already knows about the subject
- learning new information from books, interviews, and personal experiences
- organizing and categorizing information: charts (Fig. 8.1), maps (Fig. 8.2), and clusters (Fig. 8.3)
- asking who needs or wants to learn this information
- asking why the reader wants or needs to know it

Drafting

- writing a summary of what has been learned from memory
- going back to sources to jog the memory
- writing a more complete summary
- choosing an informational form

Revising

- sharing drafts with each other
- answering questions peer group members ask

Category	Characteristic 1	Characteristic 2	Characteristic 3

FIG. 8.1. Data chart.

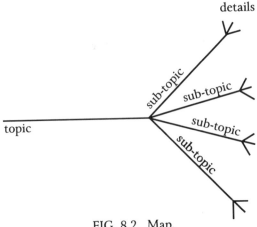

FIG. 8.2. Map.

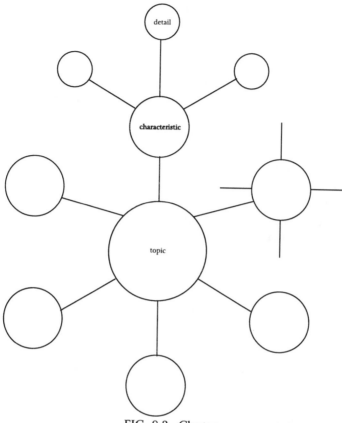

FIG. 8.3. Cluster.

- adding quotations that support what the writer wants to say
- rethinking reader concerns

Editing

- inserting subheadings
- inserting graphics
- cleaning up grammar and spelling as appropriate for target reader
- documenting sources through credits, acknowledgments, or bibliography

Publishing

- sharing the final piece with classmates
- sharing the final piece with its intended reader

To help children draw on their multiple intelligences to share information, try the following:

Intrapersonal Intelligence. Ask children to make a list of things they know how to do well: games they are good at, chores they do well, hobbies they have. Ask them to make a list of subjects they know a lot about: pets they have, something they studied in an earlier grade, something they have read about in several books.

Verbal/Linguistic Intelligence. Ask children to read three books or articles on the topic about which they have chosen to write.

Interpersonal Intelligence. Ask children to talk to one or more people who are experts on the topic about which they have chosen to write.

Logical/Mathematical Intelligence. Ask children to divide their topics into sections. Ask them to put those sections in some sort of sequence (chronological or order of importance, for example).

Visual/Spatial Intelligence. Ask children to make graphics or draw pictures that help explain the paragraphs they have written.

Body/Kinesthetic Intelligence. For "how-to" pieces, ask children to demonstrate the process about which they are writing. For historical or general information pieces, ask them to act out a scene.

Musical Intelligence. If appropriate, ask children to find a song from a historical period about which they might be writing.

DEVELOPING COMPETENCE WITH INFORMATIONAL WRITING

Because informational writing focuses on content, it is sometimes hard for students to remember they are experts writing to a reader for a reason. As teachers, we need to help our students identify readers who need the information they have learned. We also need to help them choose a form that will both fit the information they have to share and help the reader comprehend.

Helping Children Identify Readers and Purposes

- Once students have a topic they want to write about, ask them to brainstorm people who don't know the information they already have. From that list ask them to identify one or two who might want to learn. Ask them to list reasons their target reader might need the information they have to share.
- When students have chosen their topics, make a list on the board of those topics. Ask classmates to sign up for a topic they would like to read. Pair children in reader/writer partners. Ask readers to tell writers why they chose the topic they did. (Do this until all reader/writer partners have had a chance to talk.)
- Work with another teacher to provide readers for your class writers: younger schoolmates or peers in another classroom, for example. Brainstorm reasons younger schoolmates might like to learn the information the writers have to share.
- Send home a list of topics about which students are planning to write. Ask parents to sign up to be readers on two or three. Ask parents to write a brief note to their writers explaining why they signed up for that topic.
- Once students know who their reader is going to be, ask them to talk to the reader in person or on the phone about the reasons the reader wants to learn about their topic. Ask writers to decide whether they should write seriously

or with humor, informally or formally—depending on who their reader is and why that reader wants/needs the information.

- Instead of reviewing for a test, have students write reports in groups for each other on various concepts needing to be reviewed. Have groups trade reports and critique each other's work.
- Have students write instructions for some aspect of a favorite pastime or hobby. Have them share their instructions with a classmate who wants to learn the hobby. Ask the reader to critique how well their instructions worked and whether they enjoyed reading about the hobby; then have the writer revise instructions as needed.

Helping Children Choose A Form

Informational writing comes in many forms: reports, brochures, procedures, classifications, descriptions, essays. But whatever the form, informational writing has certain structural characteristics that make it recognizable: often, in fact, the structure is obvious in the text. Headings, subheadings, lists, introductions, all tell the reader what the main ideas are. Graphics in the form of tables, charts, and pictures support the prose explanations and offer quick summaries to the reader. Sources are often an important part of informational writing as well. When teachers encourage students to experiment with real forms—including graphics—informational writing comes alive. Students get excited.

- Introduce students to a variety of informational forms: pamphlets, magazine essays, how-to instructions. Discuss for what each form is particularly good.
- Help students think through which form matches their own reader's purpose best.
- Show students how to include subheadings with their writing.
- Encourage students to include pictures, graphics, and diagrams with their writing.
- Provide students with frames for informational writing. For example, give them a "fill-in-the-blank" report form or bibliography to follow.
- Teach students to quote, paraphrase, and summarize.
- Have students read several sources on one topic. Have them choose which source they found easiest to understand. Ask them to tell why they liked it. Ask how they might use a quotation to support what they want to say.
- Have young writers write a class report. First, have children read a variety of books of their choice on one topic, dinosaurs, for example. When children have finished reading, make a giant chart synthesizing what individual students learned. Next provide a skeleton of a report for organizing the information on the chart. Last, write the report together on an overhead projector. Type it and make it available to the class to read.

CHILDREN WRITING TO SHARE INFORMATION

To illustrate, let's look at some examples of informational writing written by children. The expert stories (Figs. 8.4 and 8.5) were written by third graders and illustrate informational writing done based on life experience. The report on sharks and lionfish (Fig. 8.6) was written by a second grader and illustrates informational writing done from research.

In the Classroom

Paula:

Since we do expert stories early in the year, I have my third graders do most of their prewriting orally. They talk with each other about what they know that other children

```
    I love to go fishing. I go to ashhurst lake some
times. So far I have got three fish from ashhurst
lake. But the first step is to find a low spot if
you want to no why it is becues if you get a fish
it will be pretty esiy for you to get it out of
the lake. When you get your real ready you have
to cast out your real to where you want it. Then
the hard part comes you have to whait and whait
and whait. But the good part is you get a snack
to munch on. One of the fish that I got had blue,
green, pink, red, white and yellow with dots.
```

FIG. 8.4. Neil's expert story.

```
    I'm very good at drawing.
    I can draw the very best when I have a book or
magazine to look at. What I love to draw are
characters from cartoons or video games. My
favorite chracters are sonic tails and knuckles.
I drawed a picture so nice my older brother took
it to High school with him. I have 4 hole books
filled up with drawings. Every time we go to the
hobby store at the mall I buy some drawing paper.
Drawing is my favorite thing to do on rainy and
snowy days.
    The steps of drawing
    The first step of drawing is you will need a
good and sharp pencile and and something to color
with. Take your time don't rush through it if you
take your time your picture will turn out great!
```

FIG. 8.5. Joe's expert story.

> Some little sharks may be eaten by bigger sharks like a hammerhead shark. The sharks will get very very crazy when the water gets churned up, it causes an eating frenzy. The Lionfish is a member of the scorpionfish family. When the lionfish stings another fish that fish will never bother the lionfish again!
>
> The shrimp has ten legs, but it doesn't have any claws. Shrimp live on the bottom of the sea. Shrimp like the sandy places.

FIG. 8.6. Emily's shark report.

might like to learn about. Then they each choose a specific person in the class who wants to learn more about whatever it is they are expert at. Then they begin writing. Sometimes they ask parents or friends questions that fill in gaps in their own explanations. When they do this, they simply list the other person as a source at the end.

When the children share their rough drafts with each other, they get really excited. They realize they are all experts at something. They realize they have real information to share with their peers. The excitement carries them through the final draft when they rewrite their pieces to give to the person they specified as their reader as they got ready to write.

Bernadette:

Even in second grade, research is an important part of informational writing. I want the children to learn how to read a book and use the author's information in their own writing without plagiarizing. I usually teach research as part of another unit we're studying. For example, I recently taught research while we were doing our "Oceans and Fish" unit.

First, I read a paragraph to the class about a topic from the ocean, "sharks," for example. Then in small groups the children discussed what I had read to them. After the groups had finished talking, they told me what they had learned, and I wrote the ideas on the board exactly as they said them. Then I explained that what they had just done was paraphrase what we had read. Next I read one sentence from another subject, "waves," for example. I asked the children to tell me in their own words what that sentence meant and write it down. In this way we were learning to do research without using the author's words. The children were excited by this.

Another day, I had the children read one paragraph from a subject of their choice concerning oceans and fish. Then I asked them to use their own words to write several sentences about that topic. It worked! We had no plagiarizing, and second grade research became real to the children. Later, we shared what we had learned with each other from the research we had done. The children became their own teachers and were introduced in a developmental way how to research for themselves.

THE INFORMATIONAL WRITING ROAD

When children write to share information with others, they set out on a writing road that stretches from their expertise to someone else's interest. This road can be fun because it allows students to draw on knowledge they already have or research a subject they are interested in and educate themselves. This road builds confidence by helping children realize how much they have learned about a chosen topic that other people do not know.

CHAPTER SUMMARY

When writers write to share information they possess, they write informational pieces for readers who want to learn. The informational writing process focuses on gathering and organizing information for a particular reader with a particular purpose. When teachers offer opportunities to write about information students care about to readers who care about the same information, children get excited about learning and sharing. Beginning writers sometimes need help identifying topics about which they are already experts or would like to become experts. Emergent writers sometimes write to share information together in a group.

APPLICATIONS

1. Find a sample of informational writing you have used to learn something in the last few months. Analyze who the writer was and how he or she became expert in the topic. Analyze your purpose for reading the piece. Analyze how well the text fit your purpose.
2. Find a sample of informational writing you think your students would enjoy. Analyze its target reader and its purpose. Analyze its form and how the writer made use of outside sources.
3. Make a list of topics you are expert on. (Look back at the suggested topics in "Establishing Comfort.") Choose one you think your students would be interested in learning about. Tell why you think they would be interested.
4. Draft an informational piece for your students on the topic you chose in #3 above. Choose a form you think is appropriate. Share your draft with a child. Revise according to the response you get.

9

Trying to Change Things

Dear Student at Knoles Elementary School:

While you wait for your ride after school, you decide to take a walk. You go across the baseball field, glad to be out in the warm spring day. It's quiet in the forest, so quiet you hear your tennis shoes slide softly across the pine needles that cover the trail. Between the tops of the ponderosas you see blue, blue sky. Up over your head, a chickadee buzzes happily. Ten feet ahead an Abert squirrel, its feathery tail held high like a flag, scurries across the trail, swerving to avoid a faded Coke can. The breeze that feels so good on your face and bare arms plasters a dusty napkin on your jeans. You reach down to pull it off and you count three cigarette butts by your feet. A couple of yards to the side of the trail a plastic six-pack ring rests among the lavender wild iris.

I'm sure you've been on this trail, or else you've been on the sidewalk that runs along Butler Avenue, or you've been on the playground or the baseball field: glad to be outside, only to have your mood ruined by litter. You probably know some of the terrible stories of birds dying from trying to eat cigarette butts or squirrels cut on pieces of metal. You may even have seen a wild animal in trouble sometime or other. You probably know the dismal facts about the time it takes for nature to break down this litter: years for cigarette butts, decades for paper, centuries for plastic and aluminum, eons for glass. So you can imagine what the forest and the area around the school are going to look like in a hundred years when your great-grandchildren open the time capsule at the Public Library.

Of course some people are trying to clean up the mess. The Forest Service puts Smokey the Bear on TV to get us to be careful about fire in the forest. Michael Jordan does a commercial to tell us not to throw away old batteries carelessly. The Environmental Protection Agency helps pass bills like the Clean Air Act to get businesses to clean up after themselves.

Maybe you'd like to help clean up the mess around the school. If you would, here are two clean earth acts you can do right now!

Act 1: Whenever you go outside ...

- put your own litter in your pocket.
- take a bag with you and pick up litter you walk by.

Act 2: Get your group to help (the band, your volleyball team, your class) ...

- adopt an area of the school grounds to keep clean of litter.
- adopt a half-mile of Butler Avenue to clean up once a week.

When writers write to try to change something, they begin with a problem they have and readers who have the power to make the changes. When I wrote my letter, I wrote because I was tired of the litter problems on my street. I live a half block from an elementary school, so I decided the older children in the school had the power to help me clean up our area a bit. Because I did not have money to pay them, I had to think about ways of convincing them to agree with me and help me on their own.

We find persuasive writing in social action literature, in philanthropic literature, in religious literature, in advertising of all sorts. Children are exhorted in print not to smoke or to take drugs. They are asked to recycle, to save the rain forest, to go to church, to raise money for a mother in the community who needs an expensive operation. They are the targets of advertisements selling cereal, computer games, and tennis shoes.

Let's look at two more examples of persuasion that are very different from my letter. The first is from *Children Discover*. It's an excerpt from a two-page list of descriptions and pictures from the Nature Conservancy (1995) called "How YOU Can Help" (p. 16).

Much has already been done to save animal and plant species—by people just like you. But there's a lot more that needs to be accomplished if some of your favorite plants and animals are to be seen by your grandchildren.

What can you do?

PUT UP BIRD   **URGE YOUR PARENTS**

houses. Set out   to use natural pesticides

bird feeders. Grow   on garden plants and crops.

flowers in window   Dispose of anti-freeze and

boxes to provide   oil properly.

food for insects

and birds.

In this piece the author from the Nature Conservancy wrote because he wanted to change how children act toward conservation of plants and animals. The writer began by giving children a reason to conserve (so their grandchildren can see their favorite plants and animals) and proceeded quickly to give concrete suggestions of things children and their parents can do differently.

A second piece is quite different. Take a look at this excerpt from *American Girl* (1995, pp. 24–25). It's a quiz called "When You Lose Your Cool," and it's set up in three parts: questions with A, B, C, D options for answers; a section called "How Did You Answer?" that explains what each answer option represents; and a section called "Making It Better" that suggests four steps for handling anger in a productive way.

Is the way you handle ANGER hurting or helping you?

Take this quiz and find out!

Every girl has her own way of getting mad. What's yours? Circle the answer that's closest to the way you would respond to each situation.

1. Your sister borrows your best shirt and gives it back covered with stains. You
    A. yell, "What a klutz! You can't even keep a shirt clean!"
    B. run the shirt under water as tears stream down your face.
    C. say nothing. Your parents will be furious if you start arguing.
    D. take back the headband you gave her for her birthday.

In this piece the writer wanted to change how girls deal with anger. She began with a quiz to help readers identify their own style of dealing with anger. Next she explained why the four styles she offered in the quiz are all less than helpful. Last she offered steps girls can take to deal with their anger in a productive way: "Anger is helpful when it leads you to change what's bothering you. To do that you need to talk about how you feel. Follow these steps to say what's on your mind." (p. 25)

These three pieces of writing, although quite different from one another, illustrate persuasive communication: a writer who has something he or she cares about enough to try to change, a reader who can help the writer with the change, arguments tailored to convince the reader, and concrete suggestions for change. Let's take a look at each one of these principles more closely.

A Writer Who Cares and Readers Who Can Help

I wrote the letter to children who walk by litter every day and either add to it or do not seem to notice it because I wanted them to help me clean up the area around the school. The Nature Conservancy writer wrote to children who think they cannot do anything to help plant and animal species to survive because his mission was to get everyone to help save nature. The writer of "When You Lose Your Cool" wrote to girls who handle anger in unproductive ways because she was concerned about violence in our homes and communities.

Arguments Tailored to Convince

I used emotional and factual arguments, and I reminded children that picking up litter is part of a bigger issue. The Nature Conservancy writer used pictures to convince: of smiling children, of famous people, of endangered plants and animals, and of an extinct species—Steller's sea cow. He also used examples of real people who have helped to convince: four famous people and three groups of children from elementary schools. The writer of "When You Lose Your Cool," used scenarios and analysis to convince.

Concrete Suggestion for Change

My letter offered four concrete actions children can take at Knoles Elementary School: two personal actions and two group actions. The Nature Conservancy writer listed 12 things children and their parents can do right at home. The writer of "When You Lose Your Cool" offered a four-step plan for dealing with anger in a productive way.

As teachers, then, our challenge is to help children identify things they would like to change, different arguments that will convince these readers, and concrete suggestions for change. Let's take a look at how to accomplish these goals.

ESTABLISHING COMFORT WITH PERSUASIVE WRITING

Children do not usually think of writing to try to change things, so as teachers we can establish comfort with this kind of writing by helping students identify how they encounter persuasion all the time.

- Have students tell stories of times they convinced their parents to change their minds.
- Have students tell stories about convincing their friends.
- Tell stories from your own classroom about students who convinced you.
- List examples of persuasive campaigns going on in the school: save the rain forest, recycling, using fluoride.
- Have students list their favorite commercials.
- Have a contest for the most persuasive reason the class should get an extra recess.
- Have students write a persuasive letter to a friend, convincing the friend to change his or her mind about something.
- Have students write their own commercials for a favorite product and sell the product to the class.
- Have students design their own persuasive posters for a favorite school campaign. Put the posters in the hall.

Readers and Topics

Because persuasive writing results from a commitment to change readers, the first challenge for children is to identify people or procedures they want to change. In persuasive writing, topics and readers are intimately connected: once a student knows what he wants to change, the who follows naturally; once a student knows who she wants to change, the what follows naturally.

- Have students identify conflicts in their relationships: with friends, with parents, with teachers, custodians, coaches, principals. Steer them away from abstract conflicts among adults in the larger society. Have them list whom the conflict is with and what they wish would change.

- Ask students to make a wish list of three things they would change in your town if they could. Put the answers on the board. As children see what other children want to change, they will think of even more topics.
- Ask students to brainstorm who has the power to change the items on the wish list. Beside each item on the wish list, write the name of someone who could make the wish come true. Write what the person would have to do to start the change.
- Ask students to make a list of three things they think people around them don't care enough about. (Contexts might be the family, the environment, health, children's rights.) Share. Brainstorm people children would like to convince to care more. Brainstorm what actions people could take to show they care.

BUILDING CONFIDENCE WITH PERSUASIVE WRITING

When writers write to try to change things, the process focuses on the reader more than it does in other kinds of writing. Prewriting focuses on identifying what the conflict is between the writer and the appropriate reader: who the reader is with the power to change things and what that reader believes that is different from what the writer believes. Drafting focuses on gathering arguments that will work and brainstorming suggestions for action. Revising and editing often focus on choosing the most effective form and making the final draft readable. Publishing occurs when the persuasive piece is given to the target reader. The activities that follow will help children write to try to change things.

Prewriting

- Identifying the conflict and the reader. From the topics/readers students chose earlier, have them pick one by determining which one has the greatest chance of actually changing.
- Analyzing the reader to determine what he or she believes. Ask students to predict answers to two questions: What does this person think about my issue? Why does he or she believe this way? Have students interview their readers, asking the two questions to which they predicted answers. If interviewing the real reader is impossible, ask them to interview someone who genuinely agrees with their target reader. Ask them to compare their own predictions with the answers they got in the interview. Ask them to share any surprises.
- Identifying effective arguments. Have students list what they believe and why. Have them list what their reader believes and why.
- Gathering support for the arguments. Have students look for ways to support their side of the argument reading, by talking to people, and by remembering personal experiences.

Drafting

- Getting arguments down on paper. Ask students to write about their feelings about their issue. Have them identify feelings their target reader can identify with and feelings they would be better off keeping to themselves. Ask students to summarize the facts they know or have learned about their topic. In small working groups have students brainstorm people who agree with them. Ask them to interview one person who agrees and get permission to use that person's name. Based on what they observed in their reader interviews, ask students whether they think the person they are writing to will respond more to the facts they have gathered, the feelings they wish to share, or the opinions of others. Suggest that they emphasize facts, feelings, or opinions accordingly (while including a bit of the other two categories).
- Making suggestions. Ask students to answer the question "What do you want to happen?" Ask them what their reader could do tomorrow to start moving toward the desired result.
- Writing a rough draft.

Revising

- Choosing a form. Have students decide whether their readers would respond better to a letter, a poster, an advertisement, or a pamphlet.
- Sharing drafts with each other. Pair students and have them role-play reader and writer. Encourage students to argue back with the writer. Have students brainstorm answers to the new arguments.
- Adding more support. Have students list the feeling, fact, and people arguments they used to make sure all categories have been covered. Have students go back to the "gathering support" stage of drafting. Have them find two more arguments they can use.

Editing

- Inserting pictures or graphics as needed.
- Cleaning up grammar and spelling as appropriate for the target reader.
- Documenting sources through credits, acknowledgments, or bibliography.

Publishing

- Sharing the final piece with classmates.
- Sharing the final piece with its intended reader.

To help children draw on their multiple intelligences to try to change things, try the following.

Intrapersonal Intelligence. Ask children to make a list of things that make them mad. Ask them to make a list of things that make them sad. Ask them to put stars by items on their lists that can be changed.

Interpersonal Intelligence. Ask children to identify people they know who could change 3 of the starred items on the list they made for "intrapersonal intelligence." Ask them to choose which of the three people they think they could convince the most easily. Ask children to identify emotional arguments that would convince the reader they have chosen. Ask them to identify an outside authority that reader would be impressed by.

Verbal/Linguistic Intelligence. Ask children to read a book or article about the issue about which they have chosen to write.

Logical/Mathematical Intelligence. Ask children to identify facts that might persuade the readers they have chosen. Ask them to list those facts most important to least important.

Visual/Spatial Intelligence. Ask children to find or draw pictures that might convince the reader they have chosen.

Body/Kinesthetic Intelligence. Ask children to role-play their arguments: have the writer play his or her reader and another child play the writer.

DEVELOPING COMPETENCE WITH PERSUASIVE WRITING

Because persuasive writing focuses on changing a reader's beliefs or actions, its success depends on a writer analyzing a reader's beliefs, choosing arguments that will work, and making concrete suggestions to start the process of change. In order to write effective persuasion, children must be able to understand why their readers feel the way they do so they can offer suggestions for change that will be accepted. At first this task may seem difficult, but children do this kind of analysis intuitively when they approach Mom, Dad, or Grandma in different ways to ask permission for the same privilege.

Helping Children Analyze Readers

- Ask students what special privilege they would like to have for the coming weekend. Have them role play with each other asking Mom, asking Dad, asking a grandparent.
- As a class, brainstorm feeling, fact, and people arguments they could make to the school board to get a new piece of playground equipment.
- As a class, brainstorm a list of things that need changing around the school. Brainstorm a who/what list to match at least two of the items on the first list. Discuss arguments that would work in one situation but not in another.
- Have the class make a Venn diagram (Fig. 9.3) showing differences and similarities between the two sides of one of the issues just mentioned. Focus on finding similarities that can be used to open the discussion.

Helping Children Identify Arguments

Classical rhetoric identified three kinds of effective arguments in persuasion: emotional, logical, and appeals to authority (see Crowley, 1994). As teachers we

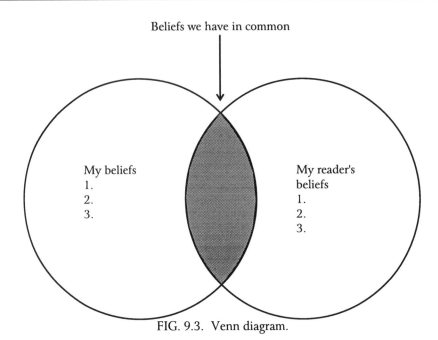

FIG. 9.3. Venn diagram.

can help students use a variety of arguments by helping them think in terms of feelings, facts, and people.

- Analyze persuasive campaigns going on in the school—recycling or the D.A.R.E. program—for types of arguments used.
- Analyze a favorite commercial for types of arguments.
- Analyze a letter to the editor for types of arguments.
- Have children brainstorm arguments for their own writing using 3 categories: facts, feelings, people. Ask them to gather arguments in categories that are weak: facts from books, feelings from inside themselves, people from talking to others.

Helping Children Make Concrete Suggestions

Although it is often easy to figure out what we want the end result to be, it is sometimes harder to figure out what has to happen to reach that result. This process is particularly hard for children. To begin to develop this capacity, have children start with the result they want and work backwards step-by-step to where they are now by asking the question: "What would have to happen before that could happen?" For example, if the desired result is a longer recess period, the process might look like this:

Result: 15 more minutes at recess
Before that could happen: The principal has to agree.
Before that could happen: The teacher as to ask the principal.
Before that could happen: The teacher has to agree with the class.
Before that could happen: The class has to find a way to get their work done in 15 less minutes.

In this example, then, students could see that in order to start the process of changing the recess time, they must make concrete suggestions about how to get their work done more quickly. Once they get the idea as a whole group, ask children to brainstorm "Before that could happen" in small groups for each other's problems.

IN THE CLASSROOM

Becky:

When I teach persuasive writing, I ask my students to focus on personal issues. We brainstorm conflicts they have with friends or parents that could be discussed in a letter. Then when the students know what they want to write about and who they want to write to, we start the process of figuring out why the other person wants things the way they are right now and why the student wants things to change. One way I've found to help my students think their topics through is by giving them a frame [Figs. 9.4 & 9.5] that lists reasons as pros and cons. Then when they get ready to write, I suggest that they think of solutions to the cons. After they've published their letters by giving them to their parents or friends, we take some time to find out whether the letters worked or not. Sometimes they do, and the students get excited about the power that writing has.

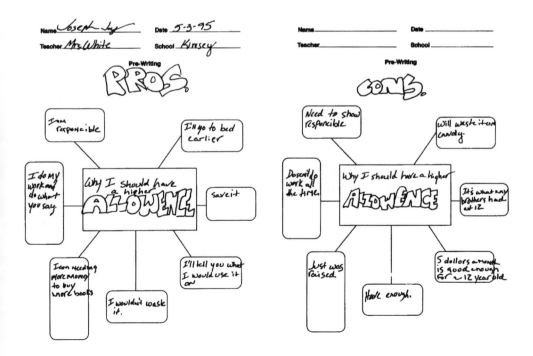

FIG. 9.4. Joseph's "pros and cons" frame.

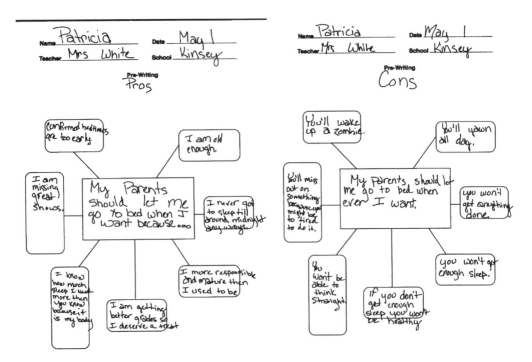

FIG. 9.5. Patricia's "pros and cons" frame.

CHILDREN WRITING TO TRY TO CHANGE THINGS

These pieces illustrate children writing about things they'd like to change to readers who have the power to help them. Figures 9.6 and 9.7 are letters written by two sixth graders to their parents based on the frames included in Figs. 9.4 and 9.5. The last piece (Fig. 9.8) is a letter to the editor written by a fourth grader. Notice the different kinds of arguments Kevin uses in his letter. He chose his topic from local concerns and did most of his research on the Internet.

THE PERSUASIVE WRITING ROAD

When children write to try to change things, they have set out on a road that leads from their own view of the way things ought to be to readers who disagree with them or who do not care. It is a bit rockier road than personal writing or informational writing, but it is a rewarding road because it allows writers to take action toward something about which they feel strongly. It is a good road to travel in learning to write because it is closely connected to the writer's life.

CHAPTER SUMMARY

Persuasive writing exists to convince other people to change what they believe or how they act. As reader-based writing, it focuses on who the appropriate reader is, what kinds of argument will convince that reader, and what suggestions will

May 10, 1995
Dear Mom and Dad,
I have written this letter to ask you if I could have a higher allowance. I know you probably think five dollars is high enough allowance already, and that it was just raised. I know I have wasted it on candy and other meaningless things in the past.
But I won't do that. I'll save it and tell you what I'll use it on and how much it will cost. I'll be responsible and do my work on time. I'll even go to bed earlier. A kid my age needs and wants things to buy.
Thank you for reading this letter.
Your Son,
Joseph Jay

FIG. 9.6. Joseph's persuasive letter.

Dear Mom,
I know how much sleep means to you. Like you, I believe everyone needs a certain amount of sleep. Believe me, 8:30 p.m. is too early. I know that you let me stay up a little later but that is still too early.
The reason I writing this letter is too tell you that I am old enough to go to bed when I want. I will do more chores and even make dinner. I promise that I will get all my homework and chores done.
Besides, now I am old enough, mature enough, and responsible enough to stay up late. I know that you may disapprove of this. I have thought this over, so please think this over, this is very important to me.
Love,
Patricia

FIG. 9.7. Patricia's persuasive letter.

6/27/96

Dear Editor:

My name is Kevin Scott. I am nine years old and going into the fourth grade at Sechrist Elementary School. My interests include sports, animals, and occasionally computers.

One day, when I was at computer camp, I looked up "The Grand Canyon" on the Internet and found information on many interesting things. When I was surfing the 'net, I also found some information that bothered me. I read that some developers are trying to build a commercial development called "Canyon Forest Village."

CFV will include:

- 5,000 hotel rooms
- 500,000 square feet of retail space
- 2,600 homes, apartments, and condominiums
- 15,000 people that would use almost 2 million gallons of water per day

CFV is a bad idea because it will ruin the Grand Canyon's delicate ecosystem. It will also increase pollution levels by bringing hundreds of thousands of cars into the canyon each year. CFV will turn the South Rim of the Grand Canyon into the largest commercial development in the history of Arizona and will destroy its natural charm.

I feel terrible that this may happen to the Grand Canyon and I really don't want them to ruin one of Arizona's natural landmarks. I want to ask everybody, especially the Forest Service, to say NO to Canyon Forest Village.

Sincerely,

Kevin Scott

FIG. 9.8. Kevin's letter to the editor.

help the reader start the process of change. Even very young children are accustomed to using persuasion to get their way, so this kind of writing can be fun and rewarding for elementary students. When topics and readers are carefully chosen, persuasive writing is a natural!

APPLICATIONS

1. When have you been successful at convincing someone to change: at home, at school, in the society? What kinds of arguments worked? Why?
2. If you could change one thing at your school, what would it be? Identify who has the power to make the change. Identify three arguments you could use: an emotional, a factual, and an authoritative argument.
3. List the 3 times you were maddest this month. Identify what needed to be changed in each of those situations and who had the power to change things. List the 3 things you worry about the most. Identify what could change to make you quit worrying and who has the power to make those changes.
4. Choose one of the conflicts you identified in #3. Make a Venn diagram of your position, the other person's position, and the points of similarity. Brainstorm arguments you could make that might convince your target reader: facts, feelings, and people.
5. Use the "Result"–"Before that could happen" exercise on this conflict. List concrete actions your target reader could take to begin the change process.
6. Draft a letter to your target reader. Role-play your draft with a partner: have your partner read the letter to you; you respond as your reader. If you want to, revise your letter and send it.

10

For the Love of Writing

The Two-in-One Mystery

Jamie frowned. She tucked her straight brown hair behind her ears and looked under the planter. The flower seeds had just come up, like soft green feathers. She looked in the coils of the garden hose, careful not to bother the lacy spider web with the toe of her tennis shoe. She even looked in Chloe's cardboard house again.

"Chloe," she said, "where is your red ribbon?"

Chloe, who was a clothespin doll, didn't answer.

"This is the last straw!" Jamie made a face and plopped down on the torn pillow she kept on the porch. "First your blue blanket disappeared. Then it was your yellow yarn hair. Now it's the red ribbon. This is a mystery."

Chloe smiled her ink smile.

"Somebody's taking your things!" Jamie gritted her teeth and stood up. "I bet it's that little pest Katy. She always wants to play with your things."

Jamie clipped Chloe to the sleeve of her t-shirt and stomped next door through the freshly cut grass. She knocked on the screen and waited.

"Hi, Jamie," said Katy's mom. "Katy's had the flu for a week, so she can't play."

"Oh," said Jamie.

"Maybe tomorrow," said Katy's mom.

Jamie nodded and headed home. "Katy's been sick, Chloe," she said. "I'm sorry I thought she took your things." Jamie pushed her bangs out of her eyes and frowned. "Maybe it's Socks. That cat's always hiding stuff behind the curtains."

Chloe smiled up at the sky from Jamie's sleeve.

"If Socks did it, I won't give him a treat for a week!" Jamie walked in the house and let the door slam shut.

Socks was lying on the window sill in the warm sunshine, but none of Chloe's things were behind the curtain.

"I'm sorry, Socks." Jamie reached out and stroked his soft back. "You're a good cat." She unclipped Chloe from her sleeve and looked into the ink eyes. "So who's taking your things?"

Chloe just smiled.

"And why are you smiling when you should be mad? This is a two-in-one mystery!"

Of course, Chloe kept smiling.

Jamie sighed and looked out the window to the porch. On the pillow she saw a little brown bird.

"Look!" Jamie held Chloe up to the window.

As they watched, the house wren pulled out a piece of pillow stuffing. Then it flew up under the roof.

"The robber," whispered Jamie.

Carrying Chloe in her hand, she tip-toed out onto the porch. Pretty soon, the bird came back. It got another piece of stuffing, and this time Jamie spotted the nest.

"Isn't it pretty, Chloe?"

One end of Chloe's ribbon hung down from the nest and flapped like the tail of a tiny red wind sock. Pieces of Chloe's yellow hair poked out from the twigs and grass. A corner of Chloe's blue blanket and tufts of white stuffing peeked over the top.

"Now we know who's been taking your things."

Chloe smiled, maybe a little bigger than before.

"And I know why you're smiling, Chloe. No mysteries anymore." Jamie smiled herself. "It's spring!"

Sometimes writers write just because they love to write. I wrote "The 2-in-1 Mystery" because I love mysteries, and I wanted to tell a story to children who love mysteries too. I started my story by thinking about the mystery story form: a puzzle that needs a solution, clues, suspects, and a sleuth. I thought about characters that could be part of my story and situations that might happen to children.

When writers write for the love of writing, they write literature. When we think of *literature*, we sometimes think of classic literature—the famous historical works we studied in school. But literary writing is more than Shakespeare and Melville. It is tall tales, fairy tales, and ballads. It is creative nonfiction (essays that are art) and sitcom scripts. It is the best-seller list. It is epigrams, jokes, and funny stories. It is movies and comic books and science fiction. From Saturday morning cartoons to MTV, literary writing is all around us. When writers write because they love to write, they usually begin with a particular form.

Take a look at this excerpt from "Buster and the Toboggan" by Sandra Beswetherick (1996).

"Why don't you go on over? Join the fun." Grandad points to the children we're watching through the kitchen window. They're sliding down the snow-covered hill next to his house.

"I'm not in the mood, Grandad." Didn't I tell Dad I was old enough to stay alone while he was away on business? He brought me to Grandad's anyway. "Besides, I don't have my Snow Skimmer." There wasn't enough room in the car to fit my brand-new sled with the ski runner and steering handle.

"Snow Skimmer? Who needs one of those?" Before I know what's happening, Grandad is down in the basement and back up again. He's carrying—oh no! Not the tobaggon! (p. 20)

Although I have never met Ms. Beswetherick, we can tell from how carefully she crafted her story that she loves to write. As she wrote, she considered the ingredients of short stories: plot, character, setting, and theme. Her plot revolves around a boy spending a forced vacation with his grandfather. Her characters are Grandad, the "I" narrator, and a dog named Buster. Her theme is something like, "It is easier to make friends than you think."

Now take a look at a poem: "What to Do if You See a Monster"[1] by Fay Robinson (1996).

If you see a monster,
look at his eyes,
look at his nose,
look at his ears,
look at his toes,

look at his knees,
look at his scales,
look at his hands,
look at his tails,

look at his teeth,
and at last,
if he's real,
get lost FAST!

Robinson loves to write poetry. From her poem we can tell she enjoys playing with words, making them rhyme and making them tell a tiny story very quickly. As she wrote her poem, she considered the characteristics of children's poetry: short lines, rhythm of words, rhyme, repetition, and humor. Because she was writing for very young children, she chose an imaginary subject (monsters) and simple rhyming words (nose–toes; scales–tails; last–fast). The picture that accompanied the poem made it funny rather than scary.

---

[1]Copyright by Highlights for Children, Inc., Columbus, Ohio. Permission to reprint one time, nonexclusive.

ESTABLISHING COMFORT WITH LITERARY WRITING

Most children have listened to family stories or watched Disney videos since before they could say "Cinderella." Young children often make up stories to tell each other or to guide "playing house." They sing songs with their own tunes and words. Writing stories and poems seems natural. So primary children will probably feel naturally relaxed with literary writing and think it is fun.

Older children, however, may have begun to feel intimidated by our culture's fascination with "stars" in the literary sky. A good way to help older children overcome their reluctance to try literary writing is to ask them to share examples of literary writing they enjoy consuming: favorite TV shows and movies, favorite songs and rhymes, favorite books. Share pieces of your own literary writing to bridge the gap between nationally famous pieces and their own writing. Activities that will help children begin to feel more comfortable with literary writing include the following:

- Ask students to tell their favorite story to a group of classmates or younger students.
- Ask students to read their favorite nursery rhymes aloud to younger students.
- Ask students to tell the story of an episode from their favorite movie or TV show to a peer partner.
- Model a story or poem of your own.
- Invite a storyteller to your classroom. Ask him or her to teach your students the basics of storytelling.
- Invite a local poet to your classroom. Ask him or her to do a poetry writing workshop with your students.
- Write a drama of your own for the class to act out.
- Invite an actor from your local playhouse. Ask him or her to give your students backstage tips.

BUILDING CONFIDENCE WITH LITERARY WRITING

When writers write for the love of writing, the writing process focuses on the form of the writing more than it does in other kinds of writing. Prewriting consists of getting familiar with a particular form and then letting the imagination wander within that form: learning how short stories, poems, or plays are put together and then imagining. Drafting consists of channeling the imagination in the chosen form: making a short story out of my imaginary trip into the past, making a poem out of love for a cat, making a play out of a fight with a best friend. Revising and editing consist of getting the form just right: making lines break at the best place or making sure the conflict is clear. Activities kids might do to write stories, poems, and plays include the following:

Prewriting

- reading new poems and stories
- re-reading favorite poems and stories
- retelling favorite stories
- daydreaming and imagining

Drafting

- finding form: a short poem, a long poem, a short story, a play, a picture book.
- following a frame for the chosen form (Figs. 10.1, 10.2, & 10.3 shared by Becky White)

FABLES   NAME_____
                                          DATE_____

TITLE OF FABLE:
AUTHOR:

SPECIFIC LESSON LEARNED:

NAME THE ANIMAL THAT DEPICTS GOOD AND WRITE ABOUT ITS PART IN THE STORY:

NAME THE ANIMAL THAT DEPICTS EVIL AND WRITE ABOUT ITS PART IN THE STORY:

SUMMARIZE THE ENDING OF THE FABLE:

FIG. 10.1. Fable frame.

Trickster Tales

NAME OF STORY WHAT COUNTRY?	WHO TRICKED?	WHO WAS TRICKED?	WHAT WAS THE TRICK?	WHAT WAS THE RESULT?

FIG. 10.2. Trickster story frame.

MYTHS AND LEGENDS

NAME_____

DATE_____

TITLE OF STORY_____

SETTING: WHERE_____

WHEN_____

CHARACTERS: WHO _____

PROBLEM_____

FIG. 10.3. Myths and legends frame.

Revising

- polishing form: adding dialogue, changing line breaks, deleting unneeded stage directions
- sharing drafts with each other
- answering questions peer group members ask

Editing

- editing to the expectations of the form: punctuating dialogue, etc.
- cleaning up grammar and spelling
- polishing line by line, word by word

Publishing

- performing the piece
- celebrating written language

To help children draw on their multiple intelligences to write literary pieces, try the following:

Verbal/Linguistic Intelligence. Ask children to read poems, short stories, plays, tall tales, whatever form you choose. Ask them to pick their favorites. Ask them to re-read their favorites until they know them by heart.

Intrapersonal Intelligence. Ask children to spend time daydreaming. Ask them to make a list of their favorite daydreams.

Visual/Spatial Intelligence. Ask children to storyboard their pieces (make a series of rough sketches that tell the story without words). Ask them to make a collage or draw pictures to go with their piece.

Logical/Mathematical Intelligence. Ask children to tell their stories in chronological order. Ask them to tell you what the most important parts of the story are and what the least important parts are. Help them give more details about important parts and less about unimportant parts.

Musical Intelligence. Ask children to find a tune for their poem or a song that could go with a poem or play. Allow them to write their own songs and tunes if they want to.

Interpersonal Intelligence. Ask children to perform their drafts to each other. Ask them to make a list of ideas they got for their own piece from hearing/watching their peers perform.

Body/Kinesthetic Intelligence. Ask children to act out their stories for the class. Have groups of children act out each other's stories. Have groups perform plays children have written.

DEVELOPING COMPETENCE WITH LITERARY WRITING

Writers who write because they love to write become competent when they take ownership of a particular form of writing. Helping children develop competence with this kind of writing, then, depends on introducing them to the structures of literary writing. Overviews of three structures follow: fiction, drama, and poetry. No matter what structures you and your students work with, provide audiences for students' literary work: perform plays, read poetry aloud, send stories to younger students, or include parents in a publishing party.

Fiction

Whether they have been read to or not, children who have grown up on Saturday morning TV and Disney movies possess an almost intuitive awareness of what a story is in popular American culture: a character, a problem, and solution. The character can be drawn from contemporary life (the Karate Kid), from history (Pocahontas), or from imagination (the Little Mermaid). Characters can be people or animals—both real and imagined (the whale in *Free Willy* or the stuffed animals in *Winnie the Pooh*). Problems, too, can come from almost anywhere. In the *Karate Kid* movies, the problem is a bully. In *Winnie the Pooh* it is finding honey. Solutions must be arrived at by the character with the problem: Pooh must get his own honey, even though Christopher Robin could ask his mom to go to the store for some; Daniel must take on the bully rather than appeal to adult authorities. To be an interesting story, the solution can not be too easy. There must be complications: Pooh must contend with bees to get his honey; Daniel must learn karate before he can take on the bully. So, we have a simple structure for fiction: a character with a problem, complications, a solution. Let's take an example:

> *character*—a shaggy yellow dog with friendly brown eyes; *problem*—needs a home; *complications*—has a hurt leg; *solution*—finds a boy who wants to be a veterinarian.

Of course fiction, like all literary writing, possesses *theme*, or meaning, as well. However, lest children fall into the "what is the moral of this story?" trap, it is best to allow themes to emerge from solutions. The theme of our sample story might be "Never give up."

Helping Children Write Fiction

- Have the class write a story together on the overhead projector. Guide the discussion of character, problem, complications, and solutions.
- Do group serial stories. Put children in groups of three or four. Ask each group to invent a character. Have groups trade characters. Ask each group to invent a problem for the new character. Have groups trade again. Ask groups to invent complications. Have groups trade again. Ask groups to invent solutions. Have groups read their stories to the class.
- Begin with a character. Ask students to invent characters: monsters, heros, real children different from themselves, historical characters, children just like themselves. Use different prompts to help them: other stories, pictures from magazines, music. In partners, have students brainstorm the kinds of problems these characters would be likely to encounter. Once a character and

a problem have been chosen, have different sets of partners brainstorm solutions and complications.

- Begin with a problem. Have students list four problems they or a friend have had to solve. Ask them to invent complications that would make the problem even worse. Using some of the ideas just mentioned, help them invent an imaginary character who might have had this problem (perhaps in another form—a bully, but not the same bully, for example). Have students brainstorm solutions in small groups.
- Begin with a happy scene (a character with a solution). Have students brainstorm what problems the character had to overcome to reach this place.

Drama

In our society, most people consume fiction in dramatic form, through TV or movies. Drama, then, is another natural form of literary writing. Children often get excited about writing a new episode for a TV show they watch, a sequel to a movie they love, or even a screenplay for a novel or short story they have read. Drama, of course, has many of the same characteristics as fiction. It is built on a character solving a problem. However, drama shows action through dialogue and stage directions. Because of their familiarity with this form, student writers often find drama a fun and rewarding form of literary writing. Small groups working together can help each other with natural sounding dialog and clear stage directions. A parent (or another child) with a video camera can even tape student dramas!

Helping Children Write Drama

- Have students write down a favorite episode of a TV show. Ask them to note places in the action where characters were speaking to each other; stage directions needed for action scenes; how particular characters were dressed; what the character's clothes communicated.
- Have students dramatize familiar fairy tales. (If possible, show an episode of *Fairy Tale Theater* to the class first.)
- Have students begin writing drama from a story they have written.
- Have students act out scenes before writing them down.

Poetry

Poetry is a form of literary writing that values the sound of language and economy of words. Because most poetry is meant to be read aloud, it often depends on rhythm and sometimes on rhyme. Because poetry is sparing in its use of words, figures of speech like metaphor, simile, personification, and hyperbole often carry much of the meaning in poetry. Classical poetry also depended on formal line structures. The English sonnet, for example, has fourteen lines usually in two stanzas, one with eight lines and a second with six. The French sestina consists of six stanzas of six lines each and a three-line concluding stanza. Although some modern poets still use the classical forms of poetry, other poets write in free verse, allowing meaning to dictate form.

Although formal poetry may seem strange and unfamiliar to some students, poetic forms are actually fairly common in our society—as song lyrics, commercial jingles, and greeting card verses. If we allow our students to begin with the familiar and work toward the unfamiliar, many children will find that they enjoy writing poetry. Brief structures like haiku and cinquain are user-friendly and can be used to introduce the concept of structure. Other patterns for poems offer opportunities for students to practice a variety of forms.

Helping Children Write Poetry

- Have students write out the lyrics to a favorite song.
- Have students write verses appropriate for holiday cards.
- Have students write a new verse to a favorite song.
- Have students write haiku, a 17-syllable poem of three lines: 5 syllables, 7 syllables, 5 syllables
- Have students write cinquain, a 22-syllable poem of five lines: 2 syllables, 4, 6, 8, 2.
- Have students write concrete poems: words in the shape of the object being described.

INVITING ALL CHILDREN TO WRITE LITERATURE

Sometimes we assume that the literary structures with which we are familiar are the same in all cultures. This is not true, of course. In Native American cultures, for example, coyote tales are a common literary structure quite unlike European story structures. These stories sometimes serve the same function that fables serve (to teach moral lessons), but the stories follow a much different structure and focus on the never-ending stupidity and immorality of coyote. Encourage children who know literary structures from other cultures to share them with the class. Ask them to teach the class to write a story, poem, or song following that structure.

IN THE CLASSROOM

Becky:

> We write a lot of poetry in my class. The kids love to hear it, and they like to write it and share it. It doesn't go through the same depth of the writing process as other forms of writing, so it's immediate for them. They write it and read it on the same day.

> Over the years I've had a lot of success with my students and poetry contests. Our district puts together an anthology every year called *Northland Portfolio*, and I've had kids published in it almost every year. A couple of years ago several of my students

submitted poems to a national poetry book, *The Anthology of Young Poets*, and one student was published in that. Last year I had four students volunteer to go and read for the Writers' Harvest held at the university and all of their parents went along.

When one student in the class gets published, it's exciting for all of them. They have a group ownership of the poem because they've all worked on it, and it makes them all feel successful. A really great thing about poetry is that I have kids from all levels and all socio-economic backgrounds get really involved in poetry. Even special ed kids succeed with poetry.

CHILDREN WRITING LITERATURE

Let's take a look at three examples of literary writing by children. Figure 10.4 is a retelling of a fable by a second grader; Fig. 10.5 is an original myth by a sixth grader; Fig. 10.6 is a poem about a little brother with cerebral palsy by a third grader.

THE LITERARY WRITING ROAD

When children write for the love of writing, they set out on a road of their own imaginations. They are free to invent, compare, and daydream. They can go forward in time or back in time. They can write short verses for a special occasion or long dramas like they see at the movies or anything in between. The literary writing road is a fun one for beginning writers because they are free to re-invent the world in any way they like.

```
                The Fox and the Goose
                  by Rachael Graves
    Once upon a time there was a little goose. She
was sleeping in a nest.
    A sneaky fox came along.
    The fox picked up the goose and he ran over hills
and rivers and streams.
    He ran to a tree and sat in the shade of it.
"Little goose what would you do if you had me
under your wing?"
    "I would say grace."
    "I will," said the fox. He said grace. And then
the goose ran.
```

FIG. 10.4. Rachael's retelling.

How the Rainbow Came to Be

One day after Serues had planted a beautiful group of flowers, Ires had been wondering why such beautiful group of flowers had to die one day. Ires came up with a plan so that the beautiful flowers could be seen by everyone all over the world. She went to the meadow and picked flowers of all different colors, Red ones, yellow ones, orange ones, pink ones, blue ones, and purple ones. She lined them in rows by colors on a sky blue blanket then she went up to the top of Mt. Olympus and stood at the very very top, then she was going to through them up in the sky. But all of a sudden it started to rain. Ires was very sad and started to cry, when Zues came and put his arm around her and said, "Don't cry my child, the rain will soon end then you can make your rows of flowers into the sky." Zues did not belive that she could do it by herself so when the rain ended she was about to through her flowers into the sky Zues made them stay up there so that Ires would not be sad. Ires named the flowers in the sky a rainbow, then Zues made Ires the rainbow goddess. Now every time it rains it is followed by by Ires's flowers.

by Janet L. Garcia

FIG. 10.5. Janet's myth.

Lyle is like catepelar that crawls on the ground he has a long body and is always slow, he eats vegetables like a caterpillar and he is always laughing.

Lyle likes to play outside and watches other people play, he has small feet and wiggles on the floor like a caterpillar.

Lyle dreams to become a cocoon and wait until he hatches to become a buitiful long Winged Buterfly that's my brother Lyle.

FIG. 10.6. Laurando's poem.

CHAPTER SUMMARY

Literary writing creates art from words. Its formal forms are fiction, drama, and poetry. Its informal forms are TV and movie scripts, folktales and ballads, song lyrics, and greeting card verses. Although students may feel unfamiliar with classical forms of literature, they will be comfortable with contemporary forms. Encouraging them to have fun with their writing as you teach them the structures will make literary writing into a favorite genre.

APPLICATIONS

1. What forms of literary writing do you enjoy? Why do you like them? Which forms did you most enjoy as a child? Why?
2. Find a copy of a favorite story or poem from your childhood. Re-read it. Analyze its structure. (A favorite TV show or movie will work if you can remember it well enough to analyze structure.)
3. If you could be a child again, what would you most like to do? Spend some time daydreaming answers.
4. Using the favorite piece you worked with in #2, draft a literary piece based on one of your daydreams in #3.
5. Analyze your literary writing process from applications 2–4. Which parts were easiest for you? Which parts were hardest? Why?

11

To Learn

When writers write to learn something new rather than to communicate with someone else, they pick and choose among the activities of the writing process. Sometimes they simply gather information and organize it (prewriting). Sometimes they put what they are learning into tentative sentences and paragraphs (drafting). Sometimes they choose readers and begin to communicate what they know to someone else. Just as teaching helps us learn, so writing to someone else helps us learn in more depth. When I wrote my first book, *Evaluating Children's Writing* (1994a), I began writing to elementary teachers what I knew about evaluation because I believed that grades were a necessary evil with which we all had to cope. By the time I had completed the book, I had learned how to use evaluation as teaching tool that could actually help us teach better. Writing what I knew taught me more than I knew when I started!

Writing is a powerful tool for learning because it draws on higher-order thinking skills like synthesis, analysis, application, and evaluation. Informational writers, for example, must gather information from many sources, evaluating the quality of the sources to decide which ones to rely on and which ones to ignore. To synthesize individual facts into coherent meaning, informational writers must first analyze how the facts fit together. When students write reports that ask them to evaluate, analyze, and synthesize facts until they are their own, they develop competence in writing as they are developing competence in content. When students write persuasive pieces in the context of a variety of content areas, they must analyze and evaluate arguments, and they begin to grasp the controversial nature of much of what they are learning in school. Personal writing adapted to content study calls for synthesis and empathy. It can help students identify the human element of factual information. Literary writing requires students to use their imaginations to think about concepts they are learning. It enables them to go beyond facts into possibility. Learning to write for communication and writing to learn content, then, are symbiotic processes that nurture each other.

WRITING AS PART OF LITERATURE STUDY

Ms. Nelson says to her third-grade class, "Children, we've read lots of Chris Van Allsburg's books, haven't we? What was your favorite?"

"Jumanji (1981)," says Jon.

"Polar Express," says Alyssa.

"The Sweetest Fig," says Walter.

"Good," says Ms. Nelson. "This has been a fun lit. study. Now we're going to write about some of the things we remember from the books we've read. We're going to write an alphabet poem. How many of you know the alphabet?"

All the hands go up. "I'm silly," says Ms. Nelson. "You're in third grade. Of course, you all know the alphabet. But I bet you don't know how to make a poem out of the alphabet, so I'll show you." She turns on the overhead projector and puts a clean sheet of acetate on it.

She picks up a marker and writes *A*. "Now," she says, "what can we think of from Chris Van Allsburg's books that begins with *A*? How about *ants*?" She writes *ants* next to the *A*. "Were there ants in any of the books?"

"In *Two Bad Ants*," says Jessica.

"Good," says Ms. Nelson. "How about antennaes? The ants had antennaes, don't they?" She writes *antennaes* next to *A*.

"Good," says Ms. Nelson. "Who can think of another *A* word?"

"Axes," says Jon.

"Good," says Ms. Nelson, writing *axes* next to *A*. "What book had axes in it?"

"The Widow's Broom," says Jon.

"Allen," says Alyssa. "From *The Garden of Abdul Gasazi*."

Together the class writes an alphabet poem:

Ants, antennaes, axes, and Allen
Brooms, Bibot, bunnies, and bells
Curious, Chris, cats, crystals, and coffee
Dog or duck??
Eiffel Tower, elves
Figs, frost, future, and Little Fritz
Gasazi!!
Hay, houses, and HIDDEN DOGS!
Ice and illustrations
Judy and Jumanji's jungle
Kangaroo and Katy
Lions!
Monkeys, Marcel, and music
North Pole
Overalls
Polar Express, Peter, presents, and pumpkins
Queen ant
Rhinoceroses, reindeer, and rain
Santa, stranger, sugar, surprises, and soup
Toothpicks, toothaches, trains, and time travel
Up: Zephyr

Van Allsburg
Witch and widow
X-press-Excellent
Young ladies
Zephyr

Ms. Nelson has used writing this poem as review to help her students recall and synthesize the books they've read over the course of their Chris Van Allsburg literature study.

Personal and literary writing lend themselves almost intuitively to literature; however, informational and persuasive writing can support literature study as well.

Personal Writing

- Have students keep a personal response journal throughout the literature study. Ask them to respond to prompts like:
  "Did you like this story? Why or why not?"
  "Tell an experience you've had that is either like the character's or different."
  "If you were this character, would you have reacted as he or she did? Why?"
  "If you were the author of this story, what would you change in it?"
- Have students write personal letters to the characters in the story.
- Have students pick their favorite author and write a personal letter to the author.
- Using the persona of a character they've read about, have students write diary entries for the time period of the story or for the following week. Share the diary entries in small groups.

Literary Writing

- Tie reading and writing of literary forms together. Write poetry while studying it; write tall tales while reading them. Have students read their own writing aloud to the class.
- Analyze literary reading for structure of writing as well as for meaning. Use the communication triangle to organize class discussions of poems or stories.
- Ask students to write book reports based on analyzing what they've read using the communication triangle. Put the book reports in a folder for classmates to look through when picking their next book.
- Have students make their own literary anthologies: a notebook of favorite poems, a collection of favorite short stories to keep over the years. Have them write their own entries for the anthology.

Informational Writing

- Ask students to research a favorite author and write a biography. Put together an anthology and place it in the class library.
- Ask students to research the time period in which a book or play or poem was written. Have the class put together a newspaper of the time period that includes a review of the book. Share the newspaper with another class.

- Have students write an informative report on background in a story. For example, a student reading *Little House on the Prairie* (Wilder, 1953) might write about sod-house construction. Have students share their reports with the class.

Persuasive Writing

- Have students write a persuasive book jacket for their favorite book. Ask the librarian to display the book jackets in the school library.
- Have students write persuasive letters from one character in a story to another character solving the conflict a different way from the way the author solved it.
- Have students write a commercial selling a book they especially like. Have a contest to see which three commercials were the most effective for the class.

WRITING AS PART OF SCIENCE STUDY

Look at the account a sixth grader wrote of an imaginary hot-air balloon ride (Fig. 11.1) to summarize and synthesize what she had learned from her geography study of Italy. It is an imagined piece of personal writing, like a personal essay, but it is based on book knowledge and imagination rather than personal experience.

Second graders wrote the descriptions of bubbles in Figs. 11.2 through 11.4 after observing bubbles in a science experiment. They are poems, but they are based on careful observation.

Sometimes we think of informational writing as the only kind of writing that can support science study, but persuasive, personal, and literary writing can support science learning as well.

```
    As I am flying over Italy in my hot-air balloon
I see vegetables of many colors and as big as
basketballs and there was a big pasture of wheat
about the size of 600 football fields. The sugar
beets were barely growing like babies and almonds
being picked. Tobacco being packed in square
bundles to ship to another place and potatoes of
red and brown colors and as big as bananas. Then
grapes about ready to eat, and that was the end
of my whole trip over the beatiful, rich, Italy.
                    By: Amberly
```

FIG. 11.1. Amberly's balloon ride.

Pretty Bubbles
Bubbles . . . . .
bubbles are
smooshed together and rainbow
streaming and popping
Large and tiny
Bubbles . . . . .
bubbles on my paper.
Written and illustrated by:
Emily Ruth Evans

FIG. 11.2. Emily's bubbles.

Big Bubbles and Small Bubbles
Bubbles . . . . .
bubbles are
fun and gooey
popping and flying
white and big or small
Bubbles . . . . .
bubbles on my paper.
Written and illustrated by:
Jose Gutierrez

FIG. 11.3. Jose's bubbles.

Informational Writing

- Ask students to research a variety of related topics: for example, common animals of the state. Have students write a report for the class on the information they learned. Make a class book for students to check out and read.
- Have students write lab reports of experiments they have done or watched. In groups, ask them to choose the most accurate report.
- Have students read a biography of a famous scientist and write a report for a classmate. Have a class quiz on all the scientists.

```
        Colorful Bubbles
        Bubbles . . . . .
            bubbles are
     humongous and enormous
       growing and popping
     rainbows and outrageous
        Bubbles . . . . .
       bubbles in my hair.
    Written and illustrated by:
      Ashley Katherine Baker
```

FIG. 11.4. Ashley's bubbles.

Persuasive Writing

- Have students write essays on both sides of scientific theories: evolution, the big bang theory, the extinction of dinosaurs, theories of the formation of the Grand Canyon. Hold a class debate based on the essays.
- Have students write persuasive predictions before they do science experiments to convince their group they are right. Have groups choose the best prediction. After the experiment, compare predictions with results.
- Have students write letters of support for their favorite project to the science fair judges in your school.
- Have students write travel commercials that they might see on TV for places they are studying in geography.

Personal Writing

- Have students conduct an experiment on themselves (with changing diet or homework practices or exercise, etc.). Have them keep a journal of their observations and then write their personal conclusions.
- Have students pose problems from their own lives that could be resolved through experimentation. Have them write personal statements of why they want answers to these questions.
- Have students choose a state they would like to visit. Have them research their state and plan an itinerary for their trip: where they would go, what they would see, how long they would stay, and so on. Ask them to write a letter to their parents proposing such a trip.

- Have students write their own "science" autobiography to you, telling things like experiences they have had studying science, how they feel about science, and why.

Literary Writing

- Have students dramatize important scientific discoveries for their parents: what life was like before the telephone and how the telephone changed people's lives, for example.
- Have students write descriptive poems for younger children about scientific concepts: a series of poems about the planets of the solar system, for example.
- Have students write a mystery for each other that depends on knowing a particular scientific fact for its solution.
- Have students write a rap of facts they need to recall for a science test. Have them share their raps with the class and pick three they would like to memorize.

WRITING AS PART OF SOCIAL STUDIES

Two second graders wrote the trip stories in Figs. 11.5 and 11.6 as part of a social studies unit on pioneers. The stories make the notion of a long trip concrete by tying it into children's personal experiences. This writing helped kids think of pioneers as real people making long trips that were even harder than the ones they had experienced.

My Trip to Arizona
By
Elijah Mitchell

When I was five years old, my family moved from California. I liked it in Arizona. I miss my best friend, Al. He sent me a Nerf crossbow. It was hot and tiring on the trip. We had to go back and get the rest of our things in California. When we got to California we noticed that someone got into our house. The boxes were open but nothing was taken. My dad had to sleep in the hallway so no one would take anything! I know this because I went to stay with him at the house. When I was asleep, it snowed!

FIG. 11.5. Elijah's trip.

The Trip to Oklahoma
By
Danielle Cox

My family went on a vacation to Oklahoma. We went through El Paso, then to Amarillo. We checked into the motel. It was the Mundalein. We stayed there for a week. Then we saw the bombing site. We went to Texas and stayed at my Aunt Pat and Uncle Tom's house. Uncle Tom took us to the zoo. We saw all the animals. Uncle Tom took us to Old New Mexico where we saw a glass blower. Then we went back to the house.

We played in the sprinkler. We did handstands with our mouths open and our eyes closed. Then we went to Carlsbad Caverns. We saw all of the walls.

Then we went to Flagstaff. It was a long time. Then we saw our house. We were all very tired.

The End

FIG. 11.6. Danielle's trip.

The story in Fig. 11.7 was written by a second grader as part of a study about national heroes. By writing about their own heroes, they were able to imagine George Washington and Abraham Lincoln as real people rather than as storybook figures.

Personal writing and informational writing seem to lend themselves naturally to social studies, but literary writing and persuasive writing can offer new dimensions to social studies as well.

My hero

My hero is my brother becaus hes a nice person. And he saved me from getting squashed becase the garage door was coming down on me. My Sister and Mom and Dad becase thay are a good person to be like. And Miss McNees and Mrs. Whisler becase thay are also a good person to be like.

Danielle

FIG. 11.7. Danielle's hero.

Informational Writing

- Have students research different aspects of one topic. For example, if the class is studying the Anasazi Indians, have one group study diet, another tools, a third social organization, a fourth housing. Make a class encyclopedia to leave for the next year's group.
- Have students write a newspaper that a group of people they are studying might write. For example, if the class is studying Mexico, divide the class into teams to write articles that might appear in a Mexican newspaper: on the weather, on commerce, on politics, etc. When the newspaper is finished share it with another class.

Persuasive Writing

- Have students write persuasive letters back and forth between historical figures: George Washington to King George, Abraham Lincoln to Jefferson Davis, and so on.
- Have students write persuasive letters for or against particular current event issues: the celebration of Columbus Day, the voucher system for school attendance, etc. Have them write their letters to someone they know who takes a different stance than they do.
- Have students write political advertisements they might see on TV.
- Have students write commercials for everyday items from days past: sod houses on the prairies, Eli Whitney's combine, the pony express, etc. Ask the class to role-play consumers and judge the effectiveness of the commercial.

Personal Writing

- Have students play "You Were There" in writing. Ask them to write diary entries about what they would have done had they been involved in a particular historical situation.
- Have students write diary entries for a historical person involved in the time period the class is studying: a child on the Oregon Trail, for example.
- Take field trips. After returning to school, ask students to write about what they found most interesting on the field trip and why. Ask them to connect what they saw with their own lives and write a letter home about the field trip.

Literary Writing

- Have students write stories or songs for their parents that could have been written during a time period they are studying.
- Have students dramatize important historical events for another class.
- After studying a famous person, have students make up folk tales about the person's childhood to illustrate an important quality the famous person

possessed. (Offer the story of George Washington and the apple tree as an example, perhaps.)

WRITING AS PART OF MATH STUDY

The story in Fig. 11.8 was written by a sixth grader as a review of multiplication. To solve this puzzle, readers must use their multiplication facts. Sometimes it seems that math is the one content area with which writing has nothing to do. But as the following little story shows, even literary writing can be adapted to support math learning.

"Mom, I want to have a Birthday party, "I begged." "Nicole have you fed the dog," asked mom. It seems like she just doesn't want to listen to me, I thought. "I guess I might as well give up on a Birthday party" I sighed. "Nicole feed the dog!" mom called. As I got up to feed the dog I found a piece of paper with a grocery list exept it was for 2 dozen donuts. "I wonder what those are for," I thought as I shuved it in my pocket. "I'll have to look at this later." As I fed the dog I bumped into the closet and I heard something fall. I opened the closet and found a box with 12 strings in it. I kept wondering what all this stuff was for. Strange stuff kept happing. For example Mom was cleaning the house yesterday. (she never cleans up) Also when she went to the store she bought a lot of food. (usally she just gets what we need.) I walked to my bedroom and shut the door. Something is going on and I have to find out what! As I spread out all my information, I thought, "What would mom do with 2 dozen donuts." She hates donutes. Then it clicked, "A couple years back my brother had a Birthday and every body had to eat donuts off a string! That was it mom was throwing a party for my brother. No, wait his birthday was a while back! Wow! Could it be!

FIG. 11.8. Jane's mystery.

Would mom throw a suprize party for **Me**! Maybe, but I have to figure out how many people would come! I raced out of my room and down the hall. "John! John!" I shouted my brother's name over and over. I knocked on the door, not waiting for him to answer I burst in his room. "John rember a couple years ago when you had your birthday and everyone ate donuts off a string?" "Yeah, so what?" John answered as he turned his music up. I rushed to turn it back down. "John how many donuts did you each have?" I asked very axiosly. "I don't know!" John snapped back. "Go away and leave me alone" He shouted. I grapped the remote and said "Tell me and I'll give it back!" "Fine! You win. Let's see . . . Well, we each ate two off the string and then the next morning we also had two each." I dropped the remote and ran out the door! Oh, no I forgot something! I stopped half way down the hall and shouted, "Thanks, John!" Then I ran back to my room and shut the door. Lets see . . . there is 12 in a dozen . . . . And . . . Thats it I got it!! NO!! I forgot I have to eat donuts too!! When I finally figured out how many friends were comming it seemed like mom had done it just right. All my best friends were comming. I could hardly wait.

I can hardly wait for you to figure out how many of my friends are comming.

FIG. 11.8. continued.

The little story in Fig. 11.9 is a retelling by a second grader of a story Ms. Whistler used to introduce the concept of how different number operations work together. But literary writing is not the only kind of writing that supports math learning. Informational, persuasive, and personal writing can also be used.

Informational Writing

- Have students summarize a concept they have just learned for someone else in the class. Ask them to trade papers and critique each other's summaries.

> ## The King and his Advisors
>   Once upon a time there was King that had a bondel of gold and he was not happy. So he called Cont Subtraction so he came and said I shal make you happy so he took all his gold away. But the King was still not happy. So he wint to get all the gold. And then he called Sir Divishin. And came and said I will divide your gold. And give som to every pore persin. But the King was still not hppy. So he called Sir Adition so he came and said I will get more of everything you have. But the King still wasint happy. So he called cont multiplidkashon he said I will split the gold in half. But the King was still not happy. But with all the Advisors together he was a happy King from that day on.
>   ## The end

FIG. 11.9. Danielle's arithmetic story.

- Ask students to write questions they still have at the end of an explanation of a new concept. In groups, ask them to write answers to each other's questions.
- Have students research the use of math in a job/career they're interested in by interviewing an adult who does that job. Ask children to write a report on what they find out and share it with the class.
- Ask students to write explanations of math concepts they learned the year before. Pair them with younger students and have them teach the concept using their explanation.

Persuasive Writing

- Have students write letters to younger students persuading them of the need to learn particular math skills such as the multiplication tables.
- Have students write letters to each other "to use or not to use" calculators in school.

Personal Writing

- Have students write a math autobiography to you relating their early experiences learning to do arithmetic. Ask them to tell how they feel about math and why.

- At the end of a lesson or unit, have students write personal notes to you or to each other asking the questions they still have about the material covered.

Literary Writing

- Have students write story problems for each other involving math concepts they are learning.
- Have students write mysteries for each other which involve math calculations in the solution.
- Have students dramatize for each other the importance of math in the jobs their parents do.

WRITING TO LEARN/LEARNING TO WRITE

Just as the four categories we have been using to describe writing often blur into hybrid forms, so writing to learn and learning to write often blur. To use writing to support content learning and content learning to support learning to write, try the following activities:

- Have students write holiday stories for younger students. Ask them to draw on their own experiences with the holiday for the story. Ask them to use the stories to persuade the young reader to take a particular action over the holiday.
- Have students write a class play to perform for another class. Ask them to base the play on information they have learned in science or social studies.
- Have students choose a piece of their own writing they particularly like. Ask them to rewrite that piece for another reader. Ask them to rewrite the piece in another category. (For example, if they have written a diary entry to themselves, ask them to write an informational letter to a friend based on the content in the diary entry.)
- Provide opportunities for students to write to outside readers like a pen pal in Russia or an elderly person in a nursing home. Help them analyze what common ground they have with this reader. Show them how to build writing bridges between themselves and an outside reader.
- Have students choose larger conflicts with outside audiences: in the school, in the town, in the society as a whole. Have them react to appropriate issues in the newspaper or a national magazine (a discussion of implementing dress codes in school, for example). Ask them to write letters that use informational, personal, and persuasive techniques.
- Have students consider tone and voice in a persuasive piece of writing they have done for science: Will humor work better or a shock effect? Will a sad tone or a problem-solving tone be more effective? Have them rewrite a paragraph or two in a variety of tones to a variety of readers.

- Have students consider structure in a piece of persuasive writing they have written for social studies: Will it work better to start with a statement of the problem or with a story? Should the suggested action be mentioned first or last?
- Have students consider sentence structure in a piece of personal writing they have done for literature study: Will short sentences or long ones fit with the mood of the story better? Why?
- Have students write a booklet for their parents for a special occasion. Have the booklet contain a poem, a thank-you letter, or an autobiographical story their parents might like to recall.

IN THE CLASSROOM

Paula:

I try to incorporate writing into all our other work. For example, we do author studies for reading. At the very beginning of the year we study all of Chris Van Allsberg's works. We study Leo Lionne (1969) and a lot of the other little stories that you read to little children as they are learning how to read. We study what the stories are really about, and we look at the illustrations. Then we talk about how the pictures fit the stories. We study the authors' styles, and then we get into writing our own narrative stories.

Becky:

In my district children are very separated, very compartmentalized in elementary school. But life is not compartmentalized; life is a theme, and everything builds on everything else. When you weave writing throughout the curriculum, then kids get a better sense that connectedness is what life is about. Take the subject of science, for example. When I use expository and literature and different types of writing in science, my kids are still learning. They are learning science *and* writing.

As I am teaching writing in the school year, I use two approaches. I have both a separate period for writing from time to time with just strictly narrative topics, and then at other times I do writing across the curriculum. But after writing in a subject area I always like to come back to narrative writing because I like to maintain that tie with writing as fun. In sixth grade they enjoy writing about themselves. They like telling their own stories. That doesn't stop, of course—even as adults we like telling our own stories. So I have different approaches at different times.

Sometimes, like with biographies, both approaches fit together. We had a separate writing time because we did the whole process, but we tied it into reading. The students read a biography of their choice, and we did a whole unit on biographies: their genre, characteristics, and guideline. Then they wrote a biography of their own. They chose someone who was special to them and interviewed them. Then they went through the whole writing process with it and we had a publishing party at the end.

Right now we're doing a unit in social studies on the continent of Asia, and we will do some writing projects in relation to several diverse countries we study. The balloon ride project is one I really like to use because it gets students to synthesize facts and lets them have fun with their imaginations at the same time. I find that poetry works that way too. Poetry permeates my curriculum: there's no subject it won't work with. Writing ties everything we do together.

ROLLING DOWN THE WRITING ROAD

When writers are comfortable, confident, and competent, when they have reasons to write and readers to write to, travel on the writing road begins to smooth out. The wheel rolls evenly down the road toward whatever destination the writer chooses. The writer can write to a close personal reader or a distant formal reader. She can write a convincing piece or a piece that makes her reader laugh. He can relate his own experience to the facts of the world to explain to someone else something he has already learned. She can write about something she knows a lot about or about something she wants to learn. Writing groups and writing process blur into learning content. Mechanics disappear into reader expectations. Readers and writers form a community of sharing about the world. The wheel rolls across unexpected territory, making its own road to take writers places they never dreamed they would go.

CHAPTER SUMMARY

Different kinds of writing fit more naturally than others with particular subjects; however, a wide variety of writing can be used to help support all content learning. For example, personal writing and literary writing are natural components of literature study; informational writing seems to support social studies and science study; math study may seem separate from writing. However, because writing supports higher-order thinking skills, all four types of writing can support all types of content study.

When writers write to learn, different parts of the writing process sometimes become more important than others. For example, when writers are writing to teach themselves something, prewriting and drafting (gathering facts and organizing them) may be more important than revising and polishing. However, when writers write to learn something so they can teach others, revising and polishing may become important communication tools. Writing to learn and learning to write, therefore, are not mutually exclusive categories. Sometimes writers write to learn for themselves and end up sharing what they have learned; sometimes writers write to share what they know and end up learning new information.

APPLICATIONS

1. Analyze your own writing-to-learn history. In what content areas do you remember writing? What forms did you learn? To what readers did you write? Which of your experiences would you like to repeat for your own students? Which would you like to change? Why?
2. Tell the story of a piece of writing you did that taught you content. What was the purpose of the piece? How did writing teach you things you wouldn't have learned by reading?
3. Choose a piece of your own writing (one of the pieces you did for an earlier chapter, a piece you are doing for another class, a piece you are doing in your daily life). Analyze it as a piece of communication. Analyze how you might rewrite it so you would learn something you don't already know. (For example, you might set a short story in an earlier time period so you would need to study social customs of the past. Or you might change the reader of a persuasive piece so you would need to research a different angle of your conflict.)
4. Choose one of the previously suggested writing activities in Literature Study or Social Studies. Do it yourself. Adapt it so you could use it as a model with your students.
5. Choose one of the previously suggested writing activities in Science Study or Math. Do it yourself. Adapt it so you could use it as a model with your students.

PART III
THE TEACHING-WRITING PROCESS

12

Learning to Teach Writing

I went to college in the 1970s, and we weren't taught how to teach writing. It was something we were all just expected to do. It was very much a bumbling process for me, and I am embarrassed to tell you how I used to teach writing. I would pick one of the topics in the Language Arts textbook and write it on the board. I'd say, "This is what we are writing on today. You are going to write about your favorite sport." Or I'd tell them, "You are going to write about your hobby," or something like that. Then they were on their own, and I'd expect them to come up with a good product. The writing I taught was not thought out; it was not enjoyable. I am embarrassed to say I did this for a very long time.

After several years of this I learned the writing process, and I found a method of writing that created a whole different atmosphere in my classroom, not to mention a whole different product that my students were putting out. I started to teach my students to prewrite. I began to set the stage mentally for writing and help the children determine who to direct their writing toward, who would be their audience. I started helping them pick which word to use.

Now I am seeing myself grow each year because I am learning from my students. I am learning to relinquish control of writing and allow writing to become more student oriented. I watch these children grow as writers by trying and failing and reworking their writing. I watch their success too. Seeing all this, I am moving forward too. I sometimes feel, "Well this didn't work," but then I regroup, and I try something else, because I am not going to give up teaching writing. I know this is my chosen path and so it has been fun to be aware of that and then just blunder my way through. That in itself is causing me to keep growing.

—*Becky*

Becky's experience of learning to teach writing over a period of years is not unusual; in fact, it's the norm. A few years ago, Elizabeth Stroble and I observed three groups of teachers who had come to our Writing Project Summer Institute to discover how quickly they implemented the writing process in their classrooms (see Bratcher & Stroble, 1994). What we saw as we followed these teachers for 3 years was a process of growth. In the first year after they attended the Summer Institute, most of the teachers kept teaching exactly as they had in the past, overlaying writing activities on top of old teaching plans. In the second year, they changed how they taught writing during language arts, instituting some form of the writing process. It was not until the third year that most teachers began to

149

experiment with writing and content teaching. Although while our formal study stopped after 3 years, we kept up with some of these teachers informally for 3 more years. The growth continued! So, far from feeling embarrassed by her struggles with the teaching-writing process, Becky should feel proud of her growth over the years.

COMFORT, CONFIDENCE, AND COMPETENCE IN TEACHING WRITING

Just as children establish comfort, build confidence, and develop competence as they learn to write, as teachers we establish comfort, build confidence, and develop competence as we learn to teach writing. Just as comfort, confidence, and competence in learning to write blur into writing for many reasons, comfort, confidence, and competence in teaching writing blur into teaching for many purposes.

Comfort in teaching writing comes from teaching things we like. For example, if I like to write poetry or keep a journal myself, I feel comfortable teaching poetry or journaling, and I can be enthusiastic with my students. Confidence in teaching writing comes from teaching things we know how to do, whether we enjoy them or not. So if I know the rules of outlining, I can teach outlining with confidence, even if I do not often outline my own writing. (The Personal Inventory in Application #1 will help you determine your own comfort and confidence with teaching writing.)

Competence with teaching writing develops when teachers take ownership of their classrooms by considering the communication context in which they teach and tailoring instruction accordingly. Competent writing teachers take into account what their students know and need to learn, as well as what they themselves are comfortable and confident with. Let's look, then, at teaching writing as a communication context.

TEACHING WRITING AS COMMUNICATION

If we adapt the communication triangle to writing instruction, we draw a triangle like the one in Fig. 12.1. Let's look at each corner of the triangle to identify questions that help define it.

Teacher-author

Whenever teachers make writing assignments, they become instructional authors. Who they are as teachers of writing affects the instruction, providing an instructional voice, in fact. A series of questions can help teachers define themselves as teacher-authors of writing instruction:

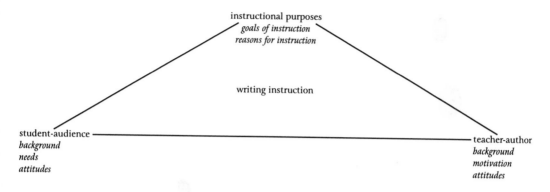

FIG. 12.1. Teaching writing as communication.

- How comfortable am I teaching writing? Do I like to write? What kinds of writing am I comfortable with?
- How confident am I teaching writing? What kinds of writing do I know how to teach? How much experience have I had teaching writing?
- Why am I teaching writing? Is my purpose my own or is it being dictated from some outside source?

Student-audience

Whenever children begin to learn to write from a particular teacher, they become an instructional audience, and who they are as learners affects the instruction. A student-audience analysis can help define the student corner of the communication context:

- How comfortable are the students with writing? Do most of them like to write?
- How confident are the students with writing? How much practice have they had writing? What kinds of writing are they good at?
- Why do these children need to learn to write? How aware are they of the need?

Instructional Purpose(s)

Instructional purpose can come from different places. Some states have mandated lists of skills or concepts districts are expected to follow. Most school districts have curriculum guides that spell out the learning-to-write goals for any particular grade level. Many schools have an articulated curriculum between grade levels. In most cases, however, these instructional goals are generic and function as guidelines, so the teacher must adapt the goals based on her self-knowledge and her student analysis. In other words, as teachers we must ask ourselves what we want to accomplish with a particular group of students in a given year. A series of questions can help to define instructional purposes for an individual classroom:

- What guidelines does my state provide for writing instruction at my grade level?
- What guidelines does my district or school provide for writing instruction at my grade level?
- What priorities do I have as a teacher of writing for my students?

PLANNING WRITING INSTRUCTION

Once we understand the communication context we are working in as writing teachers, we can set writing goals for our own individual classrooms, taking into account the needs and attitudes of our students, our own strengths and priorities, and outside expectations for which we may be held accountable. Class goals are long-range purposes we hope to accomplish over an entire instructional period, and they can be used to organize instructional planning. (It is important not to confuse *class goals* with behavioral objectives. Class goals can be broken down into *assignment purposes*. Behavioral objectives are a subset of assignment purposes.) Once class goals are clear, we can design assignments and activities that meet our goals. Of course, as we saw in the writing-to-learn chapter, sometimes class goals are symbiotic, and writing assignments can work toward more than one goal at a time. (An assignment to write a tall tale can work toward a learning-literature goal as well as toward a literary-writing goal.) As children complete assignments, we can evaluate how close we have come to meeting the class goal and decide whether we need to reteach or if the class is ready to move on. A diagram of this planning process might look like the one in Fig. 12.2.

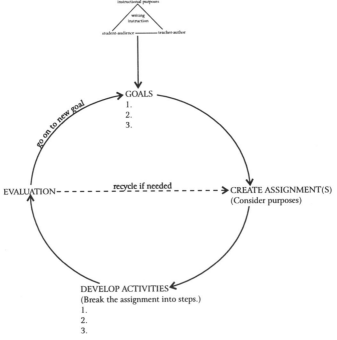

FIG. 12.2. Planning writing instruction.

Once an overall plan is in place, particular writing assignments and activities grow naturally from the plan. A planning sheet for one writing assignment might look like this:

Target Goal:
Assignment:
Student-audience:
Teacher-author:
Assignment Purposes:
Activities:
Future Teaching Plans:

AN EXAMPLE

Let's take a look at this planning process as it might apply to a classroom. Let's take a fifth-grade classroom in a midtown school in a city of 55,000 people.

Communication Context

Teacher-author: Mr. Costa has been teaching for 10 years. In that time he's taught third grade and special education classes; this is his second year as a fifth-grade teacher. He likes to write himself, especially informational writing. He teaches writing as a process, and he is especially good at teaching revising. He wants his students to enjoy writing as much as he does. His favorite subject is social studies.

Student-audience: The class is made up of 28 students: Anglo, Hispanic, Native American, and African American. Four of the children are mainstreamed students with a variety of handicapping conditions. Ten of the students test signficantly below grade-level in reading. Three of the students have parents who teach at the nearby university. Four are being tested for the gifted program in middle school. Fifteen are girls; thirteen are boys. Out of his class about a third were in Ms. Johnson's class and did a lot of writing. Another third of the class were in Ms. McBain's class and did very little writing. The other third are new to the school, so Mr. Costa has very little information about their instructional background.

Assignment Purposes: The state has recently implemented a yearly cross-curricular writing assessment, so writing instruction is a priority for the district. By the time Mr. Costa's students get to high school, they will be required to produce an acceptable writing sample in order to graduate. The state has supplied all districts with a list of writing competencies. The district has divided the competencies by grade level, and individual teachers are expected to use the competencies in their instruction. The competencies for fifth grade include personal narratives, poetry, and specialized expository reports. They also include the writing process and a variety of mechanical concerns. Because Mr. Costa believes that revision is the heart of the writing process and because he is particularly good at informational writing, he wants to be sure he shares this expertise with his students.

Chapter 12

Class Writing Goals

Because of this communication context, Mr. Costa sets five class goals for writing in his class: to have fun with writing (his own), to learn to revise (his own, district, and state), to become proficient with informational writing (his own, district, and state), to learn to punctuate compound and complex sentences (district and state), and to use writing as a learning tool (his own).

Let's look at why he set each one of these goals:

To have fun with writing: Because Mr. Costa enjoys writing himself, he wants to share the fun he has. Because he has such a diverse group, having fun together with writing can help to bring down some of the barriers he suspects are present among his students. He hopes that having fun will establish comfort for the students who didn't have much writing instruction in fourth grade. He wants to introduce a variety of writing forms with which he thinks his students will have fun.

To review the writing process, focusing on revising: Because the writing process is important to Mr. Costa, he's glad it's on the state list of skills. Mr. Costa knows that many of his students are used to cooperative learning groups, and he's confident they can learn to critique their own writing. Since he's good at revising, he wants to spend time teaching his students to revise.

To become proficient with informational writing: Because his students will go to the middle school after they finish his class, Mr. Costa has been on an articulation committee in his district, and he knows that informational writing gets more emphasis at the middle school than it does at his elementary school. As a result, he wants to be sure his students are comfortable, confident, and competent with informational writing before they finish the fifth grade.

Learn to punctuate a variety of sentence types: From his 10 years of experience, Mr. Costa knows that punctuating long sentences is still a challenge for fifth graders. He knows that when his students go to the middle school next year they will be expected to write a variety of sentence structures and punctuate them correctly.

To use writing as a learning tool: Because social studies is Mr. Costa's favorite subject, he likes to combine writing instruction with content instruction. He plans to have his students do a variety of writing in social studies, including a report on a state of their choice and a family history. Informational writing is a natural for learning content, so Mr. Costa is already seeing overlaps in his goals.

Mr. Costa's planning diagram might look like Fig. 12.3 when he begins to plan.

Planning a Writing Assignment

Early in the year, Mr. Costa begins with the goal *To use writing as a learning tool*. However, he decides he can combine that goal with the goal *To have fun with writing*. He decides to have his students write imaginary travelogues based on their study of states in social studies. He also believes he can make some progress toward *To become proficient with informational writing*. Mr. Costa might plan like this:

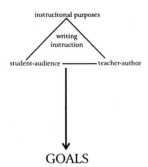

GOALS
1. use writing as a learning tool
2. review the writing process (revision)
3. have fun with writing
4. become proficient with informational writing
5. learn to punctuate variety of sentence types

EVALUATION   CREATE ASSIGNMENT(S)
                                                                 (Consider purposes)

DEVELOP ACTIVITIES
(Break the assignment into steps.)
1.
2.
3.

FIG. 12.3. Mr. Costa's first planning diagram.

Target Goal: Use writing as a learning tool

Assignment: Imaginary travelogue to a state of the student's choice

Student Audience: As he has analyzed his student audience, Mr. Costa has discovered that about a third of his students are enthusiastic about writing. He has also found out that about twenty percent of his students are terrified of writing. The others don't care about writing one way or the other. By making working groups carefully, he can spread the enthusiastic children out among the uninterested and the scared children.

Teacher-author: Mr. Costa loves travelogues. He likes to read them, to watch them on TV, and write long letters about his own trips to friends back home. He feels pretty sure he can get his students enthusiastic about travelogues because he likes them so much himself. He plans to share a letter he wrote to his wife from his trip to Alaska 2 years before.

Assignment Purposes: Because Mr. Costa began with the goal *To use writing as a learning tool*, his main purpose is to help his students learn and synthesize a variety of facts about various states (content). A second purpose he has is to help his students have fun by asking them to write travelogues rather than the reports they expect (comfort). A third is to develop ownership of writing (competence) by asking students to choose a particular state they are interested in and choosing a reader they think would like to visit that state. By putting the emphasis of the assignment on the content the children are learning, he can help them feel more confident about their writing.

Activities: modeling travelogues; choosing a topic; gathering facts (books, writing off to state tourist bureaus for promotional materials, visiting a travel agency, interviews, map study); synthesis (data charts, mapping a trip); identifying a reader; drafting travelogue letters.

Future Teaching Plans: Mr. Costa decides that if the travelogues are fun for his students, he will extend the assignment into language arts and introduce the rest of the writing process (revision, editing, and publishing to a target reader). He also decides that if students enjoy the new form, he will introduce brochures next since they will be receiving a lot of brochures when they write for promotional materials.

Now Mr. Costa's planning diagram might look like Fig. 12.4.

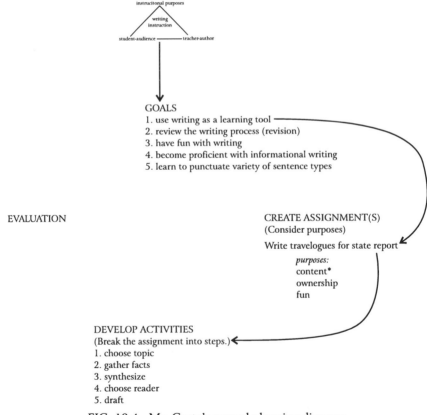

FIG. 12.4. Mr. Costa's second planning diagram.

FINDING THE TIME

Paula:

> Starting a writing program at the beginning of the year is overwhelming…You think, "I can't spend this much time." But you spend the time, and your students get better. Each day you reach another child. You're teaching intangibles, showing children how you write so they can learn to write themselves. Gradually their writing develops. You trust yourself. You trust the children. You trust the class chemistry. We do poems together and make booklets in groups. Children imitate. The children will see that writing is fun. Eventually they'll write on their own.

As Paula says, "You think, 'I can't spend this much time.'" Teaching children to write does take time. Establishing comfort with writing takes time. Very few children see their parents writing at home in the evenings because most writing in our society goes on in the workplace when children are not around. So writing may seem strange, even intimidating. For some young children writing is laborious work physically. Fine motor skills develop in children at different rates so that some first graders still have difficulty controlling a pencil. Peer groups are always awkward at first. Children need time to learn how to work in groups, and the younger the child, the more naturally egocentric he or she is, and the more time is required to learn this skill.

Once comfort has been established, the rest of the learning-to-write process takes time, too. Building confidence takes time. The writing process is a choreographed dance of skills like brainstorming and spelling, clustering and reading aloud, imagining a reader and defining a purpose. It takes time to learn each step in the dance, and it takes time to put the steps together. Developing competence takes time, too. Even helping children comprehend that writing is intended for someone else to read takes time. It takes a series of short assignments that people respond to before children really get the idea. The notion of different purposes takes time to teach as well. Writing for different purposes also takes time. Each practice assignment takes time. Full-blown writing projects like writing a class newspaper or dramatizing the trip across the Oregon Trail can take weeks to complete.

In a curriculum already packed with language arts, math, social studies, science, perhaps even music and art, is it any wonder that most reports about time spent on writing instruction in the United States are dismal? How do teachers like Paula find the time to spend?

The answer begins with *commitment*: commitment on the part of the teacher to teach children to write, a commitment that grows out of the belief that writing is a unifying vehicle for learning that cuts across all other instruction. From that commitment we begin to see how teachers find the time.

Paula says, "You think, 'I can't spend this much time.' But you spend the time." Time comes to all of us for any goal we might have only when we make it come. Without commitment there is never enough time. In the context of teaching children to write, time comes when it is planned. Paula sets aside the first hour of each day for writing with her third graders. Becky teaches thematically, building writing into each unit with the very first lesson plan. Joan makes sure writing is one of the activities she uses every time she introduces a new concept. Mary sets aside the hour after recess for writing because it settles the children down. Paula and Mary have found pieces of time in their instructional days when they wish to set a tone; the quiet time becomes a time that establishes writing comfort. Joan and Becky use other content to teach writing; social studies time becomes a time that develops writing competence. Rather than casting about for topics for their students to write about, they pull the topics out of content they are teaching.

Like writing itself, finding the time for writing is a process. As teachers we often make plans that do not work, but when that happens, rather than giving up, we simply revise our plans. After enough revisions, we hit on a plan that works, at least for a while. The next year the process of finding the time will probably go faster, but schedules, no matter how good in one context, never seem to work exactly the same way twice!

To find the time:

Commit to finding the time. Make an hour-by-hour grid of your instructional time. Prioritize the instructional goals you have for your class. Schedule writing first and work other goals in around writing. Or schedule writing as part of other instruction. Set aside time at the beginning of the day or right after lunch for writing. Watch for odd bits of time that do not appear on your grid or that otherwise might be wasted.

Make writing instruction do double-duty. Double-plan. Plan writing assignments that can be used to teach content. Plan content assignments that can be used to teach writing. Determine which of the writing-to-learn assignments can be used to establish comfort, build confidence, develop competence, or illustrate a communication reason to write. Then look at your writing goals. Determine which ones can be met with writing in the content areas and which ones need to be focused on separately.

Be selective about implementing the entire writing process. Every piece of writing children do does not need to go through the entire writing process. In fact, the full writing process is useful only when real publishing is the goal. In other words, when writers write for other people, the full writing process aids clear communication: revision improves ideas and editing improves mechanics. When writers write for themselves or informally for colleagues, collecting ideas and drafting may be the most important parts of the writing process. Have students collect all the writing they do in class in a folder. Have children choose from among those writings to find their favorites or to find pieces that have a real audience. Teach the writing process as a way of finishing those pieces for sharing.

Make fewer, but more in-depth writing assignments. Many brief opportunities to practice writing develop fluency, familiarity with pencil and paper as a means of communication. Longer, in-depth writing develops competence and familiarity with reasons to write. Create a series of short activities that build up to an in-depth writing assignment. *Do not* set writing goals like "write one essay a week" for your class! Instead, focus on instruction; determine time from learning goals rather than learning goals from time. Set goals like "take one personal narrative through the writing process"; let the learning set the time. Some classes will move more quickly than others, either because of class size or other factors beyond the teacher's control. Let learning to write be the focus, not completion of assignments.

Use writing as a tool for learning. Do not look at writing as a separate subject; look at it as a learning strategy that can be used all day long. For example, if the class attends an all-school assembly put on by the police or fire department, ask students to predict before they go what the presenters are likely to be trying to teach them. When they come back from the assembly, ask them to evaluate their predictions in a brief response to the presenters. If raising self-esteem is a goal of the school, use personal narratives and in-class publishing to give children an audience to tell their stories to. Use multiple intelligences when you teach writing to raise the self-esteem of children who may not have developed their verbal/linguistic intelligence very highly.

In the Classroom

Becky:

> Teaching writing keeps me growing. Right now I'm seeing myself grow in turning ownership of the writing back to the students. Also, I'm just writing more. Each year I learn from my students. And each year it's something new, something I didn't expect. This year, for example, I had 33 students, and the one-on-one I did the year before with 21 went to the wayside. A portion of my class was struggling with writing, and my frustration mounted. I kept asking myself, "How can I do this with so many children?" In the end I gathered groups of four writers—one good writer, two okay writers, and one weak writer—and I conferenced with the groups. For the most part it worked really well and I began to see better finished papers. I've had students return to me later and say that the writing helped them in many ways. This kind of affirmation keeps me growing willingly and happily.

CHAPTER SUMMARY

Learning to teach writing is much like to learning to write itself. When teachers know what they are comfortable and confident with and when they think of the classroom as a communication situation, teaching writing becomes a learning experience for them as well as for their students. When planning writing instruction, the communication triangle becomes a triangle around *writing instruction* with three corners: *student-audience, teacher-author,* and *instructional purposes.* Teachers consider their students' comfort, confidence, and competence as well as their own. They set class goals and plan writing assignments that meet more than one goal at once. By evaluating the success of a particular assignment, they can decide whether to reteach or go on to another goal. In order to find the time to teach writing, teachers must be committed to writing instruction. They must find ways of using writing to unify learning rather than looking at it as another subject to add to an already-packed curriculum.

APPLICATIONS

1. Take the personal inventory below to identify your own comfort and confidence zones for teaching writing.

Comfort

When I read for fun, I usually read _____ . I would classify my for-fun reading material as primarily personal, informational, persuasive, or literary writing:

If I were a professional writer, I would like to write
(a) newspaper articles
(b) poetry
(c) short stories
(d) novels
(e) political speeches
(f) religious materials
(g) my memoirs
(h) how-to books

I would classify this writing as primarily personal, informational, persuasive, or literary:

The chapter(s) I had the most fun with in this book were about _____.

The things I like most about writing are _____.

Based on your answers above, list the things you are comfortable with in teaching writing:

Confidence

When I need to, I can read _____ and comprehend well.
                                                        categories

When I need to, I can write _____ effectively.
                                                        categories

The chapter(s) in this book I already knew a good bit about were about_____.

The things I know the most about writing are _____.

Based on your answers, list the things you are confident you can teach well about writing:

2. Using the teaching-writing communication triangle and the questions provided about its components, sketch out a communication context for writing instruction in a class you are teaching now or expect to teach in the near future.

3. Using the flow chart provided in this chapter, set class goals for the class you described in #2. Identify three writing assignments for one of your goals.

4. Using the planning sheet provided in this chapter, plan one of the writing assignments you identified in #3.

5. Using the suggestions provided in this chapter, make a weekly plan for finding the time for writing in your classroom.

6. Devise a set of questions you have about instructional time management and teaching writing. Interview a classroom teacher who does a good job using class time. Share the answers you get with your classmates.

13

Teacher Evaluation of Student Writing

The Wart knew that he was turning into a fish.

"Oh, Merlyn," he cried, "please come too."

"For this once," said a large and solemn tench beside his ear, "I will come. But in future you will have to go by yourself. Education is experience, and the essence of experience is self-reliance."

The Wart found it difficult to be a new kind of creature. It was no good trying to swim like a human being, for it made him go corkscrew and much too slowly. He did not know how to swim like a fish.

"Not like that," said the tench in ponderous tones. "Put your chin on your left shoulder and do jack-knives. Never mind the fins to begin with."

The Wart's legs had fused together into his backbone and his feet and toes had become a tail fin. ... He did jack-knives as the tench directed and found that he was swimming vertically downward into the mud.

"Use your feet to turn to left or right," said the tench, "and spread those fins on your tummy to keep level. You are living in two planes now, not one."

The Wart found that he could keep more or less level by altering the inclination of his arm fins and the ones on his stomach. He swam feebly off, enjoying himself very much.

"Come back," said the tench. "You must learn to swim before you can dart."

The Wart returned to his tutor in a series of zigzags and remarked, "I do not seem to keep quite straight."

"The trouble with you is that you do not swim from the shoulder. You swim as if you were a boy, bending at the hips. Try doing your jack-knives right from the neck downward, and move your body exactly the same amount to the right as you are going to move it to the left. Put your back into it."

Wart gave two terrific kicks and vanished altogether in a clump of mare's tail several yards away.

"That's better," said the tench, now out of sight in the murky olive water, and the Wart backed himself out of the tangle with infinite trouble, by wriggling his arm fins. He undulated back toward the voice in one terrific shove, to show off.

"Good," said the tench, as they collided end to end. "But direction is the better part of valour."

"Try if you can do this one," it added.

Without any apparent exertion of any kind it swam off backward under a water-lily. Without apparent exertion—but the Wart, who was an enterprising learner, had been watching the slightest movement of its fins. He moved his own fins anti-clockwise, gave the tip of his tail a cunning flick, and was lying alongside the tench.

"Splendid," said Merlyn.

—from T. H. White (1939), The Once and Future King

THE THEORY

Evaluation is a touchy subject for writing teachers these days, perhaps because the way we usually teach writing and the way we usually evaluate it are in direct conflict. Although we now teach writing as a process, our evaluation tools (left over from an earlier era of teaching writing) often look at the products of writing without reference to the writing process or the learning process. (For a detailed discussion of the challenges of evaluating children's writing, see Bratcher, 1994a.) As a result of this conflict, some teachers shy away from evaluating writing entirely, and others feel forced to evaluate because of pressures from outside the classroom.

However, as this excerpt from *The Once and Future King* illustrates, evaluation is an integral part of teaching. As Merlyn is teaching the young Arthur to swim like a fish, he continually interweaves instruction and evaluation. *"Not like that," "the trouble with you is," "that's better,"* and *"splendid"* are all evaluations. Of course not all of the Wart's teachers evaluate as Merlyn does. His governess raps him on the knuckles, making young Arthur hate his lessons; his jousting teacher blades him with the flat part of his sword, making him feel inadequate and hopeless. As writing teachers, we can stay away from the knuckle-rapping and blading that traditional product-oriented grading represents and take our cues instead from Merlyn's way of using evaluation to promote self-reliance.

Merlyn evaluated Arthur to help him learn to swim more quickly than he could have learned on his own. Rather than just throwing the Wart in the water and leaving him until he figured it out (which he probably would have done eventually), Merlyn got in the water with him and critiqued what Arthur was doing, making specific suggestions for improvement. In this way the Wart learned to swim like a fish much more quickly than he would have done on his own. As writing teachers we can use evaluation in much the same way. With modeling, especially modeling that is our own writing, we get in the water with our students. We may not be the same kind of writer our students are (Merlyn was a tench; Arthur was a much smaller fish), but we are writers who can give expert advice to our students to help them learn to write more quickly than if they were left on their own. Effective evaluation of writing, then, grows out of communication about learning. There are many evaluation tools a teacher can use to communicate with students about learning to write (see *Evaluating Children's Writing*). However, custom rubrics are an excellent beginning place.

THE PRACTICE

Custom rubrics are easy to create from the planning sheet we looked at in chapter 12.

Prioritize your assignment purposes; transform them into evaluation criteria. Most writing assignments that you're going to evaluate have more than one purpose. Which purpose is most important? Which is least important? (It is very rare that the purposes are equally important.) Which purpose is most important for this particular group of students at this point in the year? Which purpose do you plan to spend the most time in class on? Some assignment purposes are for the teacher; others are for the students. Some purposes are quantifiable; others are affective. Quantifiable assignment purposes for the students become evaluation criteria.

Assign points or percentages to your criteria. Quantifiable assignment purposes for the students become evaluation criteria. The most important instructional purpose for students should carry the most weight on the evaluation. The least important should be incidental to the evaluation.

Break down points or percentages for the activities involved in the assignment. If we are not careful, even with custom rubrics we can fall into a "product" attitude toward evaluation. When we teach writing as a learning process, we need to be sure to include the process children go through in our evaluation of their work.

Inform students of the evaluation criteria when you make the assignment. Evaluation becomes a teaching tool when students focus on the purposes of the assignment because the purposes are the evaluation criteria. In other words, when I grade on what I want my students to learn from the assignment and they know that when they begin, most students will focus on the purposes as they write.

Teach to your purposes. The most important instructional purpose should be the one you spend the most instructional time on. Less important purposes should still receive instructional time; however, most class time will be spent on the first and second priorities of the assignment.

Encourage students to use the evaluation criteria as a focus for revision. Revision offers a second opportunity to focus students on the purposes of the assignment. Evaluation criteria can be used as the focus of a peer response group or a self-critique. When children examine their work against the list of evaluation criteria, they are really examining their work against the assignment purposes.

Evaluate on the announced criteria. Evaluation is a two-edged sword. Sometimes when we evaluate a writing assignment, we discover that as teachers we have overlooked an important purpose of the assignment. (For example, I may have assigned friendly letters with the purpose in mind of helping students understand the concept of writing to a reader, but I may have overlooked the importance of conventional spelling to readers. I may not have listed "practice spelling the most-used words conventionally" as a purpose, and thus as an evaluation criterion.) When this happens, it is tempting to "take off points" for spelling errors even though we have not focused our students' attention on this purpose or spent any class time meeting the purpose. In order for rubrics to be an effective teaching tool, we must stick to them when we grade. (Of course, we can learn from evaluation too. There's always a next time!)

Adjust future plans based on evaluation information. While it is important to have long-range goals and a plan to organize teaching around, it's equally important to be able to adjust goals and plans based on how quickly the class progresses. Sometimes evaluation of an assignment will let you know a class can move faster than you thought; sometimes evaluation will let you know you need to slow down and reteach.

AN EXAMPLE

To illustrate, let's go back to the travelogue Mr. Costa assigned his class as part of the social studies unit on states (chap. 12). As you remember, Mr. Costa had several purposes for the assignment:

- learn and synthesize facts (about a particular state);
- establish comfort with writing (by having fun with form);
- develop ownership of writing (by allowing students to choose topic and reader);
- build confidence with writing (emphasizing content).

To create a custom rubric for this assignment, Mr. Costa follows the steps just outlined.

Prioritize assignment purposes; transform them into evaluation criteria. Because Mr. Costa is using the travelogues primarily to teach social studies, his priorities for this assignment look like this:

1. learn and synthesize facts (about a particular state);
2. build confidence with writing (by emphasizing content);
3. develop ownership of writing (by allowing students to choose topic and reader);
4. establish comfort with writing (by having fun with form).

"Build confidence" and "establish comfort" are not quantifiable: thus, they are not evaluation criteria. Mr. Costa will evaluate his teaching strategies by the comfort and confidence he sees among his students. The evaluation criteria for the rubric he is designing look like this:

1. Content
2. Synthesis
3. Topic and Reader
4. Form

Assign points or percentages to evaluation criteria. Mr. Costa wants to be sure his students look up information on their states and synthesize the facts they learn into an imaginary trip, so the first two priorities will make up 70% of the grade. He wants his students to try the travelogue form, but since his main purpose for the form is to have fun, he does not want to grade too heavily on adherence to form. By the same token, since this assignment is early in the year, he is introducing the concept of a reader for the first time: he wants reader choice to be part of a beginning awareness rather than a big part of the grade. (Later in the year, his emphasis may change.) His percentages look like this:

Content	45%
Synthesis of facts	25%
Topic and reader	20%
Form	10%

Break down points or percentages for the activities involved in the assignment. Some of the activities children did for this assignment required participation with the class as a whole; some of them required independent work. Mr. Costa categorizes the activities like this, marking independent work with an asterisk:

Content	*Synthesis*	*Form*	*Topic & Reader*
class research	class model	class model	choose topic*
write for materials*	data charts*	draft*	choose reader*
personal research*	plan "trip"*		
interviews*			

He decides to use 100 points for this assignment. His rubric looks like this:

choose topic	10
write for materials	10
personal research	25
interviews	10
data charts	10
plan "trip"	15
choose reader	10
draft travelogue	10

Inform students of the evaluation criteria when you make the assignment. When Mr. Costa announces the assignment, he puts the rubric on the chalkboard and reminds his students that although they all want to have fun writing their imaginary journeys, the main reason they are doing the assignment is to learn about a state. He emphasizes that he wants them to gather accurate information and combine the facts they learn in a sensible fashion (prewriting and drafting).

Teach to your assignment purposes. Mr. Costa spends several days modeling fact gathering and synthesis. The class researches Washington, DC together and writes an imaginary class trip travelogue as a group. He shows children how to write off for promotional materials from the state they have chosen and mails their letters for them. He takes the class to the library and provides a specialized classroom library he has gathered over the years. He teaches a map-reading lesson and makes travel atlases available. He organizes a field trip to a travel agency, and encourages students to talk to people who've visited the state they're researching. After students have gathered their facts, he shows them how to do data charts (Fig. 8.1) and a trip plan. He helps children brainstorm readers who might like to go to their state and reminds them how travelogues are put together by reviewing his with them.

Encourage students to use evaluation criteria as a focus for revision. Because writing process and revision are not purposes of this particular assignment, Mr. Costa does not spend a lot of time on this step. Instead he simply puts the rubric back on the board and asks children to look at their drafts before they turn them in to him for grading to make sure they have good facts and a sensible story of a trip. He asks them to tell him who they chose as their reader.

Evaluate on your purposes. When Mr. Costa evaluates the travelogues, he concentrates on content and synthesis. He looks at form and reader and makes a few comments but does not deduct points in these categories unless he thinks the student ignored them.

Adjust future teaching plans according to evaluation. After he has evaluated their travelogues, Mr. Costa decides the assignment was a success. His students had fun with writing and learned a lot of social studies as well. They seem comfortable and confident. He decides to extend the assignment into language arts and show children how to use the writing process to get their letters ready to share with their readers. He also decides he will examine the sentence structures his students use in their final drafts so he can plan instruction for the *Learn to punctuate a variety of sentences types* goal. Further, he decides he can go on to other forms of informational writing. He decides to have his students do brochures instead of book reports.

Mr. Costa's planning cycle is now complete for this assignment. It looks like Fig. 13.1.

ESTABLISHING COMFORT WITH EVALUATION

When Merlyn first evaluates the Wart's attempts to swim, he says, "Put your chin on your left shoulder and do jack-knives. Never mind the fins to begin with" (White, 1939, pp. 39–40). Later he gives instruction about the fins. By giving specific suggestions and not evaluating everything at once, Merlyn manages to keep the Wart comfortable, in spite of his negative evaluation: *"Not like that."* As writing teachers we can do the same thing, giving specific suggestions and ignoring some writing problems until others are conquered.

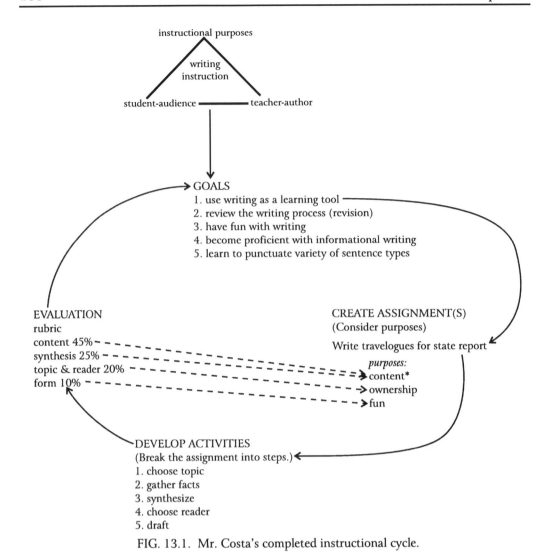

FIG. 13.1. Mr. Costa's completed instructional cycle.

Give Specific Instructions for How to Improve as Part of the Evaluation.

When Mr. Costa reads Torey's draft of his travelogue letter to his father, he discovers that Torey has omitted the information he found out about the Great Lakes from his "trip" to Michigan. So Mr. Costa deducts 5 points from the category *Plans trip* and tells Torey to add a stop-off at the Great Lakes to his travelogue.

Allow Students to Rewrite Their Papers.   Of course, giving instructions for improvement and not allowing students to rewrite will lead to frustration rather than comfort. If we teach writing as a process, it should be a process, right? That means that a teacher evaluation is not an endpoint to writing. Torey should have a chance to try again with Mr. Costa's suggestion. What better carrot for rewriting than more points?

Sometimes teachers are afraid that allowing rewrites will create a lot more work. It will not. It may create a little more work, but comparing a revised paper that you have already evaluated once to a rewrite is a very quick job, particularly when the revision is focused on a specific criterion. The rewards of seeing the writing improve far outweigh the few extra minutes required. Just as Merlyn has the satisfaction of seeing the Wart swimming better, Mr. Costa has the satisfaction of seeing Torey's travelogue synthesize more information.

To Begin With, Focus Evaluation Tightly. Suggestions for improvement can be overwhelming if we evaluate everything at once. With custom rubrics we can tailor evaluation to particular items of instruction and ignore details until it is time for them. Just as Merlyn tells the Wart not to worry about his fins right at the beginning, so Mr. Costa's rubric tells his students not to worry about mechanics at first. Merlyn deals with the fins when the Wart is ready; Mr. Costa deals with mechanics after his students have finished revising. Editing comes before travelogues are shared with chosen readers.

Sometimes as teachers we evaluate students on things we have not taught, making students tense and uncomfortable. We think, "They should have learned that last year." But that's a knuckle-rapping attitude. Evaluation that's communication about learning ties instruction and evaluation together.

Do Not Evaluate Every Piece of Writing Your Students Do. Beyond evaluating only on what we have taught, we establish comfort with evaluation with our students by only evaluating pieces of writing on which students have worked hard. Practice pieces can be checked and given "credit," "no credit," or +, ✓, –. This checking provides accountability for students who look on assignments that are not "graded" as unimportant. Pieces that students have worked on with great care can be evaluated with equal care, providing feedback on learning and guidance for future improvement. Mr. Costa does not evaluate his students' letters requesting information on their states. A child who writes for materials receives 10 points. A child who does not write gets no points. If he sees a letter that is not acceptable, he gives it a "–" and works with the child until the letter can be mailed. Then he changes the "–" to a "✓."

BUILDING CONFIDENCE THROUGH EVALUATION

When Merlyn first gets in the water with the Wart, he says, "Education is experience, and the essence of experience is self-reliance." Self-reliance is as important for our students as it is for Wart. But in order to be self-reliant, students need to feel confident.

Give Students the Evaluation Rubric When You First Make the Assignment.
Ask them to help design the rubric. When students know from the beginning what the purposes of the assignment are, they can be more self-reliant because they know where to focus their intellectual energy; they do not have to worry

about "what the teacher wants." When the class works together to design the rubric, students feel sure they know what the purposes are and they have ownership of those purposes.

Focus Revision on the Rubric.   Revision is often an abstract concept for student writers. "Make your writing better" is hard to translate into action. Peer revision groups often deteriorate into statements of what "I like" and what "I don't like." But the evaluation rubric can make a great organizer for peer input. Have students think about what the most important criterion is (the reason you made the assignment in the first place, the one that carries the most weight in the evaluation) and comment on the success of the paper regarding that criterion. For example, if *Writing to the reader* is an evaluation criterion for the extended travelogue assignment, Torey's peer group can ask him to point out stops along the way that his father might really enjoy. They can ask him to explain why his father would be eager to go to those places. (Perhaps his father loves ferry boats and would like to ride across Lake Michigan to Manitowoc, Wisconsin.)

DEVELOPING COMPETENCE THROUGH EVALUATION

As the Wart's swimming lesson progresses, Merlyn continues to introduce new concepts. At first the Wart simply follows Merlyn's lead; then he takes ownership of his swimming and follows Merlyn in his own way. As writing teachers we can use evaluation to challenge our students, and we can continue to challenge even our very best students by showing more than we talk about and by encouraging them to write in their own ways.

Build Evaluation Criteria as the Year Progresses.   As a class moves through a teaching year, assignment purposes should become increasingly sophisticated. Evaluation becomes a tool for helping that to happen. Custom rubrics, for example, might contain different criteria as the year progresses, or they might accumulate criteria. For example, *process* might be 70% of an early rubric; late in the year *process* might still be part of a rubric, but it might be worth only 10%. Personal narrative form might be 20% of a rubric the first time it is used and 50% after it has become familiar. If rubrics threaten to become overwhelming, a series of shorter primary-trait rubrics that focus on two or three characteristics at a time can feed into a portfolio checklist. For example, I might evaluate *revising* on my students' personal narratives, *choosing and adapting for a reader* on persuasive letters, *punctuating compound sentences correctly* as an editing exercise on thank-you letters to a guest speaker, and later on all three.

Ask Students to Identify Which Pieces They Want You to Evaluate.   Portfolios provide opportunities for students to show off their best work. When students choose the pieces of writing to put into their portfolios, they evaluate their own writing. To use portfolios as an evaluation tool in your classroom, follow these guidelines.

- Have students keep a writing folder which contains everything they write.
- Occasionally (every couple of weeks or so) have students look through their folders for a piece they like enough to work on some more. Have students finish this piece by revising, editing, and sharing with the class.
- Evaluate the finished pieces; encourage rewrites.
- Have students put the final pieces into their portfolios. Ask students to write an author's self-statement to explain why they chose the piece they did and what they believe the piece illustrates about their writing.
- At the end of each grading period and at the end of the year, have students write another self-statement about what they have learned about writing, using their portfolio pieces to illustrate.

Help Students Evaluate Their Own Work.   Assign points to class-generated rubrics or personal rubrics (chap. 4). Ask students to arrive at a grade for their writing. In conferences negotiate the grade to be recorded. You may find students being harder on themselves than you would be!

TEACHERS USING RUBRICS

Teachers adapt rubrics to all sorts of assignments. The rubric in Fig. 13.2 is one Paula Nelson uses to look at expert stories (chap. 8) from her students at the

GRADING RUBRIC

This project is graded on the following things:

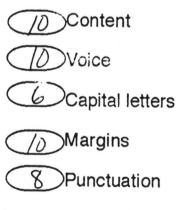

⟨*10*⟩ Content

⟨*10*⟩ Voice

⟨*6*⟩ Capital letters

⟨*10*⟩ Margins

⟨*8*⟩ Punctuation

Each category is worth 10 points.

Total Score *44/50*

FIG. 13.2. Paula's expert story rubric.

beginning of the year. The rubric in Fig. 13.3 is one Becky White uses for a science project that fulfills purposes in both science and language arts. This project uses several kinds of writing to explain a body system.

In the Classroom

Paula:

> When I grade writing, I develop a rubric that reflects any skills I am trying to teach with that particular writing project, for instance content and voice. Sometimes I have a separate place on the rubric which grades the technical aspects I'm trying to teach, like capitalization or margins or punctuation. I usually make a basic outline of maybe 50 points divided into different categories that are fairly easily graded just by reading over the essay or the piece once or twice. I like to have my rubric cover a broad spectrum to be able to include content and spelling and handwriting and two or three mechanics so I can apply those grades in my gradebook. When we spend as much time as we do on a writing project, I need to be able to substantiate it with more than one grade in my gradebook.

> For third grade we have just a straight language arts grade—A, B, C, D, or F and then an effort grade that goes along with it. I average all of my writing grades, technical

Body Systems Booklet/Expository Writing
Explanation of Points Awarded on Body System Booklet

(25)	
REPORT ON CHOSEN BODY SYSTEM: Mechanics:	
Spelling, Punctuation, and Verb-Tense Agreement	5
Information that includes major parts and their functions	9
Written to a sixth-grade audience	6
Introduction that invites the reader to continue	5
(25)	
FICTION STORY: Use of system's parts as main characters	5
Although fiction story, use of info from report and classroom learning	6
Description and detail	9
Mechanics (same as in report)	5
(20) (spelling = 5)	
RAP: Continuous rhythm and beat	7.5
Informative: true facts presented in a fun style	7.5
(15) (spelling = 5)	
BIO POEM: Keeping to the pattern of the poem	5
Using facts that relate to the body system researched	5
(15)	
DIAGRAM: Clear and neat drawing	7
Major parts correctly labeled	8

FIG. 13.3. Becky's science project rubric.

and content and everything, to come up with the grade that I put on the report card.

Also, in accordance with our district assessment plan, we are keeping portfolios. I like to keep examples of all of their finished products in their portfolios, starting from their very first day at school when I take a base line writing sample. I put each one of their finished writings into the portfolios so I can compare those as the year goes by. Then I use the portfolios in parent conferences and at report card time. I look for improvement.

Becky:

I use a system of grading that builds up over the year. The first paper is more content, more let's get interested in writing, and that's what I grade on. At first the points are minimal—just to get us started. Then the points possible increase and then I start adding mechanical things, like the addition of paragraphs, quotation marks. I give points for their first and second draft, their prewriting, and their revision sheets. They also get points for neatness, being finished on time, and sharing at the publishing party.

I total the points, make a copy of the rubric, and send it to the parents. I keep the original on file. Then at the end of the nine weeks we go through the gradebook, and a total of those points turns into an average amount. It's hard to look at a number grade like that, but I know what went into it, and I know the parents are seeing what went into it too. I also have my students add a couple of letters about their writing—the process they've gone through and what we're doing and what a publishing party is. I'm not happy with the report card like it is, but this is what I do with it.

CHAPTER SUMMARY

Sometimes writing teachers avoid evaluation altogether because of product-oriented "knuckle-rapping" grading. However, evaluation is an integral part of instruction, providing students with feedback on their learning so they can keep progressing. When we look at evaluation as communication about the learning-to-write process, we can help our students feel comfortable and confident as well as become competent. This communication stance results in evaluation that is closely tied to instruction and that allows students to keep learning even once the evaluation has been made. Custom rubrics, rewriting, and portfolios support evaluation as communication in the classroom.

APPLICATIONS

1. Discuss your feelings about evaluating children's writing. If possible, trace your feelings back to experiences you had in school yourself.
2. Discuss how you might use evaluation as a teaching tool with the children you currently teach (or plan to teach).

3. Using the assignment you planned in application #4 for chapter 12, design an evaluation rubric following the steps outlined in this chapter.
4. Explain how you determined the distribution of points on the rubric you designed in #1. (Why did certain activities get more points than other activities? Which activities grew out of which assignment purposes? Which assignment purposes grew out of which class goals?)
5. Using the rubric you designed in #1, design instructions for a peer group to help member writers revise to the rubric.
6. Using the class goals you identified in application #3 for chapter 12, make a list of assignment purposes that are more sophisticated than the ones on your evaluation rubric from #1. Put those purposes in a logical order for instruction and evaluation as the year progresses.

14

Tuning Teaching

It is late September. Outside the music building the wind catches the train whistle and blows it all over town. Inside I am sitting on a piano bench in a practice room beside the university's piano tuner/technician. I am on sabbatical, the first year in twenty I have not taught writing.

"Watch me," says Charles.

He places the heavy gray level on the edge of the slip and pushes it along the old ivory piano keys. As he moves it left to right, bass to treble, it clicks once in a while.

"The key heights are uneven," says Charles. "A good pianist can feel that. Put your fingers there. Feel it?"

I feel uneasy. I don't know how to do this. I've never noticed uneven keys before. I want to learn, though, so I take a breath and run my fingers over the keys. The edges of the high keys catch my fingertips.

Charles places his corded right hand on one of the low keys and with his blunt fingertips estimates in thousandths of an inch the difference between it and its neighbors. He chooses a tiny blue circle of paper from a box filled with green, white, pink, and blue paper circles. Lifting the wooden key, he slips the paper punching over the post. "Feel it now," he says.

I reach out and touch the keys. They are smooth and even.

"Now you try," he says.

I begin to relax, to feel comfortable. Charles is sitting next to me, and he has showed me what to do. I place my fingers on the next low key and feel for the difference. I reach for a blue punching and slip it over the post. Charles puts his fingers on the keys and shakes his head.

"Not quite," he says. "Try a pink one."

I change the blue punching for a pink one. This time the keys are level.

For the next hour I work on leveling the keys of the practice piano we are rebuilding. I feel and guess, feel and guess. At first most of my guesses are wrong, so I try again. But after about thirty keys I begin to get the feel. Once in a while I choose the right color circle on the first try.

It is May. Just outside the open garage door, a chickadee whistles and buzzes in the blue spruce. The hedge that separates my driveway from my neighbor's is covered with tiny white flowers. I look up from the ivory keys to the exposed strings of the 1904 Leland upright that almost fills my single-car garage. Steel piano wire travels a familiar path: from treble tuning pin across cedar soundboard down around hitch pin and back up to next treble tuning pin. White felt hammers wait ready to strike the strings into sound, pushed up by slender wood jacks when fingers push down on key tops.

In September when I looked for the first time inside a piano, all I saw was a tangle of wood and wire. But after nine months of afternoons apprenticing, I see a pattern, a design, parts that work together to make a whole. I can do this. I am confident. The afternoons have been a break from writing, and I enjoy learning. But this learning has been different from any I have ever experienced.

At the beginning I thought it was going to be the same. Charles gave me a book about piano tuning and repair to read. I took the book home, conscientiously adjusted the light over my left shoulder, and began to read. Two hours later, my head pounding with confusion, I decided I had made a mistake: I was not cut out to be a piano tuner.

But when I told Charles, he smiled. Taking the book from me, he said, "Never mind. I'll show you."

And he did. Sometimes three, sometimes four, sometimes five times. Without rancor, without frustration, without expectation of anything else.

I raise another key that is too low and choose a green paper punching. I replace the key, measure it against its neighbors. It is even. I consider my apprenticeship. I am surprised at how much I have learned. I have come all the way from uncertainty about clockwise and counterclockwise as they relate to the motion of a screwdriver to a solid grasp of the workings of an upright piano. How have I learned so much in such a relatively short time—and with such joy in the learning? For I have enjoyed this learning. How has Charles taught me?

He never told me about the parts of the piano. He never lectured to me on the proper use of my tools. He did not make me read the book. Instead, he showed me. I watched him repair a harpsichord in a practice room. I helped him restring the Steinway in the conference center ballroom. I listened as he tuned piano after piano on campus. Never once did he say, "Let me tell you how to repair a piano." Always he said, "Let me show you."

I still have a long way to go. "If you want to be a competent piano tuner," Charles said yesterday, "it will take you another year or two to really learn how and years more to get good at it. Nine months is not enough."

I play the bass notes on level keys and study the lost motion in the backchecks. I picture the soft touch of Charles' hand on the key. In my mind's eye, I see the proper amount of movement: the wink of the green felt when I touch the key. I place the wire tool that looks like it belongs in a dentist's office in the tiny hole in the wooden capstan and turn gently. Tuning, repairing, getting comfortable, getting confident, the time needed for competence—it all converges on teaching. At the end of the summer I'll put these tools in a box and go back to my classroom, but I'll go back with a vision of a different way to teach writing. This year I've been tuning my teaching.

THE THEORY

Apprenticing is a very old way of learning that has survived into our day. In the Middle Ages craftsmen of all kinds apprenticed to learn their trades. Today piano tuners still apprentice. So do mechanics and house framers. Doctors do internships to learn specialties. Big corporations educate new college graduates with on-the-job training. Teachers serve a brief apprenticeship in student teaching. When I apprenticed as a piano tuner, I learned by watching and imitating.

In the late 1960s, 1970s, and early 1980s Albert Bandura, a behavioral and social psychologist at Stanford University, studied learning that comes from imitating others. He called this kind of learning *modeling*.

> Because acquisition of response information is a major aspect of learning, much human behavior is developed through modeling. From observing others, one forms a conception of how new behavior patterns are performed, and on later occasions the symbolic construction serves as a guide for action. The initial approximations of response patterns learned observationally are further refined through self-corrective adjustments based on informative feedback from performance. Learning from response consequences is also conceived of largely as a cognitive process. (Bandura, 1978, p. 140)

In other words, Bandura said that one of the main ways we learn is by watching how other people act. From watching them, we form an idea of how to act, try out our idea, and self-correct as we get negative feedback on our performance (from others or from ourselves). Because of Bandura's work and the work of other researchers, learning by example has been used as a teaching strategy in schools since the late 1960s under various names: "modeling," "imitation," "vicarious learning," or "observational learning." A survey of articles available from ERIC turns up references to modeling in the literature of teaching math, computers, reading, geography, English as a second language, and writing. In the field of writing pedagogy, we find references to modeling all the way from reducing anxiety to sentence combining.

THE PRACTICE

When we model writing for students, we talk them through the writer's process of thinking and questioning and decision making. We show them, step by step, how we write. We include them in our process by asking for their suggestions along the way. When children see us take their suggestions and incorporate those suggestions into our writing, they begin to take the process of working on writing seriously. Modeling appears as a teaching strategy throughout this book. Chapter 1 begins with a story about a swimming instructor who showed small children how to swim. Chapter 2 suggests establishing comfort by showing how to write rather than just telling how to write. Many of the suggested activities in the chapters include those that say something like "Share a sample of your own writing with your students." A number of the applications at the ends of the chapters are designed to help readers write their own models to use with students.

From Bandura's work, we can develop a heuristic for modeling that includes both observational and cognitive input for learning.

Before modeling:

- Focus students' attention on the concept, skill, or process you are going to show;
- Put the concept, skill, or process in a context (connect it to earlier writing, give an overview of how it fits in with writing you will be doing in the future);
- Label and define any new concepts or terms.

While modeling:

- Read your writing slowly;
- Talk students through the process you used, step by step.

After modeling:

- Have students go through the process you modeled;
- Provide feedback to the students (yourself or peer groups);
- Have students go through the process a second time if needed;
- Have students explain the steps of their own process to you or to their peers.

AN EXAMPLE

Not long ago Jan Larson and I teamed up to model personal narrative writing for her fourth graders. The unit lasted several weeks. Before we began the actual writing instruction, Jan introduced the concept of "I-voice" to her students. As part of their literature study, the class read several first-person narrator stories, *Island of the Blue Dolphins* by Scott O'Dell (1960) and *A Taste of Blackberries* by Doris Smith (1973) among them. Notice how Smith told her story with an I-voice:

> Jamie and I snagged our way into the thicket of the blackberry patch. I picked a dark berry and popped it into my mouth. The insides of my cheeks puckered.
>
> "They need a few more days to ripen," I said.
>
> Jamie had got stuck and had his thumb in his mouth. He took it out with a smacking sound and put his "shh" finger to his lips. Someone was coming.
>
> "I'll bet Jamie and them will be sorry they didn't come," a voice said. I was "and them."
>
> Jamie and I made faces at one another and pressed our lips together to keep quiet. (p. 1)

Because the class was accustomed to writing in journals after recess each day, Jan began making journal prompts personal: my favorite birthday, the best present I ever got, my favorite toy when I was young, my experience with pets, a trip I won't ever forget, the birth of my sister/brother, a great time my friend and I had once.

When Jan felt confident that her students understood the concept of "I-voice," we decided to share our own personal stories. Jan shared a story of a special trip she made to her grandparents' house when she was about 10. I shared the story of the birth of my brother (chap. 7). Then we talked to the children about how we decided on our topics. Jan talked about starting with a trip she wanted to tell about and thinking of a reader who would like to hear the story (her 17-year-old daughter). I talked about starting with a reader (my niece) and deciding on a story she would like to hear. We introduced the "who-why-how" triangle for writing (chap. 4). The triangle for my story looked like Fig. 14.1.

Next, we asked children to work on triangles of their own, using their journal writings to start stories from. Pods (working groups who sat together in Jan's class) looked at individual triangles and made suggestions. Once we were confident that all the children had triangles to work from, Jan introduced clustering as a way of remembering details. The basic cluster we started with looked like Fig. 14.2. Next we talked the children through adding details. The detail cluster I shared with the children looked like Fig. 14.3. After children had made their own clusters, we talked to them about putting ideas in order by numbering bubbles on their cluster. My ordering looked like Fig. 14.4.

Throughout the process of making their clusters, Jan and I walked around the room, looked over shoulders, and answered questions. Jan pulled a small group together and showed confused children how to separate main ideas from details in their clusters. I worked with a small group on adding more details by asking questions. When all the cluster maps were finished, we asked the children to write their personal narratives.

When they had finished drafting, Jan and I modeled revision using partner checklists we had devised that included questions about I-voice, target reader, purpose, sensible order, and interesting details. I read my story again, and we asked children to look at the checklist with us. Children suggested details that

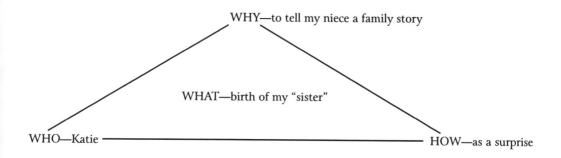

FIG. 14.1. Suzanne's who-why-how triangle.

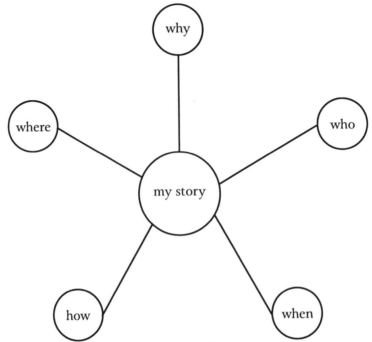

FIG. 14.2. Basic cluster map.

FIG. 14.3. Suzanne's cluster map #1.

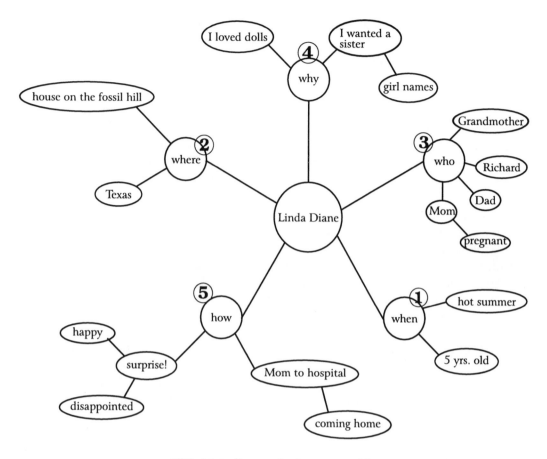

FIG. 14.4. Suzanne's cluster map #2.

were missing from my first draft (what I had thought a baby would be like, what color the baby's eyes were, etc.) that they would like to know. We did the same thing with Jan's story. Children suggested words that might need to be changed for Jan's reader (a young child). When children read their stories to their pod partners and filled out their own partner checklists, they had a concrete idea of what to do.

After partners finished making revision suggestions, children wrote a revised draft. The next step was editing. Jan targeted three errors for children to look for in each other's work: capital letters, spelling, and periods at the end of a sentence. Because these were familiar concepts from earlier minilessons, Jan reminded the children of charts on the wall they could use to remember the rules. Then she put the children in groups of three, appointing each child one responsibility for the group. (One child looked for capital letters in all three papers; one looked for spelling; the third examined period placement.) Once editing was complete, children made final copies, and we had a publishing party. Jan collected the final copies and made a book for the school library. At the end of the personal narratives unit, we asked children to make a list of the steps they went through to write their personal narratives.

A WRITER AMONG WRITERS

Modeling with our own writing is a teaching strategy that is sometimes difficult for us to implement because so few of us experienced it as students. "Telling" teaching was what we experienced. We do not know how to go about "showing" teaching. Sometimes we feel uncomfortable, intimidated even, by the idea of sharing our writing with our students.

After I spent a year learning to tune pianos by watching Charles, I decided to write with my students to show them how to write rather than simply tell them how to write as I had for so many years. At first I was nervous. I wasn't a very good writer, and I knew it. I could write flawless five-paragraph essays for school, and I had managed to write a successful doctoral dissertation, but I didn't like my own writing. It bored me. However, as most of the writing my students were doing bored me too, I decided we might all learn a better way to write together. I took a deep breath and stepped out from behind the safety of my desk. I invited my students to step out from behind the safety of their old habits of writing. They did, and together we began to write. In fairly short order we became a community of writers. I became one among them— a writer among writers.

When I first took the risk of stepping out from behind my desk, I did so because I was convinced I had found a better way to teach my students to write. Six years later I know I was right because my current students write better than my previous students did. However, I've discovered benefits for myself that I never dreamed of. Now I show writing not only for my students, but also for myself. There are wonderful side benefits teachers reap from modeling writing for their students.

We Learn to Write

Learning to write well is a lifelong pursuit. Look at the complete works of almost any published writer, and you will find a difference between the early works and the mature works. Even a writer as good as e.e. cummings got better as he continued to write. As teachers, when we write with our students, we get better, too. Our students provide us with a real audience and teaching writing provides us with a real purpose. As we write, we find our writing voices.

We Experience Comfort, Confidence, and Competence

At first I was nervous about sharing my writing with my students. As I got responses from them, however, I began to relax and become confident that this new strategy was working well. As I asked for their feedback, I began to learn ways of making my writing better. Gradually I developed competence, both as a teacher using modeling as a strategy and as a writer. As we establish our own comfort, we understand more clearly how to establish comfort for our students with their writing. As our own confidence builds, we find ways of increasing our students' confidence. As we take ownership of our classrooms and our writing by analyzing and responding to the communication situations we are in, our students watch us and analyze their own communication situations.

We Join the Community of Writers We Are Building in Our Classrooms

As we write with our students we experience what they are experiencing, and they experience what we are experiencing. The mood changes from one of expert passing along information to one of experienced learner making suggestions to inexperienced learners. Students relax, and we relax. Effective communication seems more important than perfection. Prewriting and revision become natural, part of the work of trying to communicate more clearly with our readers. Editing and publishing happen as a matter of course because we are working in a community of writers who help one another and are eager to hear each other's work.

Evaluation Is Easier

Evaluating writing is a complex task. Even when different children write on the same topic, it is almost impossible to compare their papers. One student has excellent content but no voice; another has a clear grasp of writing to a reader but does not spell conventionally; a third prewrites entirely in his head. Nevertheless, when we write with our students, we understand the task we have set for them from the inside out. It becomes easier to articulate assignment purposes. When we write with our students, we know where the hard parts are, where the easy parts are, what is important, and what is a side issue. We look forward to reading our students' writing because we are curious to see what they did with the assignment. Evaluation becomes a celebration of creativity and a strategy for improvement rather than a scavenger hunt for errors.

HINTS FOR HOW TO

As exciting and as beneficial as it is, writing with students can be a daunting undertaking, particularly if we fail to keep our instructional purpose for modeling clear. It is easy to fall into a performance mode with modeling and simply shift writing stress from our students to ourselves. But modeling is not the same thing as performance. In other words, our models do not have to be perfect. In fact, imperfect models actually do a better job at showing students how writing happens than do perfect models. As with learning to write, there is a process of learning to model.

Break in Slowly. Do not try to write every single writing assignment with your students when you first try modeling. Choose assignments with which you are comfortable and confident. Begin with pieces you would like to write anyway, and pieces you can use for another purpose as well as modeling for your students. For example, if I want to model reader and purpose with a friendly letter, I write a letter I need to write anyway that I can share with my students (to my mother perhaps).

Model as You Go Through the Process. Show your students how you write step by step, not expecting yourself to have a finished product before the students do. Prewrite as they prewrite. Draft as they draft. Ask children to help you revise and edit. Share your final piece when they share theirs.

Build a Modeling Portfolio over the Years.   The second year you model writing, use the pieces you wrote the year before. Model a finished piece from year 1 as prewriting for the same assignment in year two. Choose new assignments to write with your students in year 2. Do the same thing the next year until you have a complete modeling portfolio. Start over. As you get bored with assignments, create new ones to write with new groups of students. As you get more experience with modeling, you have old pieces to use and new pieces to keep you interested and challenged with your students.

TEACHERS MODELING

Teachers write with and for their students in many ways. Figure 14.5 is the journey story model Bernadette Whistler wrote for her students in their pioneer unit (chap. 11). She said about it, "Sometimes I just sit down the night before I give a writing assignment and write my model as fast as I can. I just want to show my students what I want them to do. My models aren't always the best pieces of writing I can do, but they accomplish my purpose."

In the Classroom

Becky:

> After writing with my students a few years, I began to see myself as a writer, solving problems and working through things with writing. I never felt that way before. Now writing is so ingrained in me that I am able to now teach it and try to bring this feeling about in my students as well. It's a real important process in our lives to be able to write and solve problems in writing, and I feel like I am able to bring this to kids—lead them to it. Writing has just become an integral part of my life—at school and at home. The bottom line.

Paula:

> Right away from the very first day in school I share my writing with my students. I have some of my pieces posted in the room. You can make them look so nice with a word processor, so I have them with a nice presentation posted in the classroom as posters.

> At first some of the children are hesitant about writing, and if I say, "Let's write a story today," the answer is, "I don't want to do that."

> So I say, "Well, I like to write, so you tell *me* what to write." I turn on the overhead projector and they start telling me a story and I start writing it down.

> Pretty soon we're laughing and talking and thinking about how we can stretch this story or explain what we want to explain better, or get rid of whatever we don't want

I remember when I was 6 years old. My family lived in Cheyenne, Wyoming. The land there is really flat and the mountains were so far away that I always thought they were blue! There was lots of wind and no bugs. Cheyenne was cold in the winter and nice in summer.

Being 6 years old, I was in 1st grade. I had some special friends at school. One of them's name was Cita. She had a kitty that we played with.

One day my dad came home and told my mom, me and my brothers and sisters: "Guess what? We're moving to Tuscon, Ariz." My brother Mark asked if that was in another country. I had never heard of it!

I was sad to leave my home with the basement and bedroom and my bunny. He was beautiful and white. I cried because I was afraid to go.

We took four days to travel by car to Tuscon. My dad, who was always so good to us kids got tired of "are we almost there daddy. I'm tired. I'm hungry. I have to go to the bathroom!"

When we drove into Tuscon we saw some really strange thins. There were tall green things with arms that reached up to the sky. There were pointy stickery things on them. I knew what trees looked like and these were not trees!

The house we moved into had lots of spiders and bugs. We nicknamed it the "bughouse." I once walked by a wall and around a corner. As I walked a huge spider jumped onto me from the wall. I screamed: "Mommy!"

The mountains in Tuscon were so close to us, they were brown! Yucky brown. My mountains in Wyoming were blue, beautiful blue. Tuscon was hot and full of plants that poke you if you touch them. Cheyenne had beautiful flowers and bushes.

I missed my home for a long time. But we lived in Tuscon til I was 18. I made lots of friends there and learned to love the desert! I just didn't touch the cactus. My mom and dad still live in Tuscon. I'm glad we stayed.

FIG. 14.5. Bernadette's journey model.

in the story. We're all working on that together, and I make a mess on the overhead. They laugh and have a good time. They say, "You left out the word *the*, Mrs. Nelson." Sometimes I do it on purpose and sometimes I do it inadvertently, but writing with them is very important to setting the whole atmosphere in my classroom that I want to set.

CHAPTER SUMMARY

Modeling how to write with our own writing is a teaching strategy as old as apprenticing. Effective models set the stage by focusing students' attention on the characteristics we want them to imitate. Effective models also include a slow step-by-step explanation and illustration with our own work. After modeling, students need an opportunity to practice what they have seen and articulate their own process. When we write with our students we join the community of writers in our classroom because we experience what our students experience. We become better writers ourselves and evaluation is easier.

APPLICATIONS

1. Discuss your feelings about writing with your students. Do you think you will model with your own writing (if you don't already)? Why or why not? How do you think modeling would change (or has changed) the mood in your classroom? Would this be a good change for you or not? Why?
2. Evaluate yourself as a writer. What parts of the writing process would you feel good about showing your students? What kinds of writing do you feel confident enough with to show your students?
3. Extend your self-evaluation from #2. What parts of the writing process would you like to learn more about as you teach your students? How might modeling help you learn? What kinds of writing would you like to learn with your students? How might you begin learning?
4. Go back to one of the pieces of writing you did to use as a model in chapters 7–10 (Applications). Analyze the process you used to write that piece. Create a step-by-step model of your process you could share with your students.
5. Based on the model you wrote for #4, design a writing assignment for your students. Identify the purposes for that assignment. Design an evaluation rubric for that assignment.
6. How did the fact that you had written a model affect the rubric you designed in #5?

Appendix

A QUICK REVIEW OF EDITING RULES (FOR TEACHERS ONLY)

What this Appendix Is; What it Is Not

- A teacher review, not elementary-age student instruction.
- Individual minilessons, not a self-contained study of grammar.
- A starting place to review rules, not a handbook. (For an excellent handbook see Gordon's *The New Well-Tempered Sentence*, 1993.)

How this Appendix Is Organized

- Self-diagnosis.
- Brief review of particular editing rules with samples, practice, and application.
  parts of speech
  agreement
  verb tenses
  capitalization
  building blocks of sentences
  sentences
  punctuation
  correcting awkward sentences

- Answer keys to self-diagnosis and practice exercises

How to Use this Appendix

- Take the self-diagnosis.
- Identify one or two concerns you want to focus on in your own writing.
- Go to those sections and review. Then do the practice exercises and applications to your own writing.

- Write out the rules for those concerns in your own words.
- Write a new paragraph which contains sentences illustrating the correct use of the rule on which you are working.
- Make up a personal method for remembering this rule when you write.
- Make up a personal system for finding these particular errors when you are proofreading.

EDITING SELF-DIAGNOSIS

Correct any editing errors you find in the following paragraphs (see p. 208).

In his book, *The Roots of the Self*, it is explained by Robert Ornstein (1993) how we each became who we are and he offers scenarios that help readers see themselves objectively. First he says there are basic building blocks of the personality, these are genetic and permanent in character. Ways of perceiving and interacting with the world that occurs on a continuum. These dimensions of temperament can be divided into three large categories; high-low amplification, deliberation-liberation, positive approach-negative withdrawal. Amplification has to do with how much outside stimulation a person likes. People with high internal amplification were often introverts disliking outside stimulation, people with low internal amplification enjoyed outside stimulation. Deliberation-liberation breeds organizational habits. With deliberate folks being highly organized and liberated folks being highly disorganized. According to this author approach-withdrawal describes spontaneous responses-positive or negative.

Going beyond his discussion of personality family and environment also affect our self-concept. Interactions with a sibling affects us as much as interactions with our parents and our parents interactions with a sibling affects us as much as they affect the sibling. In short a family is complex, subtle and confusing.

According to Ornstein it is smarter; therefore, to learn to work within our basic personalities than it is to try to change the building blocks of who we are.

PARTS OF SPEECH

The Vocabulary of Sentences

The parts of speech provide a vocabulary for talking about sentences. If you don't know the terms, the rules of written usage are mysterious. If you do know the terms, the rules are usually fairly straightforward (see Table A.1).

Labeling Parts of Speech

In order to label a particular word by its part of speech, you must look at what the word is doing in the sentence. (It won't work to memorize a part of speech for a particular word.) Look at the following examples:

TABLE A.1

Part of Speech	Definition
noun	person, place, or thing
examples: car, door, Tom, Chicago, book, cat, town, woman, child, kindness	
pronoun	substitutes for a noun
examples: I, me, mine, myself, they, this, you, everybody, who, whose, him	
verb	shows action or state of being
examples: write, writes, is writing, wrote, has written, go, went, jumped	
adjective	modifies nouns or pronouns
examples: short, attractive, famous, four (men), this (class), oldest	
adverb	modifies verb, adjectives, or other adverbs
examples: rarely (came), too (sad), never (alone), nearly always (mad)	
conjunctive adverb	modifies an independent clause
examples: consequently, first, furthermore, however, nevertheless, second, then, therefore, third, etc.	
conjunction	connects words or parts of the sentence
coordinators	connects independent clauses
and, but, or, for, nor, so, yet (This is an exhaustive list: there are only seven!)	
subordinators	creates a dependent clause as it connects
examples: after, although, as, because, if, since, so that, that, though, unless, when, where, while, etc. (Please note: Relative pronouns also make a clause dependent. There are 8 relative pronouns: that, what, which, who, whoever, whom, whomever, whose. Relative pronouns are subordinators, but not conjunctions.)	
preposition	is followed by a noun or pronoun, creating a prepositional phrase
examples: on (the chair), between (you and me), about, by, in, from, of, etc.	
interjection	interrupts to show emotion
examples: Wow! Oh, (I didn't know that.)	

love
   as a noun: His love sustained me.
   as a verb: I love you.
   as an adjective: He sent me three love letters.
   as a pronoun: Listen, love, I've got to tell you this.
up
   as an adverb: Look up over your head.
   as a preposition: Jack and Jill went up the hill.
   as an adjective: The up escalator is broken.
   as a noun: Everyone has ups and downs in life.
   as a verb: My landlord upped the rent again.

Editing Terms

The most important vocabulary terms for editing are *subject* and *verb* (see Table A.2).

TABLE A.2

verb	the action or (state of being) of the sentence; helping verbs create two- or three-word verbs

examples: The horse *won* the race. I *am* tired today. Jack *be* nimble; Jack *be* quick; Jack *jump* over the candlestick. Time *is running* out.

subject	the noun or pronoun that controls the verb of the sentence

examples: The *horse* won the race. *I* am tired today. *Jack* be nimble; *Jack* be quick; *Jack* jump over the candlestick. *Time* is running out

Practice

Label the parts of speech of each word in the sentences that follow (see p. 208).

1. Before we could get home, the storm broke overhead with fierce intensity.
2. You may not apply for graduation before your senior year, but you must meet the requirements every semester.
3. Politicians often kiss babies; however, the babies seldom kiss back.
4. Those little chocolate kisses are getting too expensive for my taste!
5. Holy cow! Did you see that?

AGREEMENT

Sentences must be consistent in number throughout. If the subject is singular, the sentence parts must be singular. If the subject is plural, they must be plural.

Subject-Verb Agreement. The verb must agree in number with the subject. (The *number* of people in the class *is* small. *All* of the people in the class *are* freshmen.)

Noun-Pronoun Agreement. Any pronouns must agree with their antecedents. To avoid sexism, use plurals. (*All* the students are writing *their* own essays instead of *Everyone* is writing *his* own essay. *Each* of the girls should bring *her* bike.)

Noun-Antecedent Agreement. Any nouns which refer back to a previous noun or pronoun must agree in number. (*People* going on the field trip will be asked to drive their own *cars*. Each *one* of the ten was dressed in a *suit*.)

Samples

The dogs all wagged their tail.
The dogs all wagged their tails.

A client who visits that lawyer will find that they must always wait.
Clients who visit that lawyer must always wait.

Neither of the books have come in yet.
Neither (one) of the books has come in yet.

On that side of the street is a grocery store, a post office, and a drugstore.
On that side of the street are a grocery store, a post office, and a drugstore.

The committee has met, has made a decision, and is writing their report.
The committee has met, has made a decision, and is writing its report.

Common Mistakes

- misidentifying the subject, particularly in inverted sentences or questions.
- using plural pronouns to avoid sexist language.

Practice

Find any agreement problems in the following sentences (S-V, N-PN, N-A). Correct the problems; then underline the antecedent which makes your revision correct and the sentence (as typed here) wrong (see p. 208).

1. Some of the enthusiasts brought their racquet to the exhibition match.
2. Neither encouragement nor frequent compliments was enough to make him feel better.
3. Across the street lives an old lady, her pampered Pekinese, and seventeen stray cats.
4. Where is my new skirt and coat?
5. Everyone should do their best.

Application

In a recent piece of your own writing find several long sentences. Identify subjects and verbs as well as nouns and pronouns that have antecedents. Determine if you have made any agreement errors. Correct the errors.

VERB TENSE

Verbs in writing show time: present tense or past tense. Unless the meaning requires it, verb tenses should be consistent throughout one piece of writing.

Samples

Present tense: The day is hot and dry. Molly leans out of the window wishing for a breeze. Not feeling one, she goes into the bathroom and pours cold water on her head.

Past tense: The day was hot and dry. Molly leaned out of the window wishing for a breeze. Not feeling one, she went into the bathroom and poured cold water on her head.

Common Mistake

- Shifting from present to past in the same paragraph.

Practice

Find the tense shifts below. Keeping to the sense of the passage, make the verbs consistent (see p. 209).

Still feeling hot, Molly went into the kitchen and opened the refrigerator door. As cool air rushes out, she feels relief. But not for long.
Her mother yells, "What do you think you're doing, Molly? Close that door!"

Application

Check a recent piece of your writing for any tense shifts.

CAPITALIZATION

Capitalize the first word of every sentence; capitalize proper names as well.

Samples

The only way Molly will be able to get cool is to go outside and sit under a shady maple tree.
The Flagstaff Middle School Lobos have the wolf as their mascot.

Common Mistake

- Mistaking a category for a name.

Practice

Correct any capitalization errors in the following sentences (see p. 209).

1. It is impossible to find much shade under an Aspen.
2. The mountains above flagstaff are called the San Francisco peaks.

Application

Check the capital letters you have used in a recent piece of writing. Make sure proper names are capitalized and category names are not.

BUILDING BLOCKS OF SENTENCES

Phrase

Any group of words that forms a meaning unit.

Samples

1. **Buried for 200 years,** the treasure had rusted into worthless scraps of metal.
2. The report was made **by the treasurer**.
3. **In the middle** of the stream was a huge rock.
4. We bought our tickets **at the gate**.
5. **According to the schedule,** we will be home **by ten o'clock**.

Practice

Underline phrases in the following sentences (see p. 209).

1. The runner, trembling with fatigue, collapsed on the side of the road.
2. "Get off the bed," shouted the boy at his dog.
3. Retell the story in your own words.
4. Study the directions under a bright light.
5. Snapping their umbrellas open, people ran for their cars.

Application

Find ten phrases in the last piece you wrote.

Clause

A group of words that forms a meaning unit and contains both a subject and a verb

Samples

1. *We discovered* a new restaurant yesterday. (1 clause)
2. Whenever the *breeze blew*, the *wind chimes rang* loudly. (2 clauses)
3. Every year *she digs* out a new patch of the yard and *plants* more flowers because *she's addicted* to seed catalogs. (2 clauses)
4. From the top of the hill *we could see* the road winding off into the distance. (One clause—*winding off into the distance* is a phrase.)
5. *Can you calculate* the cost?

Practice

Underline the subjects in these sentences; circle the verbs; put phrases in parentheses (see p. 209).

1. Spring usually comes at the end of March.
2. The wind begins to blow, and the tulips poke their leaves through the snow.
3. Juncos leave for Canada as hummingbirds move up from Mexico.
4. Snow melts everywhere except in the deepest shadows.
5. Best of all, we know winter is over.

Application

In the last piece you wrote locate 10 clauses and 10 phrases.

Independent Clauses

An independent clause is a clause that can stand alone. Every sentence must contain at least one independent clause.

Samples

1. *Martha was happy* when Tom went home.
2. *The girls stopped for a milkshake, but the ice cream parlor was closed*.
3. Unless I forgot something *we are ready to go*.
4. Before you came back *everything was going fine*.
5. *Foliage is as important as flowers*, giving a plant its individuality.

Common Mistake

- Not memorizing the seven coordinating conjunctions: *and, but, for, nor, or, so, yet* (see "Parts of Speech").

Practice

Underline the independent clause in the following sentences (see p. 209).

1. Although winter was over the nights were still cold.
2. Jason pulled off his coat and threw it on the ground.
3. Taco Bell is one of the fastest growing food chains in America.
4. Melissa went to Eleanor's but no one was home.
5. Jennifer moped all day because her dog had disappeared.

Application

Go back to the clauses you identified in the "application" section under "Clauses." Identify which ones of them are independent.

Dependent Clauses

Clauses that begin with a subordinating conjunction are dependent. This means they cannot stand alone but must also have an independent clause to make a complete sentence. Common subordinators include *after, although, as, because, before, if, since, though, unless, until, when, where,* and *while* (see "Parts of Speech").

Samples

1. *After I finished mopping,* I noticed that my shoes were muddy.
2. *Before you take the test,* be sure to read the new assignment.
3. *Whenever I try to sleep,* Ryan decides to practice his drums.
4. *Because today is my birthday,* I plan to take a holiday.
5. I will take care of your pet *until you get back.*

Practice

Underline the dependent clauses (see pp. 209–210).

1. Although Mr. Moore is the best drama teacher at our school, he is a terrible driver.
2. Try that dress on before you buy it.
3. When his backpack was stolen, he lost the draft of his research paper and all his notes.
4. She is worried that you will get hurt if you drive so fast.
5. Always carry an umbrella because it rains so frequently in Flagstaff in the summer.

Application

With the same sentences you have been working on in this chapter, find any dependent clauses.

SENTENCES

Ways to Join Clauses

1. Conjunctions (see coordinators and subordinators in "Parts of Speech").

My husband went shopping but *I stayed home to work in the garden.*
We get a lot accomplished because *we often split up* housework tasks.

2. Semicolons

• Alone
Semicolons can take the place of a period and join 2 independent clauses; they are never used with conjunctions.

We both work outside of our home to bring in money; we both work inside our home to maintain order.

- With conjunctive adverbs

Conjunctive adverbs (see "adverbs") are not conjunctions because they can be moved to another place in the sentence, but they often appear in the "slot" where we put conjunctions—between clauses. When a conjunctive adverb is between clauses, use a semicolon to divide the clauses.

Our division of labor is an efficient use of time; however, it sometimes causes us to be apart more than we would like.
Our division of labor is an efficient use of time; it sometimes causes us to be apart more than we would like, however.

Practice

Decide whether the sentences in the following paragraph require semicolons or if the commas are sufficient (see p. 210).

When I was growing up, my mother and father had a traditional division of labor in their home. My father worked outside of the home to bring in money, my mother worked inside of the home to maintain order. American society is different now, however, the rising cost of living often dictates two incomes. As a young woman raising a child I would have liked to stay home, nevertheless, I worked full time. We wanted to live in a house rather than in an apartment, so we needed my income.

Application

Look for sentences that could be combined with semicolons in a recent piece of your writing. Determine what kind of conjunction you are taking out. Try adding 3 new sentences that use a semicolon to join independent clauses; use a conjunctive adverb in one or two of your new sentences.

Common Mistakes

- Connecting two independent clauses with a comma (*comma splice*).

Run-on.   Two (or more) independent clauses punctuated as if they were one sentence.
   Samples:

The ancient Egyptians did not believe in the old saying, "You can't take it with you," they filled their tombs with all the things they wanted to take into the afterlife.
   Over the years most of the pyramids were broken into and looted, however, King Tut's tomb was overlooked.

- Putting a period after a dependent clause (*fragment*)

Fragment.   A piece of a sentence punctuated as if it is an independent clause and can stand alone.
Samples:

Because Marge was running late. She didn't notice the empty place on the wall.
A heavy wool bed rug that was hand woven by Paul Revere's mother and was stolen from the museum.

Practice

In the following paragraph put parentheses around any sentence fragments you find. Insert periods or semicolons where they are needed to break up any run-on sentences you find (see p. 210).

To develop your green thumb, take up gardening to feed your soul. Not to decorate your house or impress your neighbors. Study the needs of particular plants, you can get a certain amount of information from books, but often trial and error makes the best teacher. Plant catalogs, for example, tell "zones" (based on coldest annual temperature) and which plants will grow in which zones, but they fail to give other critical requirements. Like humidity, length of growing season, type of soil, and amount of shade in your yard. Ask questions and be alert, look around your neighborhood to see what does well. For example, I would dearly love to grow a bougainvillea, I see their spectacular magenta foliage less than 150 miles from my home. Six thousand feet down the mountain! Instead I plant honeysuckle, which doesn't mind the altitude in my yard. Be attentive, watch each plant to see if it's happy where you've placed it. Above all, be patient with yourself. Developing a green thumb is a learning process.

Application

Trade a piece of writing with a classmate. Search for sentence fragments and run-ons. Trade back. Check each other's work. Discuss any disagreements.

Sentence Variety.   Clauses are the building blocks of sentences. Every sentence must contain at least one independent clause. Addition of other clauses creates more complex sentences. There are four types of sentences:
Simple = 1 independent clause

We live in a big house with four bedrooms.

Compound = 2 (or more) independent clauses

We live in a big house with four bedrooms, but it requires two incomes to make the mortgage payment each month.

Complex = 1 independent clause and 1 (or more) dependent clauses

While I would like to only work part-time next year, I realize that I must wait a few more years before quitting my job.

Compound-complex = 2 (or more) independent clauses and 1 (or more) dependent clauses

I am willing to continue working because I want to stay in my big house; however, once the children are all grown, I want to move to a smaller house.

Practice

Label each sentence in the following paragraph *simple, compound, complex,* or *compound-complex.* Make one of the compound sentences complex (see p. 210).

When you set up your own home, you will probably have to face the same dilemma my husband and I faced. On the one hand, one of you may want to stay home to raise your children; on the other hand, you may need more living space than you can afford on one income. One solution to this problem is to move to a community that still has a low cost of living. One of you can get a job, and the other one can stay home for a few years, or both of you can get part-time jobs. Another solution is to win the lottery!

Common Mistakes

Many student writers use simple and compound sentences exclusively even though complex and compound-complex sentences make meaning more precise. Learn to use subordinators and semicolons!

Application

Label the sentences you used in one page of recent writing. Look at the pattern of your sentences; vary your sentence types.

PUNCTUATION

Commas

(Please note that this discussion of commas is not intended to review all the comma rules. The rules included here are the main ones needed for editing.)

Rule 1. Place a comma before a coordinating conjunction (and, but, for, or, nor, so, yet) that joins *independent clauses.*

Samples

1. We had looked forward to buying a car for months, *but* new cars were more expensive than we had expected. *(2 independent clauses)*
   We investigated pickups *but* finally decided not to purchase one. (2 verbs)
2. We wanted a vehicle that would go in town, *and* we wanted something we could take off road. *(2 independent clauses)*

It soon became clear that such a vehicle was out of our range *and* that we would have to lower our expectations. *(2 dependent clauses)*

TIP: Memorize the coordinators.

Practice (see p. 210)

1. Buying a new car can stretch your budget and can often cause stress.
2. My husband wanted a sturdy car and I wanted one that was easy to drive.

Rule 2.   Place a comma after information that introduces an independent clause.

Samples

1. *According to our mechanic*, the transmission on our old car would not last another year. *(phrase)*
2. *However*, a new car seemed like a waste of money to me. *(adverb)*
3. *Whenever we have a big decision to make*, we call a family conference. *(dependent clause)*

TIP: Find where the kernel sentence is; then ask yourself if there are words or phrases introducing that independent clause which place it in a context for the reader.

Practice

Put commas in if they are needed (see p. 211).

1. Therefore we decided to have a conference Saturday morning at breakfast.
2. After fixing pancakes to put everybody in a good mood my husband brought up the subject of buying a new car.
3. All in all the conference went well.
4. Because we had done the leg work together we agreed almost instantly on what to do.

Rule 3.   Place a comma following a dependent clause that precedes an independent clause; do not use a comma before a dependent clause that follows an independent clause. *(DC, IC. but IC DC.)*

Samples

Because we suddenly had another repair bill on our old car, we started talking about new cars.

We like the Jeep Cherokee the best *because it has the advantages of a pickup as well as the advantages of a passenger car*.

It looked like exactly the vehicle for us; *however*, it was terribly expensive.

TIP: Dependent clauses are created by subordinating conjunctions: words like *although, because, since, while*, etc. (See "Dependent clauses.")

First identify all clauses. Then examine the clause to see if the first word is a conjunction. If it is not a coordinator (you have memorized those), it is either a subordinator or a conjunctive adverb (words like *however, nevertheless, on the other hand*). To tell which it is, ask yourself if you can move the word to another place in the sentence. If you *cannot* move it, the word is a subordinator, creating a dependent clause, and you follow this rule. If you can move it, the word is an adverb that only looks like a conjunction (a conjunctive adverb), and you use the rules for independent clauses (i. e., a semicolon or period).

Practice (see p. 211)

1. Whenever you decide to buy a new car I hope you will take the time to gather all the data.
2. It is sometimes tempting to take the word of the salesman if you feel rushed to make a decision.
3. The salesman has a job to do however he's more concerned about selling you a car than he is about your family's transportation needs.

Rule 4.   Place commas on either side of parenthetical (nonrestrictive) information that interrupts the clause.

Samples

1. My father, *who has had to watch money all his life*, finally convinced us to buy a used car. (There is only one *my father*, so this information is extra, interrupting the clause *my father finally convinced us*)
2. A friend *who is now quite wealthy* said the same thing as my father. (I have many people who could be identified as *a friend*, so this information tells which friend I'm talking about; it is needed and so is not considered an interruption.)
3. My brother, *on the other hand*, never buys anything, *even an expensive item like a car*, that isn't brand new. (2 interrupters to the clause *my brother never buys anything that isn't brand new*.)
4. Probably the most important thing to check, *if you buy a used car*, is the odometer (a dependent clause interrupting the independent clause).

TIP: Think about parentheses: commas go where you would put a parenthesis mark. If the extra information is at the end of a sentence, however, you only use one comma since English never puts a comma and a period right next to one another.

Practice

Put commas in wherever they are needed (see p. 211).

1. Cars while a necessity in modern society consume a larger portion of our income than we often think.

2. Insurance is a considerable expense if for example you think about the monthly cost of a car.
3. My friend who lives in New York City has given up his car entirely.
4. My friend who lives in a smaller town following the example of our New York friend has gone to one car.

Rule 5.   Use commas to separate items in a list.

Sample

The used car we bought had *low mileage, new tires, and a current license plate*.

TIP: Although journalists now leave out the comma before the *and*, academics still use it. In other words, know your audience!

Practice (see p. 211)

Other hidden expenses include gasoline oil tires license plates and a garage.

Rule 6.   Place a comma after *said* when it precedes directly quoted material. Punctuate quoted sentences inside the quotation marks just like they would be if they weren't quoted.

Samples

The salesman said, "You're getting a real steal! If I needed a new car, this is the one I would buy."
He also said that the people who had owned the car had taken very good care of it.

TIP: Commas and periods always go inside the quotation marks; semicolons and colons always go outside the quotation marks; question marks and exclamation points can go either inside or outside depending on meaning.

Practice (see p. 211)

1. My husband replied that he would decide after a test drive.
2. I said I hope this car drives well. Even though it's not exactly what we wanted it's close enough for government work.

Comma Review

Memorize the following principles:

- Use a comma with a coordinating conjunction joining independent clauses
- Set off introductory information, extra information, items in a list, and quoted material.

Practice With Commas

Put commas where they are needed in the following paragraph. Write the number of the rule above that requires each comma (see p. 212).

Whenever I face teaching punctuation I cringe. I cringe because college students tend to turn off their brains at this juncture. Unfortunately most students have become convinced over the years that "grammar" is utterly incomprehensible. Fear takes over and ears close. The reality however is that grammar rules are often introduced to kids in school before they are ready to understand them. (Contrary to popular belief there is a system of logic operating beneath grammar/usage rules and simple memorization of a list of rules is not really the answer.) By the time students reach college they are ready to understand usage rules and when I am able to get students to listen with an open mind they frequently say "Oh now I get it!" after only a brief bit of instruction. The hallmark of effective instruction however is whether students can find samples of sentence patterns in their own writing determine which rule applies in which situation and put the rules into practice.

Semicolon

The semicolon is primarily used to separate two closely related independent clauses, often clauses which contrast with one another.

Samples

1. Building a new house can be quite *exciting; it* can also be quite expensive.
2. My daughter loves *cats; however*, I think they are a lot of trouble.

TIP: You may think of a semicolon as a combination of a period and a comma: the "period" means that grammatically the sentence requires a period; the "comma" means that the meaning of the sentence requires a comma.

Practice

Put in commas and semicolons as they are needed (see p. 212).

1. When we built our new house my daughter wanted to get a cat immediately however I told her we would have to wait a while.
2. My husband disagreed he thought we should get a cat the next day.
3. I won this argument however when I announced that they would have to take care of it.

Colon

The colon follows an independent clause: it tells the reader that the preceding clause is about to be explained further.

Samples

1. *Camping is my brother's favorite activity*: he loves getting out in nature.

2. *To have a successful camping trip, you must be prepared with the proper equipment*: a waterproof tent, a lantern, a cook stove, a water container, and a sleeping bag.

TIP: A colon does not precede a list unless the list follows an independent clause. So you would write *When you pack, please don't forget to bring freeze-dried milk, paper-packaged noodles, and matches.*

Practice

Add colons, semicolons, and commas where they are needed (see p. 212).

1. Backpacking can be fun if you have a good pack one that has a steel frame and is lightweight.
2. Safety rules like the following are important carry enough water stop before dark set up camp off the trail.
3. Don't forget to bring an inflatable mattress a toothbrush or a comb.

Commonly Confused Punctuation Marks

End Marks

1. Exclamation Point (!) = strong emotion
2. Question Mark (?) = ends a question

   Samples

1. "Wow!" he shouted.
2. What is the weather like today?

Apostrophes, Quotation Marks

Apostrophe (').   Use to show possession in a noun, not in a pronoun

John's car
his car

the graduates' diplomas
the men's hall
their diploma
That is theirs!

the dog's tail
its tail

Use to show a contraction

do not
don't

it is time to go
it's time to go

Quotation marks ("").   Use for a direct quote, not for an indirect quote.

He said, "I'm ready to go!"
He said that he was ready to go.

Extra information marks

Commas, extra,
Dashes —important extra—
Parentheses (unimportant extra)

   Samples

1. My home, which is in Virginia, is a long way from here.
2. Your paper—the best in the class—received an A.
3. Turn to Chapter 3 (pages 34–72).

Hyphen (-)

1/2 the length of a dash. It is used to join words and divide words at syllables.

The twelve-year-old child ran away.
Juxtaposition has five syllables: jux-ta-po-si-tion.

Punctuation Practice

   Each of the following sentences needs one mark of punctuation: add a colon, semicolon, hyphen, dash, or parentheses (see p. 212).

1. John was too self confident for his own good
2. John my best friend lives next door.
3. Turn to chapter three pages 37–45 and read it.
4. There was only one thing he didn't know how to be polite.
5. His temper got him in trouble often sometimes even his wife couldn't stand to be around him.

Correct all the mistakes in the following paragraphs (see p. 213).

That morning the postman was late. Tom had been waiting for two hours when the mail truck finally arrived. Tom rushed out of the house quickly for he was expecting an important letter from his doctor.

'morning' said the postman. "whats the rush."

"I'm expecting an important letter" said Tom "Its from Dr. Smith. Have you got it."

The postman shuffled through the stack of letters he held and nodded his head. Handing it to Tom with a bow the postman got back in his truck and drove off.

Tom rushed in the house slammed the door and ripped the envelope open. There it was. It was a refund check for $343.00. Tom kissed the check and he raced out the door. He jumped in the car hit the gas and roared towards the bank. Whoopee he shouted.

ELIMINATING AWKWARD SENTENCES

Placement of Modifiers

Modifying phrases should be attached to the words that they logically modify. A dangling modifier is one which is not attached.

Samples

Not: After *driving* all day, the *motel* was a welcome sight.
Rather: After *driving* all day, *we* were glad to see the motel.

Not: To *receive* the scholarship, a high *grade average* is necessary.
Rather: To *receive* the scholarship, a *student* must maintain a high grade average.

Practice

Correct the dangling modifiers in the sentences below (see p. 213).

1. At thirteen, my family moved from Texas to Kansas.
2. Skiing against the blowing snow, my face felt frozen.
3. While chasing his cat across the street, the boy's shoestring broke, and he fell.
4. Looking north, the San Francisco Peaks can be seen.

Parallelism

Grammatical units joined by coordinators should be parallel: noun to noun, adjective to adjective, phrase to phrase, clause to clause.

Samples

Not: A park ranger is entrusted with *the safety* of tourists *and* also *to protect* wildlife.
Rather: A park ranger is entrusted with *the safety* of tourists *and the protection* of wildlife.

Not: Our apartment is *small, gloomy, and needs* a new coat of paint.
Rather: Our apartment *needs a skylight and a new coat of paint.*

Not: The mayor's remarks were *tedious, disjointed, and could not readily be understood.*

Rather: The mayor's remarks were *tedious, disjointed, and confusing.*

Practice

Make the following sentences parallel (see p. 213).

1. The kitchen is 8 feet in length and 9 feet wide.
2. The hourly wage of a plumber is bigger than a teacher.
3. My father has had jobs in retail, in marketing, and once worked in a laboratory.
4. Oranges from California are larger and juicier than Arizona.
5. Racquetball is an exciting sport and one which requires agility and physical stamina.

Passive/Active Voice

When the common-sense doer of the verb is the same as the grammatical subject of the sentence, the sentence is in ACTIVE voice. When the common-sense doer of the verb is inside a prepositional phrase and another word is the grammatical subject, the sentence is in PASSIVE voice.

Active

Maria ate the soup.
(Maria, the grammatical subject, did the eating.)

The electrician replaced the old wiring.
(The electrician, the grammatical subject, did the replacing.)

Passive

The meeting was called to order by the vice-president.
(The meeting, the grammatical subject, did not call anything to order; the vice-president [in the prepositional phrase] did.)

The roof was destroyed by the wind storm.
(The roof, the grammatical subject, did not destroy anything; the wind storm [in a prepositional phrase] did).

ACTIVE voice is stronger than passive voice. Use the active voice as often as you can.

Label the following sentences ACTIVE or PASSIVE. Change the passive sentences to active (see p. 213).

1. The decision was made by the committee.
2. The old woman's utilities were paid for by the neighbors.
3. As a child, the comedian often offended his mother.

4. The teacher taught the students fractions.
5. The surprise party was organized by Anna.

ANSWER KEYS

Self-Diagnosis

Corrections have been bolded. The number that follows the correction will send you to a particular review section:

1. parts of speech
   a. vocabulary of sentences
   b. labeling parts of speech
   c. editing terms
2. agreement
   a. subject-verb
   b. noun-pronoun
   c. noun-antecedent
3. verb tenses
4. capitalization
   a. sentences
   b. names
5. building blocks of sentences
   a. phrases
   b. clauses
   c. independent clauses
   d. dependent clauses
6. sentences
   a. ways to join clauses
   b. fragments
   c. run-ons
   d. sentence variety
7. punctuation
   a. commas
   b. semicolons
   c. colons
   d. commonly confused punctuation marks
8. correcting awkward sentences
   a. placement of modifiers
   b. parallelism
   c. passive and active voice

In his **book** *The* **(7a)** *Roots of the Self* **(4b), Robert Ornstein** (1993) **attempts to explain (8c)** how we each became who we **are, and (7a)** he offers scenarios that help readers see themselves objectively. **First, he (6a)** says there are basic building blocks of the **personality. These (6c)** are genetic and permanent in **character, ways (6b)** of perceiving and interacting with the world that **occur (2a)** on a continuum. These dimensions of temperament can be divided into three large **categories: high (7b, c)**-low amplification, deliberation-liberation, positive approach-negative withdrawal. Amplification has to do with how much outside stimulation a person likes. People with high internal amplification **are (3)** often **introverts, disliking (7a)** outside **stimulation. People (7c)** with low internal amplification **are (3)** often **extroverts, enjoying (7a, 8a)** outside stimulation. Deliberation-liberation breeds organizational **habits, with (7a)** deliberate people being highly organized and liberated folks being highly disorganized. According to this **author, approach (7a)**-withdrawal describes spontaneous **responses—positive (7d)** or negative.

Going beyond his discussion of **personality, (7a) Ornstein discusses (8b)** the **effects (spelling)** of family and environment **on self-concept (2b).** Interactions with a sibling **affect (spelling)** us as much as interactions with our parents, and our **parents' (7d)** interactions with a sibling **affect (spelling)** us as much as they affect the sibling. In **short, a (6a)** family is complex, **subtle, and (7a)** confusing.

According to **Ornstein, it (7a)** is **smarter, therefore, (7a, b) to** learn to work within our basic personalities than it is to try to change the building blocks of who we are.

Parts of Speech

1. subordinator, pronoun, verb, verb, noun, adjective, noun, verb, adverb, preposition, adjective, noun.
2. pronoun, verb, adverb, verb, preposition, noun, preposition, pronoun, adjective, noun, coordinator, pronoun, verb, verb, adjective, noun, adjective, noun.
3. noun, adverb, verb, noun, conjunctive adverb, adjective, noun, adverb, verb, adverb.
4. adjective, adjective, adjective, noun, verb, verb, adverb, adverb, preposition, pronoun, noun!
5. interjection (two words)! verb, pronoun, verb, pronoun?

Agreement

1. *Some* of the enthusiasts brought their *racquets* to the exhibition match.
2. Neither encouragement nor frequent *compliments* **were** enough to make him feel better.
3. Across the street **live** an old *lady*, her pampered *Pekinese*, and seventeen stray *cats*.
4. Where **are** my new *skirt and coat*?
5. *All test-takers* should do their best.

Verb Tense

Still feeling hot, Molly went into the kitchen and opened the refrigerator door. As cool air **rushed** out, she **felt** relief. But not for long.
Her mother **yelled**, "What do you think you're doing, Molly? Close that door!"

or

Still feeling hot, Molly **goes** into the kitchen and **opens** the refrigerator door. As cool air rushes out, she feels relief. But not for long.
Her mother yells, "What do you think you're doing, Molly? Close that door!"

Capitalization

1. It is impossible to find much shade under an **aspen**.
2. The mountains above **Flagstaff** are called the San Francisco **Peaks**.

Building Blocks

Phrases

1. The runner, *trembling with fatigue*, collapsed *on the side of the road*.
2. "Get *off the bed*," shouted the boy *at his dog*.
3. Retell the story *in your own words*.
4. Study the directions *under a bright light*.
5. *Snapping their umbrellas open*, people ran *for their cars*.

Clauses

1. *Spring* usually *comes* (at the end) (of March).
2. The *wind begins* to blow, and the *tulips poke* their leaves (through the snow).
3. *Juncos leave* (for Canada) as *hummingbirds move* up (from Mexico).
4. *Snow melts* everywhere except (in the deepest shadows).
5. (Best of all) *we know* winter is over.

Independent Clauses

1. Although winter was over *the nights were still cold*.
2. *Jason pulled off his coat and threw it on the groun*d.
3. *Taco Bell is one of the fastest growing food chains in America.*
4. *Melissa went to Eleanor's but no one was home.*
5. *Jennifer moped all day* because her dog had disappeared.

Dependent Clauses

1. *Although Mr. Moore is the best drama teacher at our school*, he is a terrible driver.
2. Try that dress on *before you buy it*.
3. *When his backpack was stolen*, he lost the draft of his research paper and all his notes.

4. She is worried *that you will get hurt if you drive so fast*.

5. Always carry an umbrella *because it rains so frequently in Flagstaff in the summer*.

Sentences—Ways to join clauses

When I was growing up, my mother and father had a traditional division of labor in their home. My father worked outside of the home to bring in **money; my** mother worked inside of the home to maintain order. American society is different now, **however; the** rising cost of living often dictates two incomes. As a young woman raising a child I would have liked to stay **home; nevertheless**, I worked full time. We wanted to live in a house rather than in an apartment, so we needed my income.

Fragments and Run-ons

To develop your green thumb, take up gardening to feed your **soul, not** to decorate your house or impress your neighbors. Study the needs of particular **plants. You** can get a certain amount of information from books, but often trial and error makes the best teacher. Plant catalogs, for example, tell "zones" (based on coldest annual temperature) and which plants will grow in which zones, but they fail to give other critical **requirements, like** humidity, length of growing season, type of soil, and amount of shade in your yard. Ask questions and be **alert. Look** around your neighborhood to see what does well. For example, I would dearly love to grow a **bougainvillea. I** see their spectacular magenta foliage less than 150 miles from my **home: six** thousand feet down the mountain! Instead I plant honey-suckle, which doesn't mind the altitude in my yard. Be **attentive. Watch** each plant to see if it's happy where you've placed it. Above all, be patient with yourself. Developing a green thumb is a learning process.

Sentence Variety

When you set up your own home, you will probably have to face the same dilemma my husband and I faced. [**complex**]

On the one hand, one of you may want to stay home to raise your children; on the other hand, you may need more living space than you can afford on one income. [**compound-complex**]

One solution to this problem is to move to a community that still has a low cost of living. [**complex**]

One of you can get a job, and the other one can stay home for a few years, or both of you can work part-time. [**compound**]

Another solution is to win the lottery! [simple]

Commas—Rule 1

1. Buying a new car can stretch your budget **and** can often cause stress.

2. My husband wanted a sturdy car, **and** I wanted one that was easy to drive.

Commas—Rule 2

1. **Therefore**, we decided to have a conference Saturday morning at breakfast.
2. **After fixing pancakes to put everybody in a good mood**, my husband brought up the subject of buying a new car.
3. **All in all**, the conference went well.
4. **Because we had done the leg work together**, we agreed almost instantly on what to do.

Commas—Rule 3

1. **Whenever you decide to buy a new car**, I hope you will take the time to gather all the data.
2. It is sometimes tempting to take the word of the salesman **if you feel rushed to make a decision**.
3. The salesman has a job to do, **however**; he's more concerned about selling you a car than he is about your family's transportation needs.

Commas—Rule 4

1. Cars, **while a necessity in modern society**, consume a larger portion of our income than we often think.
2. Insurance is a considerable expense if, **for example**, you think about the monthly cost of a car.
3. My friend **who lives in New York City** has given up his car entirely. (needed information)
4. My friend who lives in a smaller town, **following the example of our New York friend**, sold one of his cars.

Commas—Rule 5

Other hidden expenses include **gasoline, oil, tires, license plates, and a garage**.

Commas—Rule 6

1. My husband replied that he would decide after a test drive.
2. I **said**, "I hope this car drives well. Even though it's not exactly what we **wanted, it's** close enough for government work."

Comma Practice

Whenever I face teaching **punctuation, I (3)** cringe. I **cringe because (3)** college students tend to turn off their brains at this juncture. **Unfortunately, (2)** most students have become convinced over the **years that (3)** "grammar" is utterly incomprehensible. Fear takes **over, and (1)** ears close. The reality, **however, (4)** is that grammar rules are often introduced to kids in **school before (3)** they are ready to understand them. (Contrary to popular **belief, (2)** there is a system of logic operating beneath grammar/usage rules, **and (1)** simple memorization of a list of rules is not really the answer.) By the time students reach **college, (3)** they are ready to understand usage rules, **and (1)** when I am able to get students to listen with an open **mind, (3)**they frequently **say, (6)** "Oh now I get it!" after only a brief bit of instruction. The hallmark of effective instruction, **however, (4)** is whether students can find samples of sentence patterns in their own **writing, (5)** determine which rule applies in which **situation, (5)** and put the rules into practice.

Semicolons

1. When we built our new **house, my** daughter wanted to get a cat **immediately; however,** I told her we would have to wait a while.
2. My husband **disagreed; he** thought we should get a cat the next day.
3. I won this argument, **however,** when I announced that they would have to take care of it.

Colons

1. **Backpacking can be fun if you have a good pack**: one that has a steel frame and is lightweight.
2. **Safety rules like the following are important:** carry enough **water;** stop before **dark;** set up camp off the trail.
3. Don't forget to bring **an inflatable mattress, a toothbrush, or a comb.**

Punctuation Practice

Each of the following sentences needs one mark of punctuation added. Match the appropriate mark to the sentence and place it where it goes.

1. John was too **self-confident** for his own good.
2. John—**my best friend**—lives next door.
3. Turn to chapter three **(pages 37–45)** and read it.
4. **There was only one thing he didn't know:** how to be polite.
5. His temper got him in trouble **often; sometimes** even his wife couldn't stand to be around him.

That morning the postman was late. Tom had been waiting for two hours when the mail truck finally arrived. Tom rushed out of the house **quickly, for** he was expecting an important letter from his doctor.

"**Morning,**" said the postman. "**What's the rush?**"

"I'm expecting an important **letter**," said Tom. "**It's** from Dr. Smith. Have you got **it?**"

The postman shuffled through the stack of letters he held and nodded his head. Handing it to Tom with a **bow**, the postman got back in his truck and drove off.

Tom rushed in the **house**, slammed the **door**, and ripped the envelope open. There it was. It was a refund check for $343.00. Tom kissed the **check, and** he raced out the door. He jumped in the **car**, hit the **gas**, and roared towards the bank. "**Whoopee!**" he shouted.

Placement of Modifiers

1. When I was thirteen, my family moved from Texas to Kansas.
2. Skiing against the blowing snow, I felt as if my face had frozen.
3. While he was chasing his cat across the street, the boy's shoestring broke, and he fell.
4. Looking north, you can see the San Francisco Peaks.

Parallelism

1. The kitchen is 8 feet **long and** 9 feet **wide**.
2. I think **the hourly wage of a plumber** is bigger than **the hourly wage of a teacher**.
3. My father **has worked** in **retail stores**, in **marketing companies**, and once in **a laboratory**.
4. **Oranges from California** are larger and juicier than **oranges from Arizona**.
5. Racquetball is an exciting **sport which requires** agility and physical stamina.

Active and Passive Voice

Passive 1. The decision was made by the committee.
Active: **The committee made the decision.**

Passive 2. The old woman's utilities were paid for by the neighbors.
Active: **The neighbors paid for the old woman's utilities.**

Active 3. As a child, the comedian often offended his mother.

Active 4. The teacher taught the students fractions.

Passive 5. The surprise party was organized by Anna.
Active: **Anna organized the surprise party.**

References

Armstrong, T. (1994). *Using multiple intelligences in the classroom*. Alexandria, VA: Association for Supervision and Curriculum Development.

Bandura, A. (1978). Self-efficacy: Toward a unifying theory of behavioral change. *Advances in Behavioral Research Therapy, 1*, 139–161. Great Britain: Pergamon Press.

Begay, S. (1995). *Navajo: Visions and voices across the mesa*. New York: Scholastic.

Beswetherick, S. (1996, February). Buster and the toboggan. *Highlights for Children, 51*(2), 20–21.

Braddock, R., Lloyd-Jones, R., & Schoer, L. (1963). *Research in written composition*. Champaign, IL: National Council of Teachers of English.

Bratcher, S. (1986). Text superstructures. *Journal of Reading, 29*(6), 538–543.

Bratcher, S. (1994a). *Evaluating children's writing: A handbook of communication choices for classroom teachers*. Hillsdale, NJ: Lawrence Erlbaum Associates.

Bratcher, S. (1994b). Understanding proofreading (or Frank Smith meets the surface error). *Visions and Revisions, 4*, 61–69.

Bratcher, S., & Stroble, E. (1994). Determining the progression from comfort to confidence: A longitudinal evaluation of a National Writing Project site based on multiple data sources. *Research in the Teaching of English, 28*(1), 66–88.

Brust, B. W., & Dorn, B. (1989). *Rattlesnakes, a zoobook*. San Diego: Wildlife Education Ltd.

Byars, B. (1991). *The moon and I*. Englewood Cliffs, NJ: Julian Messner.

Calkins, L. (1983). *Lessons from a child: On the teaching and learning of writing*. Portsmouth, NH: Heinemann.

Calkins, L. (1994). *The art of teaching writing* (2nd ed.). Portsmouth, NH: Heinemann.

Crowley, S. (1994). *Ancient rhetorics for contemporary students*. New York: Macmillan.

Daiute, C. (1993). Young authors' interactions with peers and a teacher: Toward a developmentally sensitive sociocultural literacy theory. In C. Daiute (Ed.), *The development of literacy through social interaction* (pp. 61–79). San Francisco: Jossey-Bass.

D'Angelo, F. (1976). Modes of discourse. In G. Tate (Ed.), *Teaching composition: 10 bibliographical essays* (pp. 111–135). Fort Worth: Texas Christian University Press.

Dillard, A. (1990). *The writing life*. New York: HarperCollins.

Dyson, A. (1989). *Multiple worlds of child writers: Friends learning to write*. New York: Teachers College Press.

Dyson, A. (1993). *Social worlds of children learning to write in an urban primary school*. New York: Teachers College Press.

Dyson, A., & Genishi, C. (Eds.). (1994). *The need for story: Cultural diversity in classroom and community*. Urbana, IL: National Council of Teachers of English.

Edelsky, C. (1989). Putting language variation to work. In P. Rigg & V. Allen (Eds.), *When they don't all speak English* (pp. 96–107). Urbana, IL: National Council of Teachers of English.

Foreman, M. (1989). *War boy*. New York: Arcade Publishing.

Franklin, E. (1989). Encouraging and understanding the visual and written works of second-language children. In P. Rigg & V. Allen (Eds.), *When they don't all speak English* (pp. 77–95). Urbana, IL: National Council of Teachers of English.

Gardner, H. (1983). *Frames of mind: The theory of multiple intelligences.* New York: Basic Books.

Glover, M. (1995). *Two years: A teacher's memoir.* Portsmouth, NH: Heinemann.

Goodman, K. (1976). Reading: A psycholinguistic guessing game. In H. Singer & R. Ruddell (Eds.), *Theoretical processes and models of reading* (2nd ed., pp. 497–508). Newark, DE: International Reading Association.

Gordon, E. (1993). *The new well-tempered sentence.* New York: Ticknor & Fields.

Graves, D. (1983). *Writing: Teachers and children at work.* Portsmouth, NH: Heinemann.

Graves, D. (1994). *A fresh look at writing.* Portsmouth, NH: Heinemann.

Grahame, K. (1985). *The wind in the willows.* New York: Derrydale Books.

Hairston, M. (1982). Thomas Kuhn and the winds of change. *College Composition and Communication, 33,* 76–88.

Hillocks, G. (1986). *Research on written composition: New directions for teaching.* Urbana, IL: ERIC Clearinghouse on Reading and Communication Skills and the National Conference on Research in English.

Igoa, C. (1995). *The inner world of the immigrant child.* Mahwah, NJ: Lawrence Erlbaum Associates.

Kendall, R. (1992). *Eskimo boy: Life in an Inupiaque eskimo village.* New York: Scholastic.

Kinneavy, J. (1969). The basic aims of discourse. *College Composition and Communication, 20,* 297–304.

Lacapa, K., & Lacapa, M. (1994). *Less than half, more than whole.* Flagstaff, AZ: Northland Publishing.

Lacapa, M. (1992). *Antelope woman: An apache folktale.* Flagstaff, AZ: Northland Publishing.

Lane, B. (1993). *After "the end."* Portsmouth, NH: Heinemann.

Lionne, L. (1969). *Alexander and the wind-up mouse.* New York: Pantheon.

McGilly, K. (1994). Cognitive science and educational practice: An introduction. In K. McGilly (Ed.), *Classroom lessons* (pp. 210–233). Cambridge, MA: Massachusetts Institute of Technology.

Maslow, A. (1970). *Motivation and personality* (2nd ed.). London: Harper & Row.

Morris, W. (Ed.) (1976). *The American Heritage dictionary of the English language.* Boston: Houghton Mifflin.

Murray, D. (1987). *Write to learn.* New York: Holt, Rinehart & Winston.

The Nature Conservancy (1995, July). How you can help. *Children Discover, 5*(7), 16–17.

Nelson, L. (1995). *Writing and being: Taking back our lives through the power of language.* San Diego: LuraMedia.

Nez, R. (1995). *Forbidden talent.* Flagstaff, AZ: Northland Press.

Noguchi, R. (1991). *Grammar and the teaching of writing.* Urbana, IL: National Council of Teachers of English.

O'Dell, S. (1960). *Island of the blue dolphins.* Boston: Houghton Mifflin.

Oliver, R. (1993). *Rocks and fossils.* New York: Random House.

Ornstein, R. (1993). *The roots of the self.* San Francisco: Harper.

Peregoy, S., & Boyle, O. (1993). *Reading, writing, and ESL: A resource book for K–8 teachers.* White Plains, NY: Longman.

Proett, J., & Gill, K. (1983). *The writing process in action: A handbook for teachers.* Urbana, IL: National Council of Teachers of English.

Rigg, P., & Allen, V. (Eds.). (1989). *When they don't all speak English: Integrating the ESL student into the regular classroom.* Urbana, IL: National Council of Teachers of English.

Rigg, P., & Enright, D. S. (1986). *Children and ESL: Integrating perspectives.* Washington, DC: Teachers of English to Speakers of Other Languages.

Robinson, F. (1996, February). What to do if you see a monster. *Highlights for Children, 51*(2), 5.

Root, R. (1994). *Wordsmithery.* New York: Macmillan.

Routman, R. (1991) *Invitations: Changing as teachers and learners K–12.* Portsmouth, NH: Heinemann.

Rumelhart, D. (1977). Toward an interactive model of reading. In S. Dornic, (Ed.), *Attention and performance* (vol. 6). Hillsdale, NJ: Lawrence Erlbaum Associates.

Shaugnessy, M. (1977). *Errors and expectations.* New York: Oxford University Press.

Smith, D. B. (1973). *A taste of blackberries.* New York: Thomas Crowell Company.

Smith, F. (1982). *Writing and the writer.* New York: Holt, Rinehart, & Winston.

Tompkins, G. (1990). *Teaching writing: Balancing process and product.* Columbus, OH: Merrill.

Towle, W. (1993). *The real McCoy: The life of an African-American inventor.* New York: Scholastic.

Van Allsburg, C. (1981). *Jumanji.* Boston: Houghton Mifflin.

Vick, H. H. (1993). *Walker of time.* Tucson, AZ: Harbinger House.

Vygotskii, L. (1978). *Mind in society.* Cambridge, MA: Harvard University Press.

"When you lose your cool." (1995, August). *American Girl,* pp. 24–25.

White, T. H. (1939). *The once and future king.* New York: G. P. Putnam's Sons.

Wilder, L. I. (1953). *Little house on the prairie.* New York: Harper.

Williams, S. A. (1992). *Working cotton.* New York: Harcourt Brace.

Williams, V. (1982). *A chair for my mother.* New York: Mulberry Books.

Willis, M. S. (1993). *Deep revision.* New York: Teachers and Writers Collaborative.

Wormser, R. (1993). *The iron horse: How the railroads changed America.* New York: Walker Publishing Company.

Yates, E. (1981). *My diary—My world.* Philadelphia: Westminster Press.

Author Index

Subject Index